AF505626

THE MUSEUM OF SCANDALS

Éléa Baucheron
Diane Routex

Front cover: Maurizio Cattelan, *La Nona Ora*, see p. 40

© 2013 olo.éditions, Paris

© for the English edition: Prestel Verlag, Munich · London · New York, 2013

Credits on page 176

Library of Congress Control Number: 2013936555;
British Library Cataloguing-in-Publication Data: a catalogue record for this book is available
from the British Library; Deutsche Nationalbibliothek holds a record of this publication in the
Deutsche Nationalbibliografie; detailed bibliographical data can be found under: http://dnb.d-nb.de

Prestel books are available worldwide. Please contact your nearest bookseller or
one of the above addresses for information concerning your local distributor.

Prestel Verlag, Munich
A member of Verlagsgruppe Random House GmbH

Prestel Verlag
Neumarkter Strasse 28
81673 Munich
Tel. +49 (0)89 4136-0
Fax +49 (0)89 4136-2335

Prestel Publishing Ltd.
14-17 Wells Street
London W1T 3PD
Tel. +44 (0)20 7323-5004
Fax +44 (0)20 7636-8004

Prestel Publishing
900 Broadway, Suite 603
New York, NY 10003
Tel. +1 (212) 995-2720
Fax +1 (212) 995-2733

www.prestel.com

Authors: Éléa Baucheron and Diane Routex

Editorial direction of the French edition: Nicolas Marçais
Artistic direction: Philippe Marchand
Editorial support: Énaïde Xetuor-Docin
Layout: Prestel Verlag, based on the design of Marion Alfano
Copyediting of the French edition: Aurélie Gaillot

Editorial direction: Claudia Stäuble, Dorothea Bethke
Translation from French: Fabia Claris, Robert McInnes
Copyediting: Chris Murray
Cover: Stefan Schmid Design, Stuttgart
Typesetting: Greiner & Reichel, Cologne
Production: René Fink
Printing and Binding: Tien Wah Press, Singapore

Verlagsgruppe Random House FSC® N001967
Printed on FSC®-certified paper *Titan MA* produced by Hansol Paper Co., Korea

ISBN 978-3-7913-4849-0

Éléa Baucheron
Diane Routex

ART THAT SHOCKED
THE WORLD

THE
MUSEUM OF
SCANDALS

What possible link can there be between a figure of Saint Teresa by a devout sculptor, an Impressionist painting of an open-air dance, and tattooed pigs? The answer is that they all created a scandal. Looking at works of art in terms of the controversy they caused can help us to understand a specific period by giving us an insight into its innermost prohibitions, fears, and aspirations. This book offers readers a different way into art and social history through the study of a selection of seventy works with stormy histories. Art is full of difficult subjects: sex, blasphemy, political and artistic revolution all find their way into art, to the consternation and horror of all backward-looking, conservative-minded people, who would much rather see art shut up in an ivory tower well away from real life and controversy. It is a moot point whether anything can be controversial in its own right or whether it depends on the "eye of the beholder." Artists very often find themselves chastised for being trivial and accused of corrupting the morals of their age. People are quick to pounce on the slightest departure from convention or failure to obey the rules, and in a sense this is a continuation of the trend set by Plato when he voiced his mistrust of art as an "imitation of an imitation" and of artists therefore as peddlers of illusions.

Looking at what has upset people over the ages is illuminating. In the Middle Ages, for instance, people were clearly touchy on the subject of religion, whereas in the nineteenth century it was anything about politics that raised their ire. Could you say off the top of your head what our current generation finds morally offensive? From the evidence we have assembled, it seems, as you will see, to include assaults on human dignity, exploitation of the weak (children and animals), and the commercialization of art. Sensitive subjects do not fall neatly into period or type, however: fear of sacrilege was not peculiar to our distant ancestors, for instance. That said, our period seems to be marked by its unbridled pursuit of the scandalous. Whereas in the past scandal was frowned upon in art, today it is synonymous with success and extends across all domains, including not just literature and cinema, but also advertising and television. "I shock, therefore I am" would be a fitting mantra for the twenty-first century.

But as you will discover in the pages that follow, the scandalous in art is far more than a sales gimmick. It springs from all kinds of causes and has all manner of effects: it forces people to think, and sometimes to act; it rejects preconceptions and outdated rules. Who says that art should be nothing but aesthetic contemplation?

SACRILEGE

POLITICAL INCORRECTNESS

SEXUAL SCANDALS

TRANSGRESSIONS

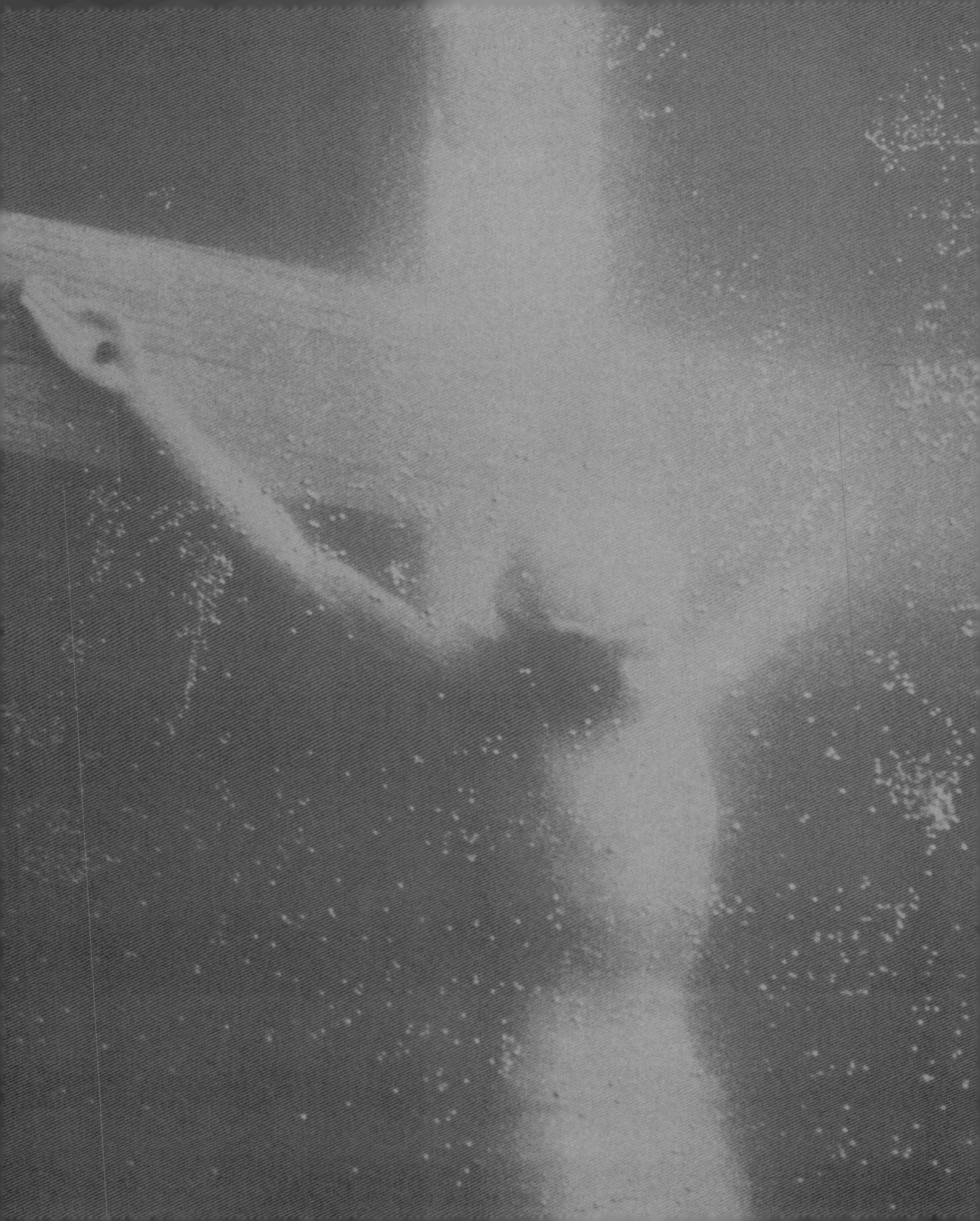

SACRILEGE

MASACCIO

FRA BARTOLOMEO

HOLBEIN THE YOUNGER

MICHELANGELO

VERONESE

EL GRECO

CARAVAGGIO

BERNINI

DIEGO VELÁZQUEZ

PAUL CHENAVARD

ANDRES SERRANO

DAVID WOJNAROWICZ

ALEXANDER KOSOLAPOV

MASACCIO

MAURIZIO CATTELAN

MOUNIR FATMI

Is art religious in origin? While many scholars contend that it is, others argue that it proceeds primarily from a love of beauty, which man later harnessed to a spiritual purpose. Whatever the truth of the matter, in ancient and primitive cultures the two were closely intertwined. Stylized pieces dating back to prehistory seem to have been linked to shamanistic rites or to have been designed to secure divine intervention. It was not long before religion imposed detailed rules on artists, sometimes going so far as to ban completely all representation of the divine. In spite of this, the various religions have generated a vast array of magnificent works of art of all kinds, from intricate mosques to giant Buddhas, and from paintings to sculptures.

Western art was initially geared to depicting a Catholic universe. In the Middles Ages, it was literally under orders to do so, with Gregory the Great, Pope Gregory I (r. 590–604), stipulating in the seventh century that art had two functions: to spread knowledge of the faith by creating and disseminating images of religious figures and scenes; and to move the faithful to devotion through such images and so elevate their souls. At this time, artists were considered craftsmen and were not free to work as they pleased but instead had to adhere to rigorous rules governing everything from materials to subjects and their treatment. Their works were rarely signed. A work was made and bought – generally by churchmen or members of princely families – to serve a specific religious purpose.

In the sixteenth century, Catholicism went into crisis as reformers established the Protestant Church. The rivalry between the two Churches led not only to killings and torture, but also to a fight for the moral high ground, which in turn led the papacy to monitor art very closely. The Council of Trent (1545–1563) set out principles designed to intensify the Counter Reformation, decreeing among other things that there was absolutely no place for profanity of any kind in a sacred work. Clerics kept a very close eye on artists, who had little freedom: any hint of originality in treatment or interpretation was seen as revealing an impious tendency to flout the rules of the Church and as demonstrating sympathy for the Reformation. Very few dared tread anything but the most well-worn paths; though, equally, many artists clearly did not feel stifled and zealously depicted and defended their faith in their works. It was not until the Renaissance that artists began to gain greater freedom and confidence. As time has gone on, religion has come to play an increasingly smaller role in society and art, and profane, lay, even anti-clerical subjects have become permissible. Blasphemy continues to vex some authorities, but these days it no longer leads to torture or the stake. It remains a highly sensitive subject, however, and believers of different faiths can be quick to take offense, as shown by the Muhammad cartoons controversy that rocked Europe and the fury that Andres Serrano's twist on a crucifix aroused (see p. 34). Whether by providing inspiration and subjects, exerting control or offering patronage, religion has been a constant influence on art.

SACRILEGIOUS REALISM

Masaccio's frescoes in the Brancacci chapel in Florence in 1427 amounted to an artistic revolution that was shocking in its treatment of religious subjects. One section, *The Expulsion of Adam and Eve from Eden,* provoked particular outrage among contemporary Florentine society, which was unprepared for such modernity.

Masaccio was never meant to provide all the frescoes for the chapel. The Brancacci family had commissioned the famous Masolino da Panicale to do the job, but he was called away on a trip and left some of the frescoes to the young painter to complete.

Masaccio had an innovative style that was different from the older painter's, however. He had already begun to follow Giotto's lead and to make use of perspective in some of his earlier works.

The Gothic art of the Middle Ages was still the order of the day. Paintings were constructed around symbols and traditional images designed to transmit a religious message rather than to represent reality. Masaccio, by contrast, made religious painting human. The size of the figures, for example, is governed by perspective and not by hierarchical order, with the result that Adam and Eve in the foreground are bigger than the angel who drives them out in the middle ground: the sinners seem to be more important than the divine messenger. There is no allegory here to convey a religious lesson; instead, the viewer is forced to confront the despair of two beings who move in a familiar world. Everything – the shadows, the perspective, the background, the despairing grimaces – adds to the realism of the scene. Masaccio's Florentine contemporaries were outraged that the divine should not have dominated. Masaccio himself was a pioneer of Renaissance humanist thought, which placed Man at the center of everything.

Masaccio died without finishing the fresco, which was finally completed by Filippino Lippi. The work came under critical fire two centuries later. Perspective was no longer shocking by 1674, but the nakedness of the figures had become unacceptable, and Cosimo III de' Medici ordered that fig leaves be added to cover the bodies.

Tommaso di Giovanni, known as Masaccio (1401–1428),
***The Expulsion of Adam and Eve from Eden,* 1427,**
fresco, Brancacci Chapel, Church of
Santa Maria del Carmine, Florence
Left: before restoration of the work in the 1980s,
showing the fig leaves added in the seventeenth century
Right: after restoration which returned the fresco
to its original state, as Masaccio painted it

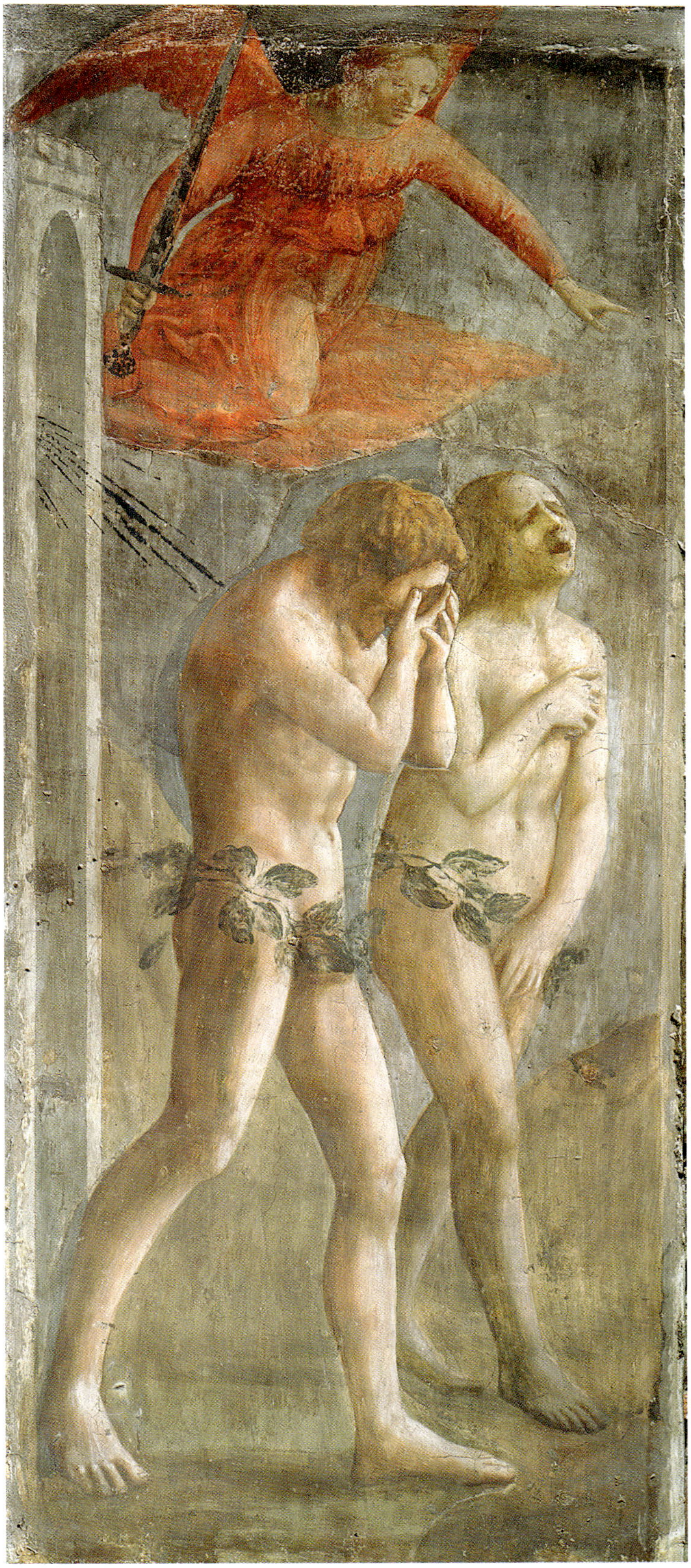

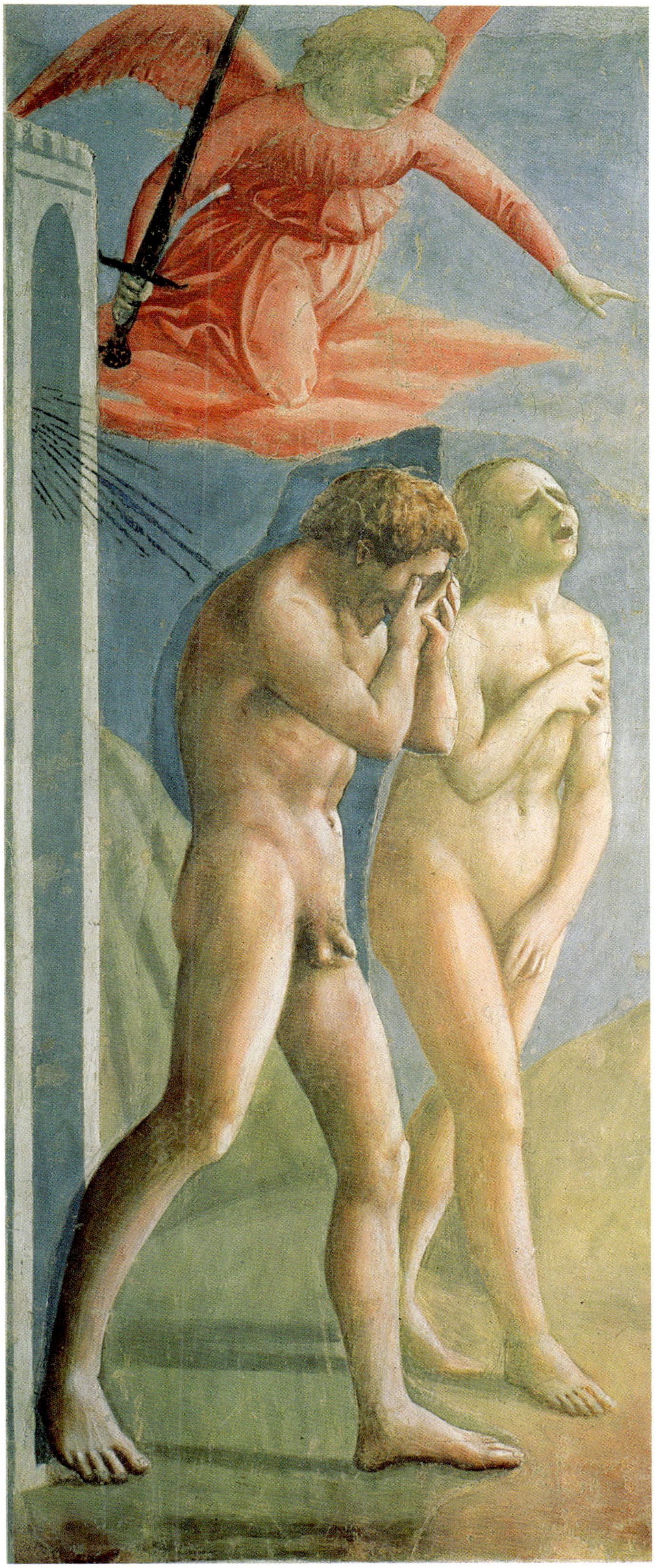

A VERY SENSUAL SPIRITUALITY

For refusing to renounce his faith, Saint Sebastian was sentenced to be shot with arrows. It was a punishment that made for a slow death, and history has it that the saint looked like a hedgehog by the time he finally collapsed. Fra Bartolomeo's painting of him of about 1514 removes almost all trace of violence and suffering and focuses instead on his unashamedly sensuous body.

Fra Bartolomeo took holy orders in 1500 and was a devout painter hardly given to sacrilege. Taken to task for not knowing how to depict nudes, he responded, however, with a painting that was to cause a stir until long after his death. It was hung in all reverence in a church in Florence but had to be swiftly removed: numerous women admitted in confession to having sinful thoughts at the sight of the saint's beautiful young male body! With its graceful, languid pose, prominent muscles, genitals barely veiled by light gauze, it was more redolent of the sensuousness of classical sculptures than of the butchery perpetrated on the saint. Only the occasional, discreet arrow and the martyr's palm presented by the angel allude to the bloody punishment inflicted on him.

The painting was to be criticized equally sharply during the Reformation, when it was seen as the very epitome of the perversion of religion by painters.

Yet subsequent depictions of the saint were to become increasingly erotic. Hands bound to a tree or a column, his body gracefully curved, his face serene or radiating divine ecstasy, Saint Sebastian was consistently represented as a beautiful, sometimes androgynous, young man. People called in vain for artists to cover his body with blood and lacerations to stop it from stimulating erotic fantasies. But this had no effect. From the end of the nineteenth century, the young martyr was even considered the patron saint of homosexuals. That too was to spark fierce controversy.

Zacchia il Vecchio (c. 1496–c. 1561), after Fra Bartolomeo (1472–1517), *Saint Sebastian,* 1526, oil on wood, 147 × 86 cm, monastery of San Francesco, Fiesole

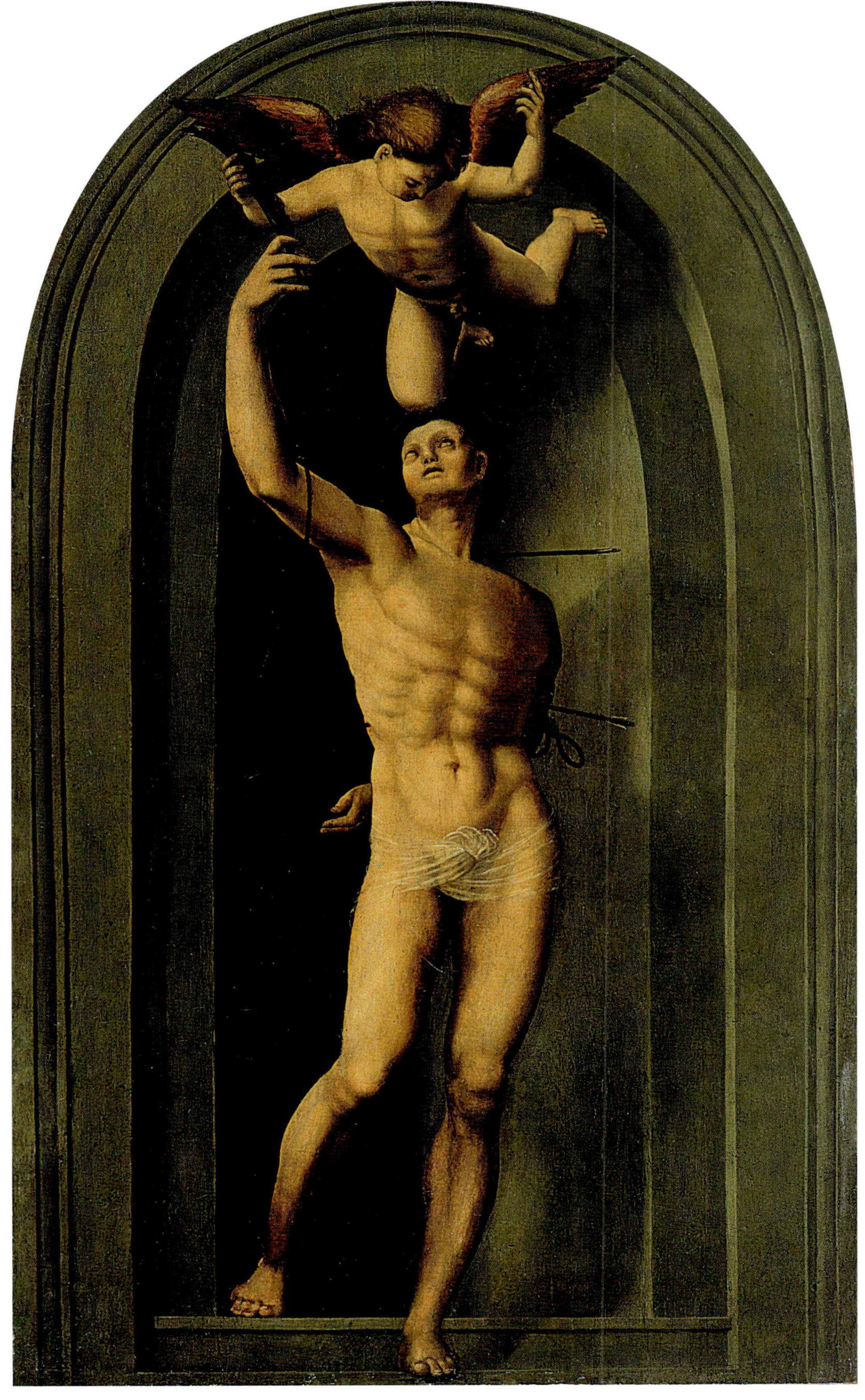

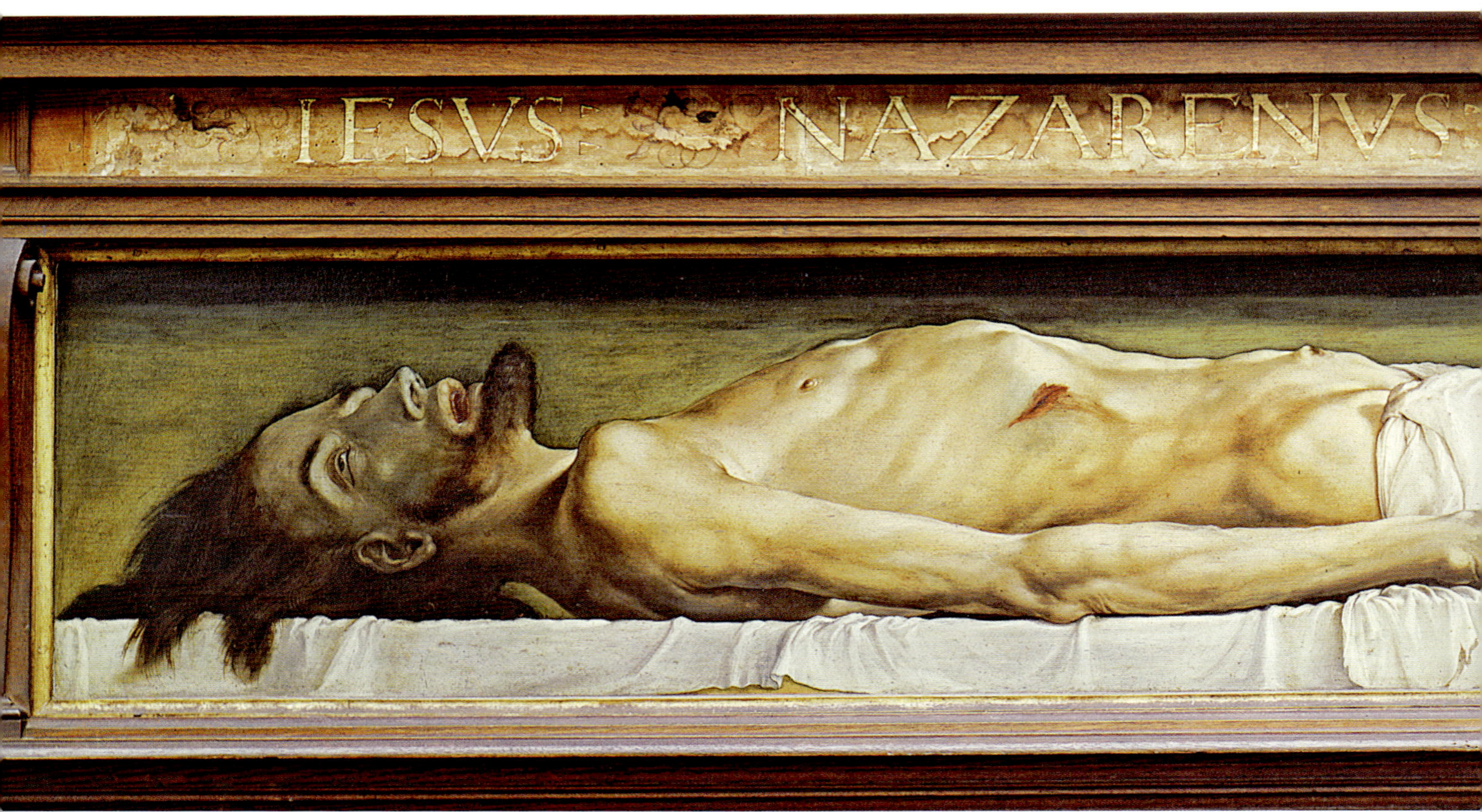

NO ONE ESCAPES DEATH

Nulli concedo, "I yield to nobody", was the motto of the great
humanist Erasmus. He would willingly explain when asked that the
first person referred not to him but to death, which spares no one.
Holbein the Younger was a great friend of Erasmus at the time and
indeed painted his portrait in 1523. His painting of *The Body of
the Dead Christ in the Tomb* exemplifies the writer's ideas vividly.

Hans Holbein the Younger (1497–1543),
The Body of the Dead Christ in the Tomb, 1521–1522,
oil on panel, 32×202 cm, Kunstmuseum, Basel

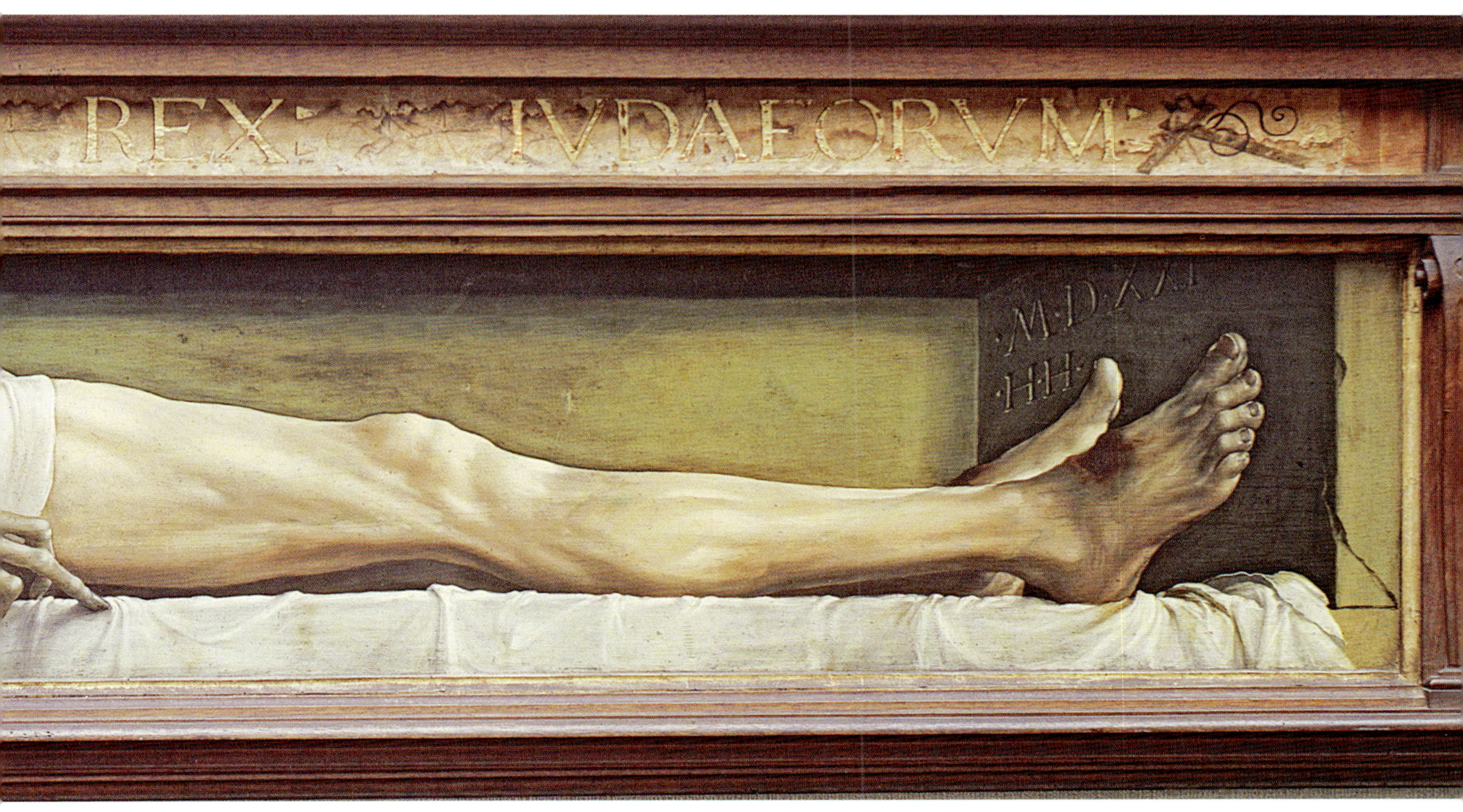

In Holbein's day the death of Christ was commonly represented in the form of a Lamentation or a Pietà in which the dead Christ is shown surrounded by weeping figures (or figure in the case of a Pietà, where only the Virgin Mary is shown). These scenes are full of pathos and viewers are inevitably moved to compassion by the sight of so much suffering. Holbein's work is all the more striking because it is a radical departure from this norm: viewers are left to contemplate this death alone, without saintly mediation. Christ's racked body, seemingly frozen in a spasm of suffering, provokes pity, but above all the painting forces viewers to reflect on the finite nature of human existence. Holbein opted to represent Christ in all his humanity here: Christ's dead body is so realistic that it is said to have been painted from the corpse of a drowned merchant. It is hard to believe that Holbein could have invented that cadaverous stiffness, that gaping mouth baring its teeth, that greenish hue, or even that half-closed eye. We know very little about how the work was received at the time, but it was apparently removed from its initial location in a church, doubtless because it was too shocking. What we do know is that a year after finishing it, Holbein repainted the background. Where there had been a semi-circular space corresponding to the niche in which the painting was originally placed, Holbein now depicted a tomb. Whatever the story behind this, viewers continue to be staggered by Holbein's Christ. The most famous response was that of the nineteenth-century Russian writer Fyodor Dostoevsky, who is known to have been transfixed by the painting on a visit to Basel, and who included a description of it in his novel *The Idiot* (1869).

HALF A MILLENNIUM OF CONTROVERSY

Michelangelo was recognized in his own lifetime for his talents as a painter, a sculptor, an architect and even a poet. Difficult though he could be, the greatest in the land fought to secure his services. After Pope Julius II commissioned him to paint the ceiling of the Sistine Chapel, his successor Clement VII asked him to paint the altar wall.

The work provoked an outcry before it was even finished. While the scaffolding was still up the master of ceremonies who came to view it with the pope declared that it was indecent, criticizing the naked bodies with their "shameful parts revealed." Michelangelo retaliated by including him in the painting as Minos, an old devil with the ears of an ass and a snake wound round him biting his genitals. A cardinal similarly took offense; and when he became pope he ordered Michelangelo to make his work respectable. Michelangelo snapped back, "Make the world a more respectable place and painting will quickly follow suit."

Michelangelo's prestige was such that he could disregard his many critics and refuse to rework his huge fresco as they demanded. Unfortunately, others were to do the job for him, notably following the Council of Trent during the Counter Reformation. Immediately after Michelangelo's state funeral, one of his circle was ordered to cover up the naked bodies and "cor-

rect" all improprieties. The poor man was known thereafter by the nickname "Il Braghettone": "the trouser maker" or "breeches-painter." He was not the only one to take on this role. In the centuries that followed, *The Last Judgment* continued to provoke a heated reaction. Some ordered it to be reworked yet again, while others defended it against any attempt to deface it. No one, however, remained indifferent

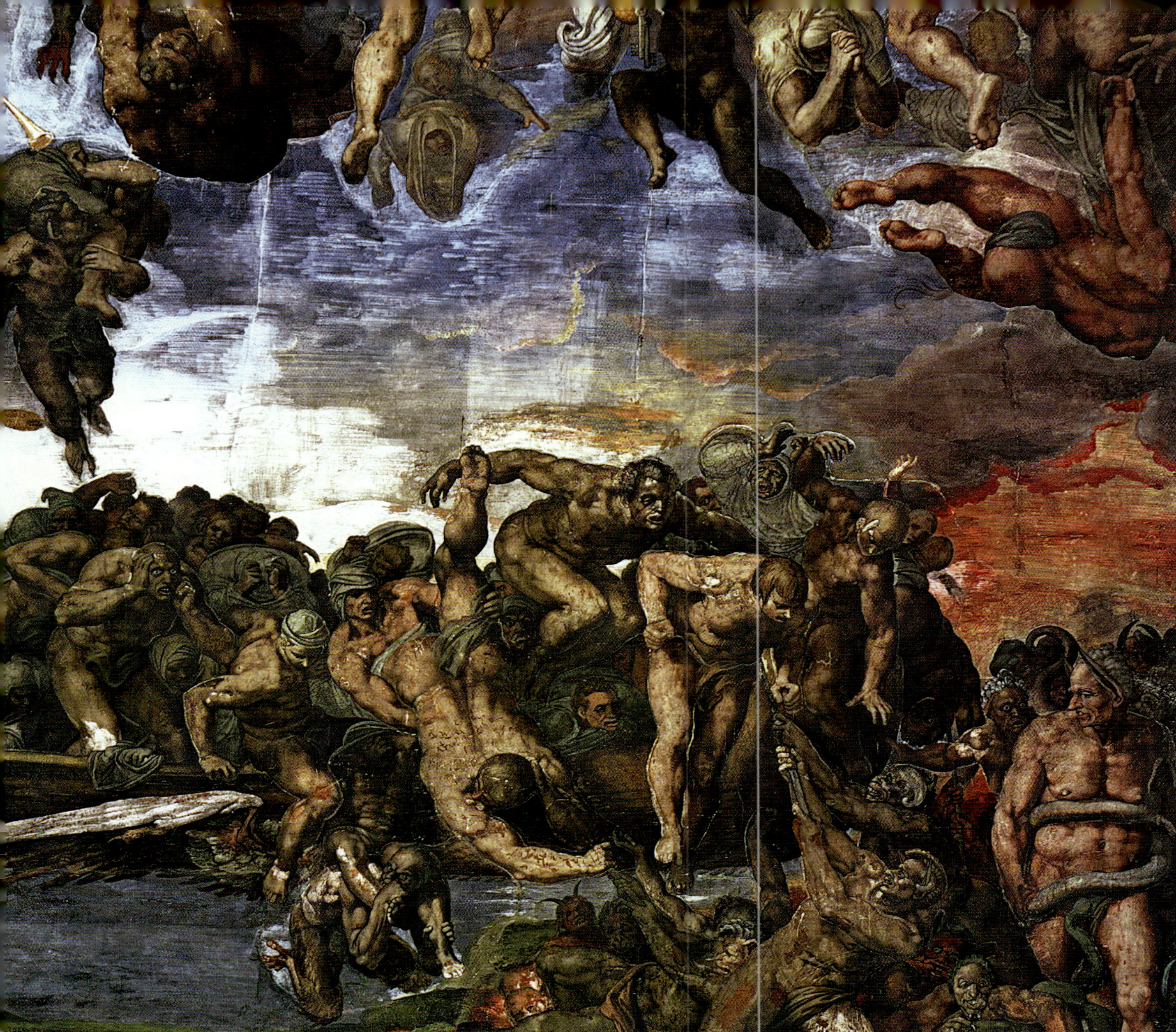

before this monumental storm of bodies in movement. People were offended by the nudity and somewhat ambiguous poses of the figures, the depiction of Christ as young, beardless, and muscular, and the violence and brutality of the torments of Hell – and at the same time people admired Michelangelo's indisputable genius. The fresco continues to provoke fierce debate even now. Restoration carried out on the fresco between 1980 and 1994 revealed an astonishingly bright and colorful painting. For many, however, this "original" version is brash and gaudy.

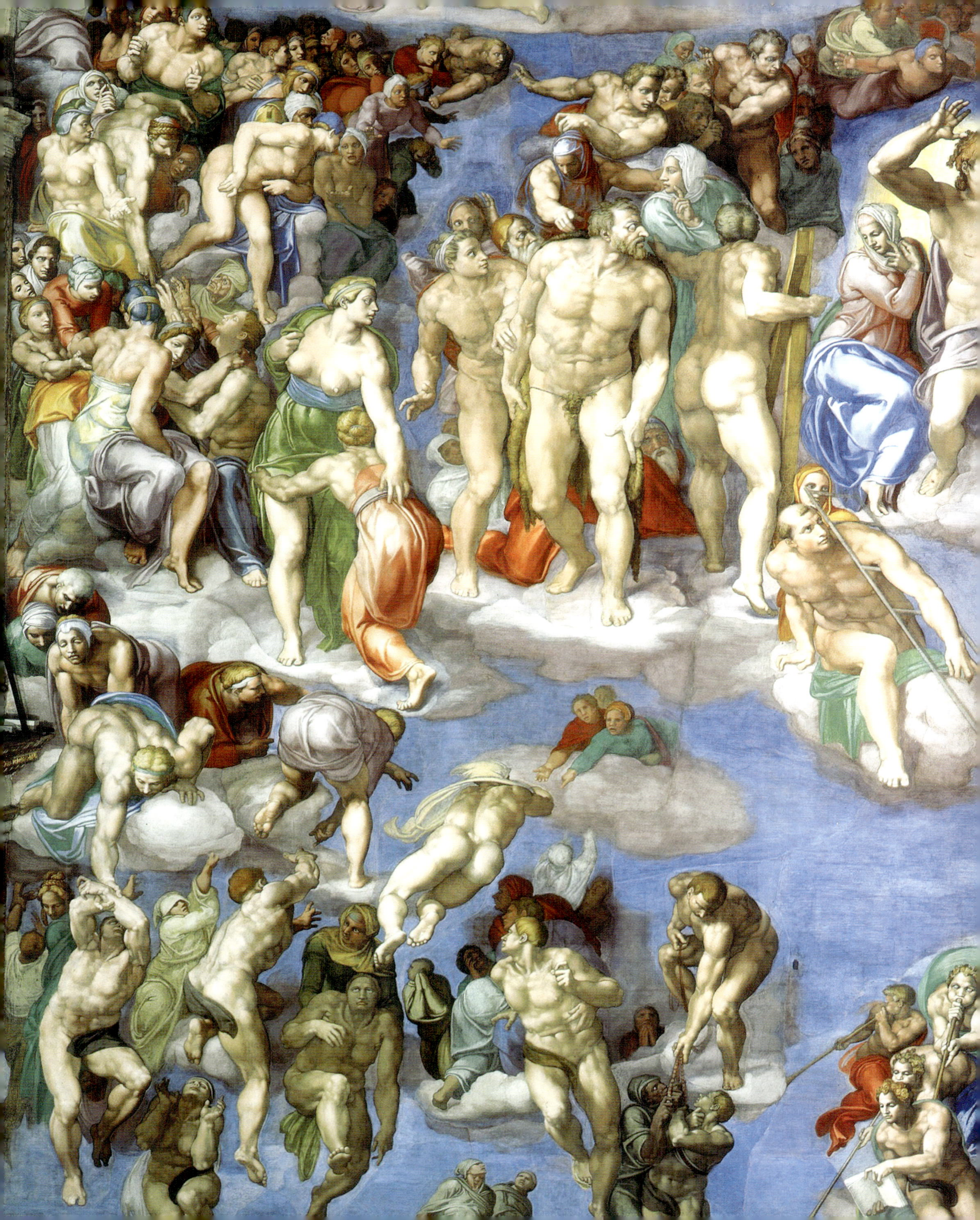

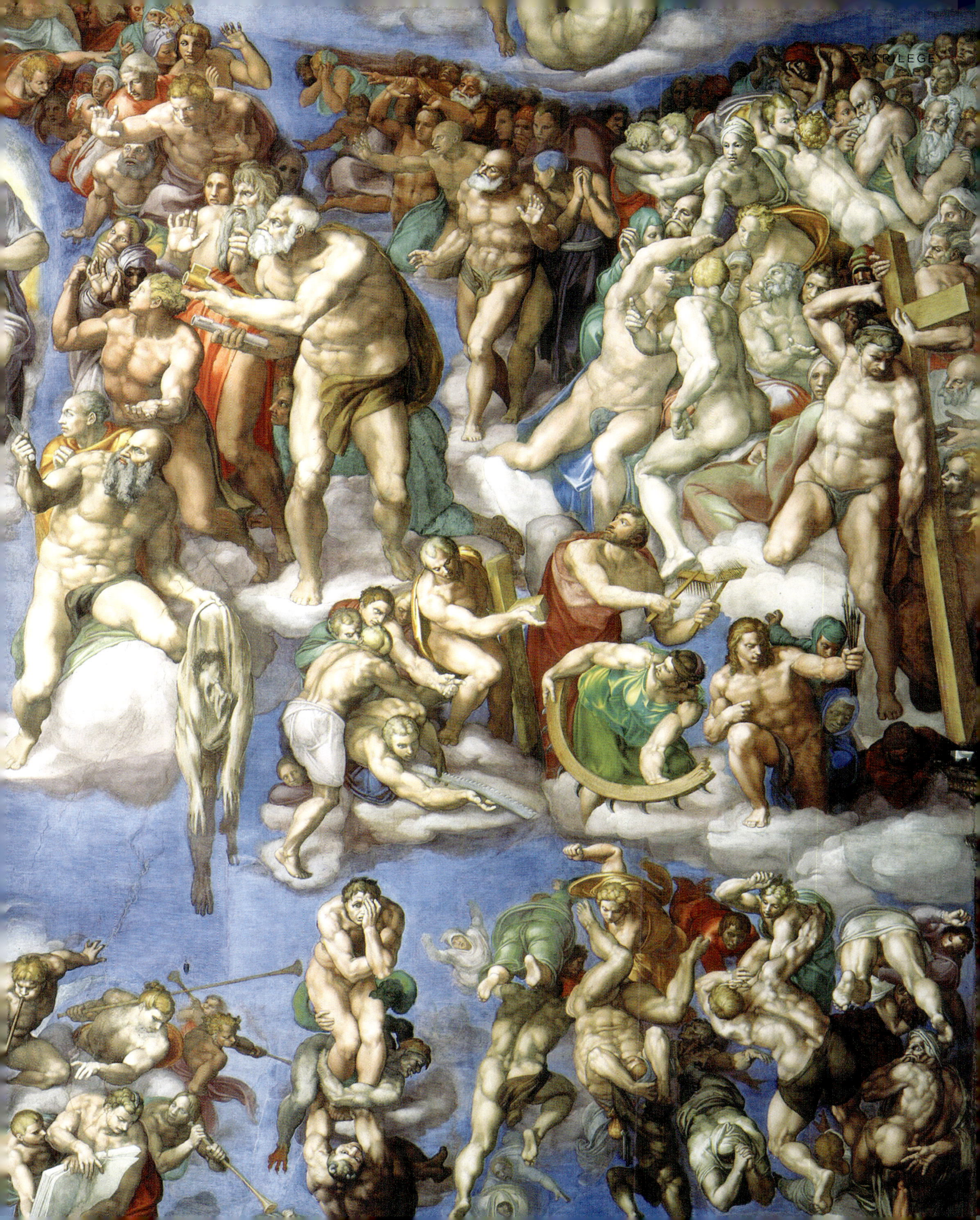
SACRILEGE

THE INQUISITION, THE PAINTER

The Last Supper: Christ and the Twelve Apostles ... but complete with a dog, a fool with a parrot, lackeys, men-at-arms with halberds, crowds of people in six- teenth-century attire, all teeming in a riot of color. Veronese portrayed Christ's Last Supper as a bustling, lavish, profane banquet. The Holy Office, known as the Inquisition, was not pleased.

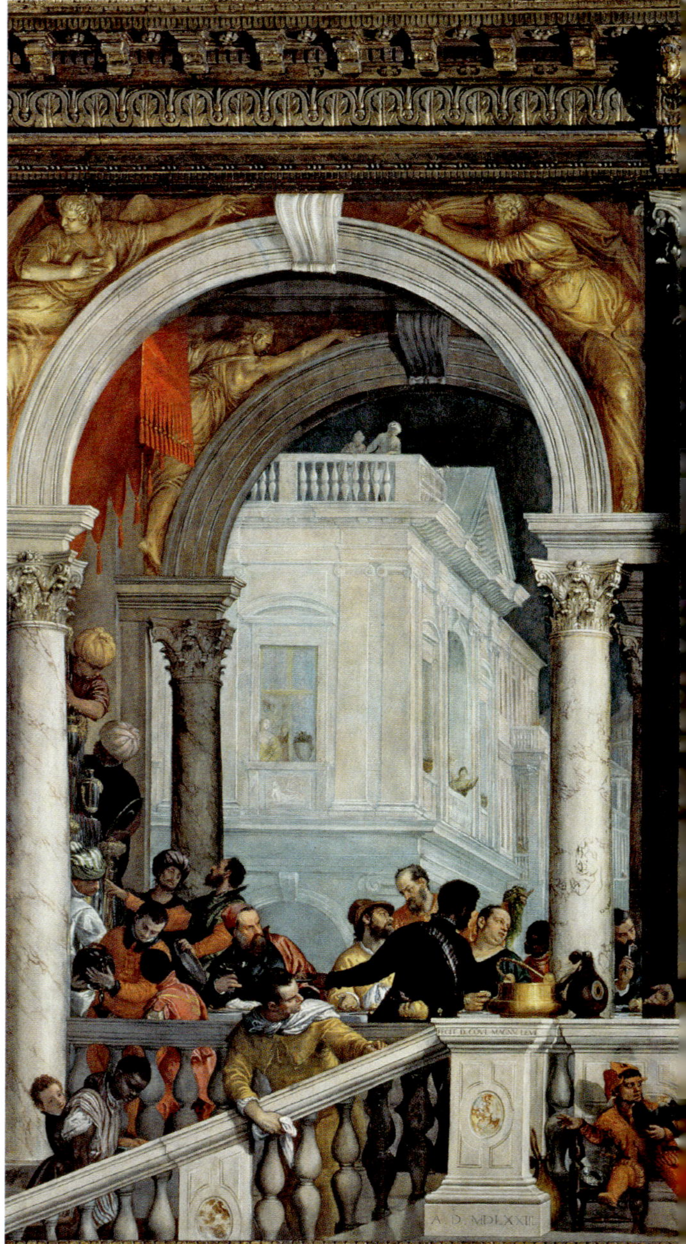

The monastery that had commissioned the paint- ing insisted that Veronese alter it and replace the dog with Mary Magdalene, but Veronese refused. The monks were outraged and complained to the Holy Office. They could not in all decency accept the dog, let alone this festive and crowded Last Supper. It was a time when the Catholic Church was fright- ened of Reformation ideas and readily identified orig- inality with heresy. People immediately mistrusted an artist like Veronese who rejected tradition. He was summoned to appear before the inquisitors, who were quick to suspect and accuse him. They too con- sidered the painting sacrilegious. By a stroke of luck, a record of the interrogation survives, and we know that the artist was asked to justify the choices he had made, defend his religious beliefs and explain his backers' interests. Veronese skillfully countered the obtuse questioning of his inquisitors, replying naively that he had simply wanted to add decorative detail to the painting, that he thought rich men had servants and soldiers. He famously went on to assert that "we painters take the same liberties as poets and fools." The inquisitors, however, failed to see the brilliance either of the line or of the painting, and Veronese was ordered to alter the painting at his own cost. Cleverly, he simply changed the title: *The Last Supper* became *The Feast in the House of Levi*.

AND THE FOOL

Paolo Caliari, known as Veronese (1528–1588),
***The Feast in the House of Levi,* 1573,**
oil on canvas, 550 x 1280 cm, Gallerie dell' Accademia, Venice

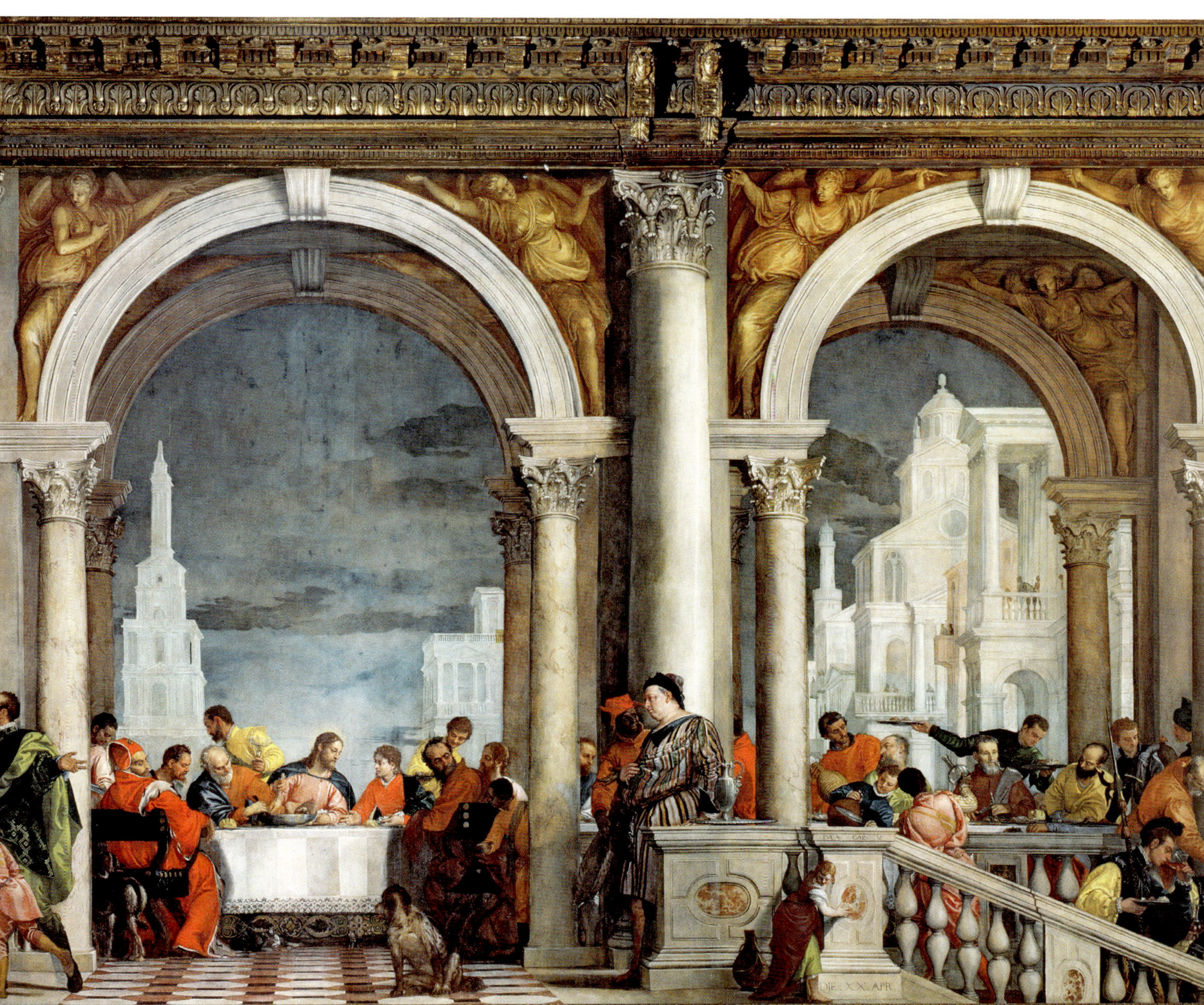

A DISTORTED SPIRITUALITY

El Greco's style was disturbing. Spain in the Counter Reformation was characterized by control, with inquisitors charged specifically with superintending art. In the Greek-born El Greco, the censors discovered a daring painter who went in for somber monochromes and elongated figures, and depicted Christ crucified with only three nails – they were bound to be incensed. Even the king was driven by a respect for rules to reject *The Martyrdom of Saint Maurice.*

El Greco's was a strong personality and when he settled in Spain after studying painting first in Greece and then in Italy, his contemporaries there described him as arrogant and mercenary. They accused him of being more concerned with profit than art in running his studio in Spain, where assistants churned out endless copies of his compositions to satisfy the growing demand. Then, as now, people did not take kindly to the mass-production of works of art.

The oddness of El Greco's drawing had been the object of criticism even when he was in Rome. It continued to disturb people not only in Spain in his own day but for centuries to come. His style gave rise to a proliferation of far-fetched theories in the nineteenth century, with people variously attributing it to the fact that he was astigmatic or even mad. Despite the evident quality of his work, people mistrusted it because of its originality. It smacked of heresy and the devout found reassurance in conformity. Acutely mindful of the injunctions of the Church, King Philip II of Spain thus found himself compelled to reject the painting he had commissioned from El Greco. For the king, El Greco's highly unconventional style of drawing, choice of palette, and treatment of the subject all represented errors of taste. Instead of being a traditional image meant to arouse pity and veneration (Saint Maurice was a Roman soldier put to death for refusing to perform pagan rites), the painting portrays a group of virile, even sensuous men in the middle of a crowd, making the image difficult to read. The monk José de Siguenza backed up the king in his rejection of the painting by declaring that artists had no business producing paintings of saints which "took away the desire to pray to them."

Doménikos Theotokópoulos, known as El Greco (1541–1614),
***The Martyrdom of Saint Maurice,* 1580–1583,**
oil on canvas, 448 x 301 cm, Real Monasterio, Escorial, Madrid

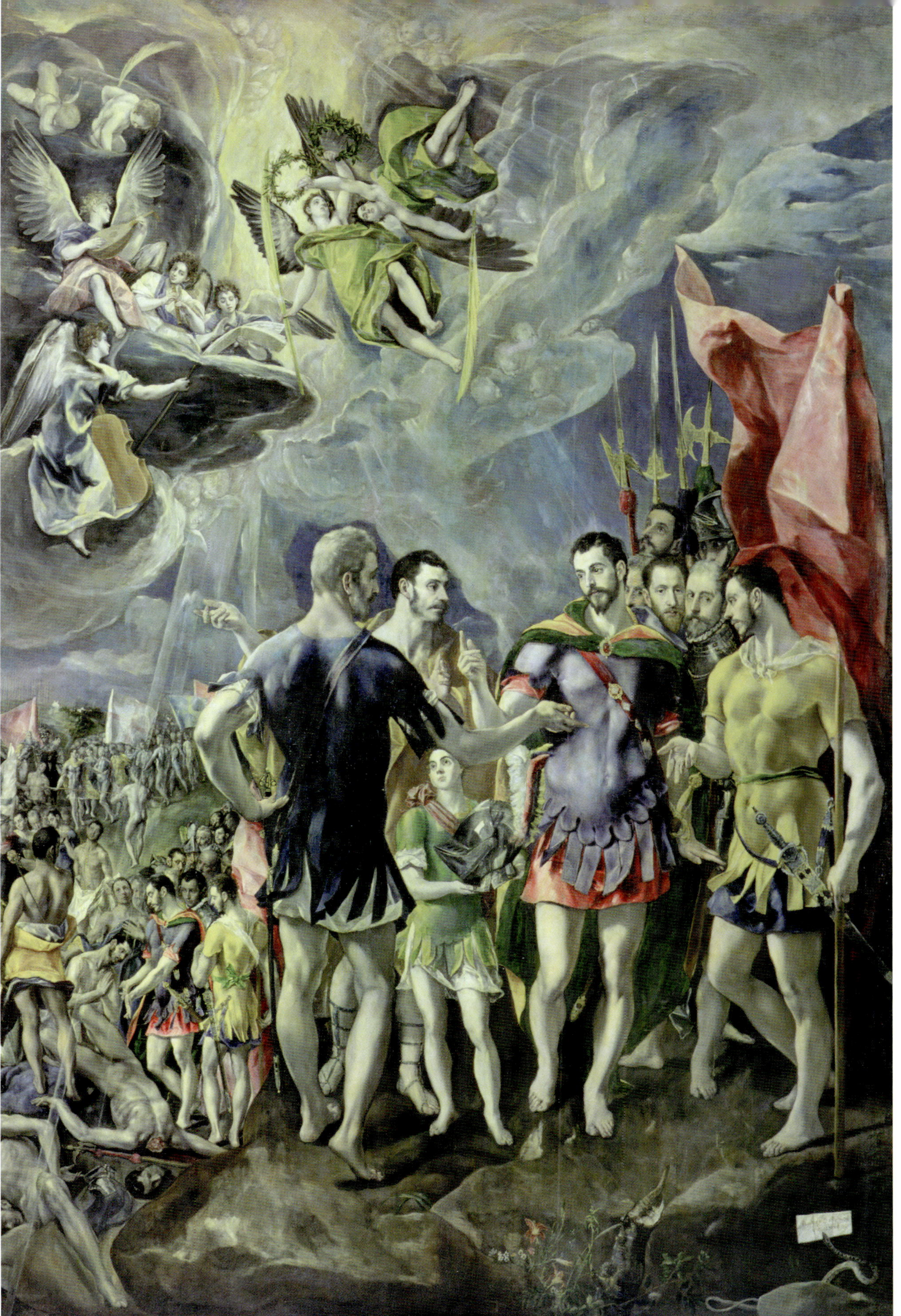

THE BIBLE FULL OF COMMON PEOPLE

The life Caravaggio led provoked as much criticism as his paintings. Despite this, he captivated aristocratic patrons and collectors in Rome, including members of the Church. He could have moved in the highest echelons of society, but he chose instead to mix with common people and find his models among them.

Caravaggio was at home with the underbelly of society. His lifestyle was seen as shockingly immoral: he quarreled, brawled, was imprisoned for minor offenses, and eventually forced to flee Rome after a fatal duel. Rowdy and unruly, he readily included his lovers in his paintings, casting young beggars and prostitutes as biblical and mythological figures. The public were not fooled. They saw the Virgin in *The Death of the Virgin* as a drowned prostitute or peasant woman fished out of the Tiber with her swollen body and shamefully exposed legs.

Caravaggio does not conjure up a flight of little cherubs covered in flowers to escort a graceful Virgin up towards a solemn heaven. Instead, he paints a common, everyday scene of death. Not surprisingly, the painting was rejected by the monks at the Church of Santa Maria della Scala who had commissioned it. Yet, however far removed from religious iconography his revolutionary treatment may have been, there was nothing sacrilegious about Caravaggio's intent. From the 1600s onwards he concentrated almost exclusively on religious painting, approaching it in his own distinctive manner, structuring the way we move through his compositions. The woman bent over in grief in the foreground acts as the first step of a "spiritual ascent": behind the dead body is a succession of three figures, each more upright and less distraught than the one before. Beyond the last, finally, rises a red drape, defying the laws of physics but laden with religious significance. A strange light from an unseen source adds to the mystical quality of the picture, offsetting the shadows and suggesting an afterlife impossible to depict. While many continued to choke with rage at Caravaggio and his work after his death, others recognized his indisputable genius and developed a new movement, Caravaggism, emulating the master's style.

Michelangelo Merisi da Caravaggio (c. 1571–1610),
***The Death of the Virgin,* 1601–1605/1606,**
oil on canvas, 369 × 245 cm, Musée du Louvre, Paris

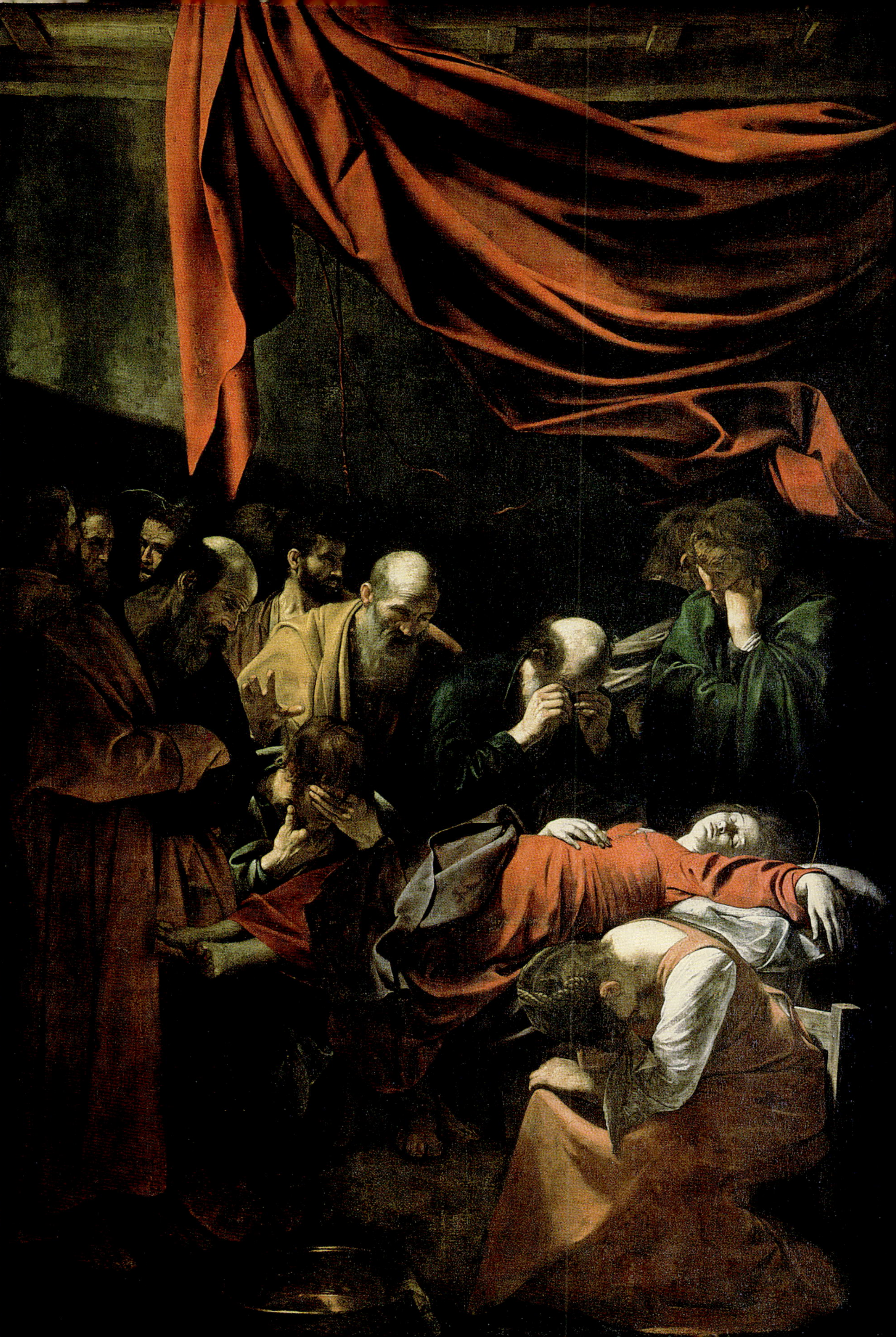

THE CARNAL AND THE SPIRITUAL

Saint Teresa of Avila is famous for the extraordinary physical and emotional ecstasy she experienced in communion with God. It was an experience that many of the faithful longed to share, but that frequently made people uneasy when it was described or depicted.

Did Bernini have a lascivious intent in this sculpture? His Saint Teresa looks as though she is in the middle of an orgasm: her body arched, her bare foot jutting out, her head thrown back, her eyes half closed, her mouth half-open letting slip a sigh. Writing on a visit to Rome in 1739, the French scholar and politician Charles de Brosses set down what many thought: "She is beside herself as the angel approaches her, threatening her teasingly with the spear in his hand, a cheeky smile on his face ... If this is divine love, I know it well." He is not the only writer to have commented on the ambiguous nature of the saint's reaction. The sculpture still provokes debate today, particularly on the Internet. Some people are scandalized by it, others find it amusing. There is a school of thought, however, which holds that it is perfectly plausible that an experience as intense as divine ecstasy should manifest itself in just this form: as an orgasmic mixture of pleasure and pain coursing through the body.

Bernini sees the experience as one verging on the sexual, yet entirely religious. He was very devout and in no way sought to shock but rather to give faithful form to Saint Teresa's own account of her experience: "I saw the angel with a long spear of gold in his hand ... I felt at times as if he were thrusting it deep into my heart, piercing my very entrails ... The pain was so sharp that it made me moan and groan in the way I have described. But such was the sweetness that came with this incomparable agony that my soul could not wish it to end, nor could it content itself with anything other than God. It was not a bodily pain. It was spiritual pain, but one which could not but involve the body to a lesser or even a greater degree" (*Life of Saint Teresa,* 1562–1565). There is nothing sacrilegious about this work, then, even though it still makes some people uncomfortable.

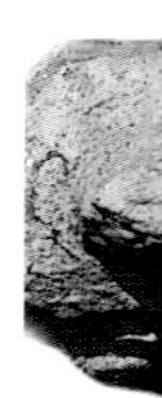

Gian Lorenzo Bernini (1598–1680),
***The Ecstasy of Saint Teresa* (detail), 1647–1652,**
white marble and bronze, 350 cm high, Cornaro Chapel,
Church of Santa Maria della Vittoria, Rome

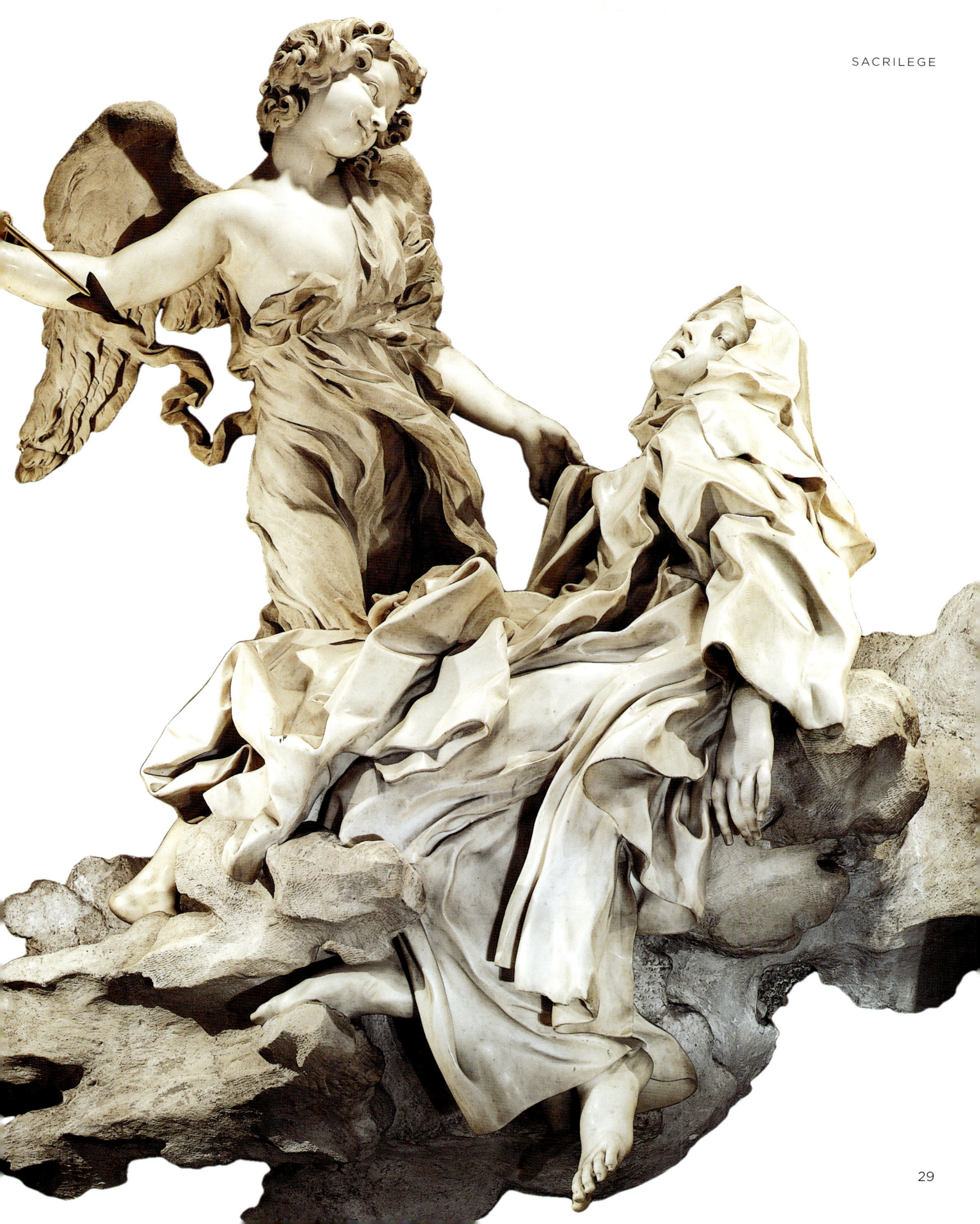

THE POPE, A MAN LIKE ANY OTHER

Velázquez is known for his moving portraits. As court painter to the king of Spain, he painted the royal family decked out in all its finery but endowed with disarming humanity. Unlike most court painters, who liked nothing better than to paint the dignity of state, Velázquez preferred to address the anguish of body and soul. It is this focus that makes his portrait of Pope Innocent X so unsettling.

The painting is suffused with violence. First there is the color, which leaps out immediately: blood red, gold, and a white that is anything but immaculate. Then there is that hard look, bordering on fierceness, that seems to burrow deep into your soul and not let go. Everything contributes to the sense of severity: the mouth with its narrow, pursed lips, the large, straight nose, the curled, claw-like hand. Apparently utterly without mercy and full of menace, this pope is at the mercy of his own body, however. Take away the hard glare of the eyes, and what is left is a slumped being with a drooping face. The strength of his gaze draws attention away from his body, obscuring the harrowing effects of old age and solitude, but behind the ostentatious trappings of ecclesiastical power sits a man like any other. This pope certainly was human, and not so innocent that he did not have a mistress, in the shape of his own brother's widow. She was outraged by the painting, chastising its lack of idealization and its shameless exposure of the pope's humanity. The pope himself chose to accept the work, however, testifying thereby to the piercing clarity of thought so evident in his gaze. On first unveiling the painting, he is said to have exclaimed, "All too true!" Perhaps he chose not to reject it in order to keep it out of public view, to keep it "in the family." Three centuries later, Francis Bacon became obsessed with the image and set about working from a photograph of it. In his painting *Study after Velázquez's Portrait of Pope Innocent X* (1953, Des Moines Art Center, Iowa), the cleric is transformed into a howling pope who looks as if he has been hurled into Hell: the unflinching power of the original portrait clearly did not escape him.

Diego de Silva Velázquez (1599–1660),
***Portrait of Innocent X,* 1650,**
oil on canvas, 140 x 120 cm, Doria-Pamphilj Gallery, Rome

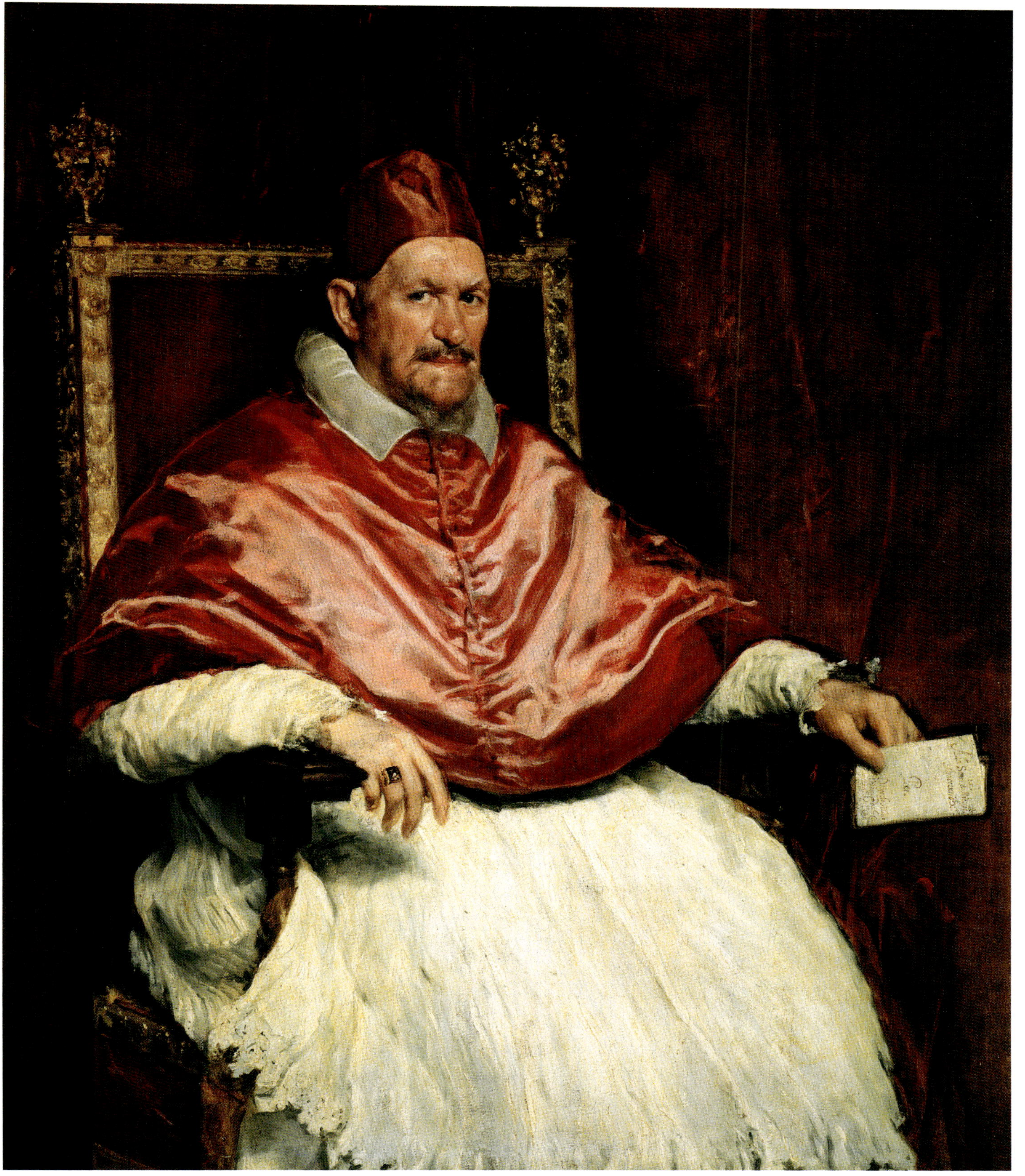

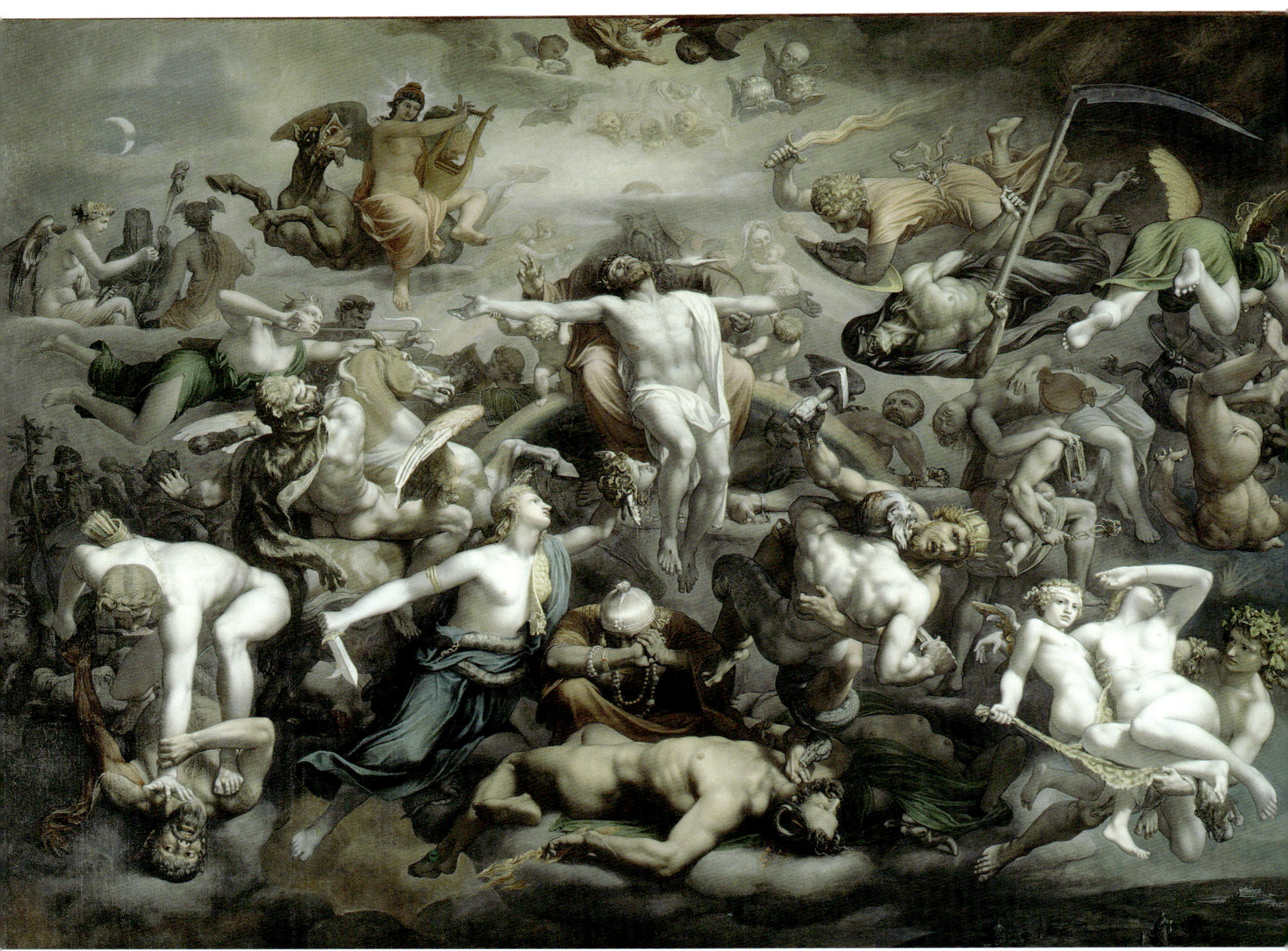

DEATH OF THE GODS

Chenavard was a strange man. Admired more for his skill with words than for the pictures he failed to produce, he was already very well-known when he exhibited his first piece at the Salon of the Académie des Beaux-Arts 1869. The crowds who flocked to see his long-awaited painting did not know what to make of the tangle of bodies that confronted them. Luckily, the exhibition booklet was on hand to explain everything – and give an entirely inaccurate explanation that was the opposite of what the painter intended.

Théophile Gautier's article on the Salon gives a good idea of the fascination Chenavard exerted: "The event of the Salon is Chenavard's *Divina Tragedia*. Chenavard is an artist-philosopher, a painter who does not paint, and there is no suggestion of mockery in this definition." Further on in the article, he discusses the subject of the painting, delivering the Salon line that it is about the death of pagan gods rendered obsolete by the advent Christianity. This may have been a wise move on Gautier's part, but it also exemplifies brilliantly the kind of censorship Chenavard had to accept in order to avoid a repetition of the fiasco of his first attempt at the project, which was to have been a fresco in the Pantheon, a work that was rejected.

Actual inspection of *Divina Tragedia* reveals an emaciated Christ falling back into the arms of God as if newly crucified, while God the Father seems barely present and ready to disappear into the mist that steals over the scene. Death lunges at the Christian Trinity, ready to cut down the already enfeebled group. The putti above are far from frolicking, chuckling, chubby-cheeked cherubs; they are more like skulls and their wings are reminiscent of the bat that attends them.

The picture provoked outrage on two fronts. The general public, on one hand, objected to all the complicated religious symbolism that turned out to be not very Catholic. Chenavard's supporters, on the other, were affronted that the museum should have misrepresented the meaning of the painting in order to make it acceptable.

Paul Chenavard (1807–1895),
***Divina Tragedia*, 1865–1869,**
oil on canvas, 400 x 550 cm, Musée d'Orsay, Paris

"GOVERNMENT-FUNDED BLASPHEMY"

At first sight, there is nothing very scandalous about this photograph. Yet its power to shock and offend has not diminished over the last twenty-five years. It makes little sense on its own, but becomes entirely comprehensible in the light of its title: *Immersion (Piss Christ)* does indeed show a crucifix immersed in urine, and the artist's own at that.

The problems started in 1988 in the United States. Andres Serrano was given a grant paid in large part by the NEA (National Endowment for the Arts), a state organization that gets its funding from the public purse. When *Immersion (Piss Christ)* was included in a touring exhibition that traveled the length and breadth of the country, journalists, curators and Christian fundamentalists joined forces to have the work withdrawn because it vilified Christ. They succeeded in their campaign. Pat Robertson, a television evangelist famous for his dubious theories about the Jewish people, went so far as to call it "government-funded blasphemy" in a television broadcast in 1989. The controversy sparked by this piece helped fuel wider debate about the public funding of art.

So much for its reception in the United States. What about in the rest of the world? In Melbourne *Piss Christ* was attacked with hammers by a group of young protesters when it was on show in a gallery there in 1997, and in Sweden in 2007 another print met a similar fate at the hands of far-right militants linked to the neo-Nazis. The most recent incident of this kind took place in Avignon in April 2011, when *Piss Christ* and another of Serrano's works were attacked with hammers and a "blunt instrument, such as an ice pick or a screwdriver" by two unidentified assailants who managed to flee the scene. *Piss Christ* had previously been the focus of a demonstration by Catholic extremists in the City of Popes, when death threats were sent to museum staff.

Despite these assaults, the American artist claims not to mean any offense by the work and to be a "Christian artist" – so much so, in fact, that, as he is keen to point out, he would dearly like to create a piece for the Vatican!

Andres Serrano (1950–),
Immersion (Piss Christ), 1987,
cibachrome print mounted on Plexiglas and framed in wood,
152.4 x 101.6 cm, courtesy of the artist and the Yvon Lambert
Gallery, Paris

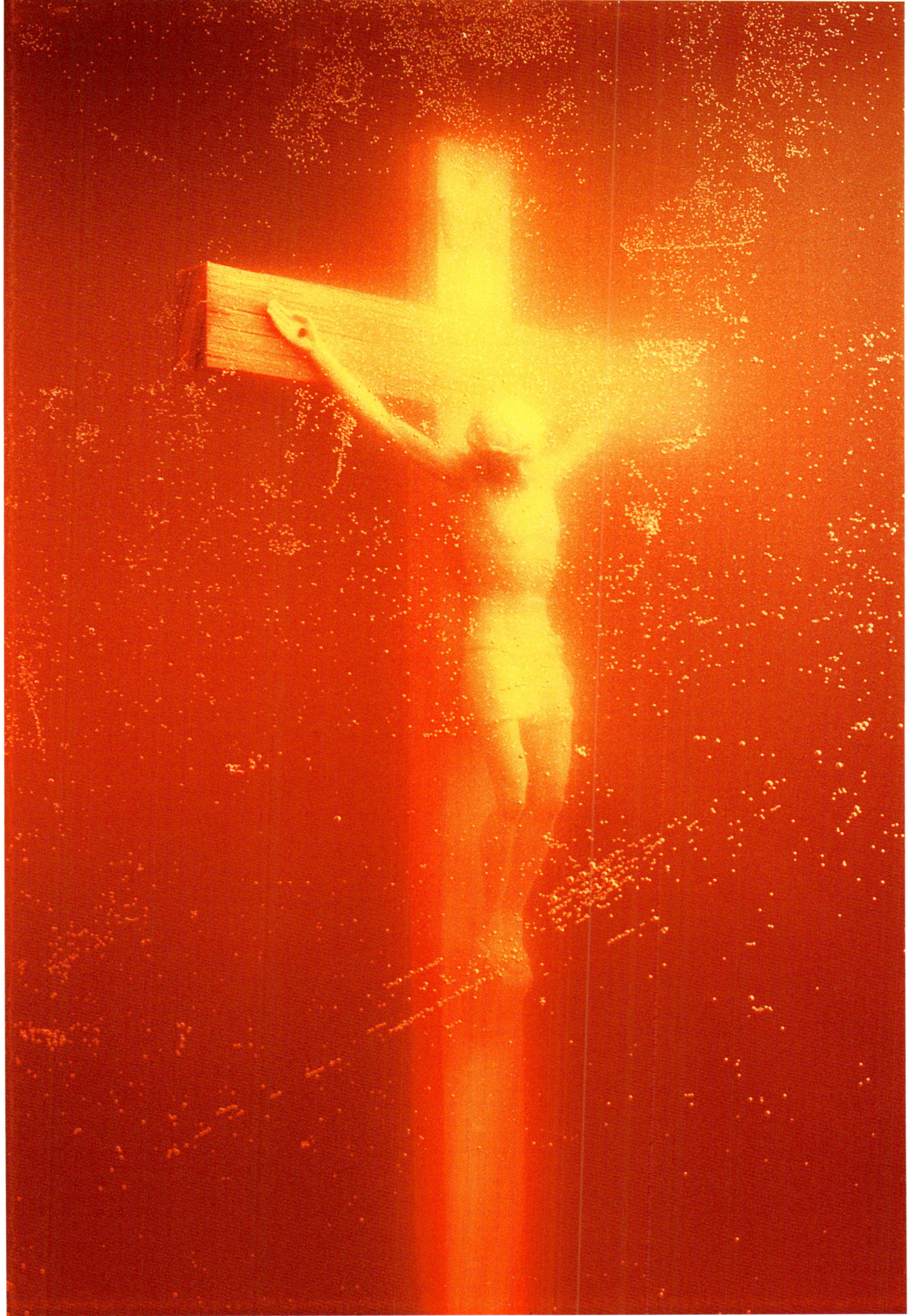

LOVE, DEATH, AND ANTS

In 2010 the National Portrait Gallery in Washington put on an exhibition called *Hide/Seek: Difference and Desire in American Portraiture*, which focused on homosexual portraits. Sadly, the homophobic reviews it prompted came as no surprise. What no one anticipated, however, was that a few minutes of video footage should provoke huge controversy.

In an exhibition that featured works by Robert Mapplethorpe, Marsden Hartley, Thomas Eakins, Andy Warhol, and Annie Leibovitz, it was a video by David Wojnarowicz, entitled *Fire In My Belly*, that caused trouble. The work consists of a series of short sequences designed to convey the pain experienced by someone suffering from AIDS. It was a homage to the love of the artist's life, the photographer Peter Hujar, who died of the disease in 1987. Wojnarowicz himself was infected and died of AIDS in 1992, at the age of thirty-seven.

So what was it that provoked the scandal? Eleven short seconds in a 4-minute video – specially shortened for the purpose – showing a mass of ants swarming over a crucifix. It was intended to symbolize the disease eating away at Peter Hujar. But the Catholic League took it as a deliberately aimed "insult" and reacted immediately with cries of "blasphemy!" Politicians got involved: several of members of Congress weighed in, asserting that it was a mis-use of tax payers' money, even when, in fact, exhibitions at the National Portrait Gallery are not funded through taxation.

Staff at the museum and its parent body, the Smithsonian Institution, issued a statement saying that they "took heed of public reaction to the work" and had no desire to offend anybody. The work was consequently withdrawn from the exhibition and the hallowed halls of the Smithsonian.

In January 2011 the director of the Museum of Modern Art in New York made a clear stand when he announced that the venerable New York institution had acquired both the 7- and the 13-minute versions of the video, the thirteenth piece by Wojnarowicz to enter its collection.

David Wojnarowicz (1954–1992),
Fire In My Belly,
1986–1987,
video, 7- and 13-minute version

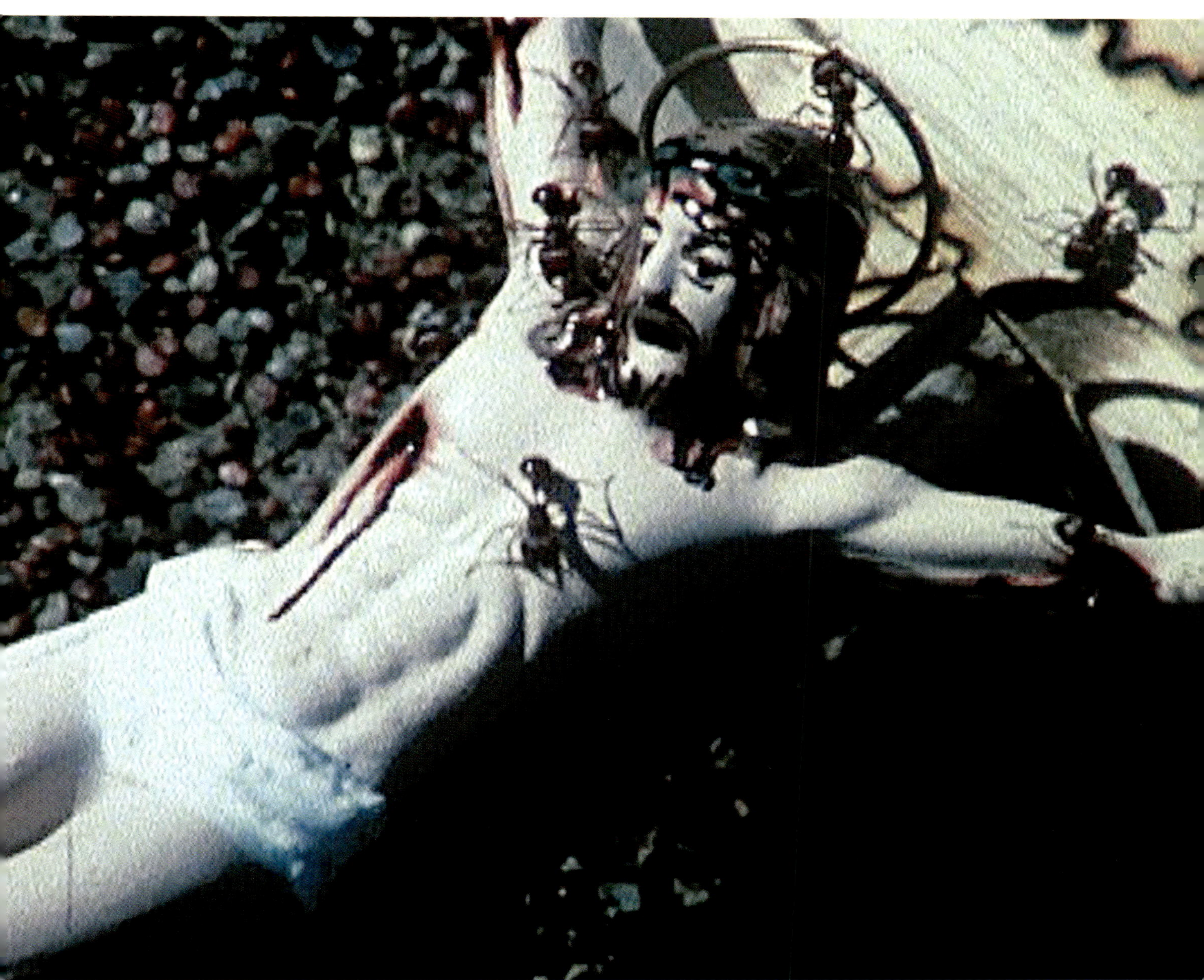

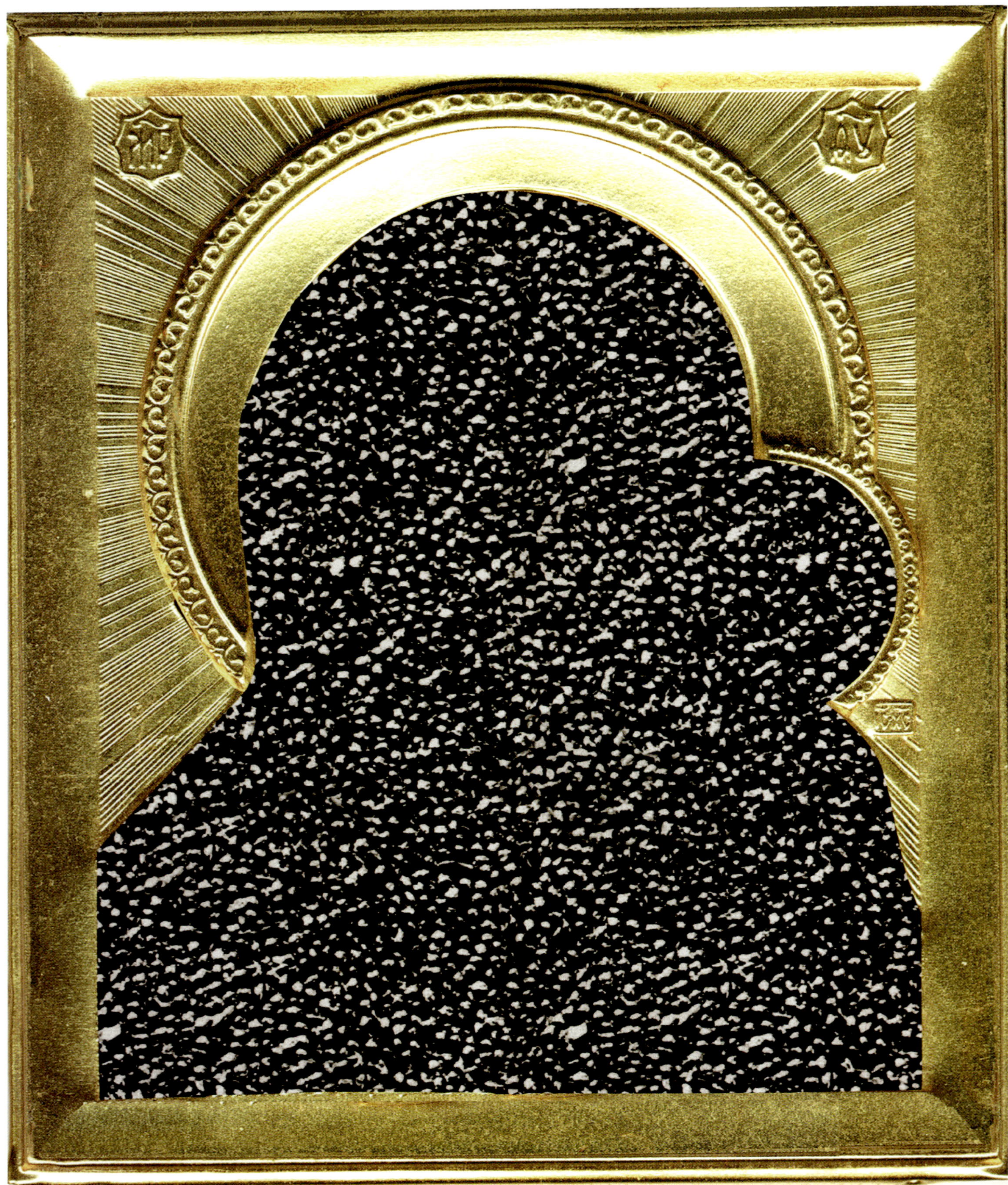

THE ORTHODOX CHURCH PUTS THE LID ON CAVIAR

In March 2007, the Andrei Sakharov Museum in Moscow put on an exhibition called *Forbidden Art 2006.* It included 24 works by Russian artists censored by the authorities in 2005–2006, and was immediately condemned by the extreme Orthodox Church as "anti-Christian."

The works were deliberately displayed so that they were difficult to see: discreetly hidden behind false walls, visible only through pinholes 1.80 m (5 feet 11 inches) above floor level. One of the pieces that attracted most criticism was Alexander Savich's *Mickey Mouse Journeys Through Art History,* in which the famous cartoon mouse finds his way into a religious painting. Another was Alexander Kosolapov's *Icon Caviar*, an icon painting of the Virgin Mary entirely covered in sturgeon's roe, emblematic of gaudy luxury in one section of Russian society. Like most of the artists in the show, Kosolapov belonged to Sots Art, a satirical political art movement born in the 1970s and a sort of Soviet derivative of Pop Art. Its members were consciously nonconformist and constantly attracted the wrath of the censors.

Outraged by what they took to be yet another piece of provocation, extreme Orthodox and nationalist groups joined together to make a complaint about the organizers of the exhibition and even to urge that they be put on trial. And astonishingly they were successful in their campaign and the trial opened in Moscow on 5 May 2009. In July 2010, Andrei Erofeiev, who had organized the exhibition, and Yuri Samodurov, former director of the Andrei Sakharov Museum, were found guilty of incitement to hatred. They were fined 9,000 euros and only narrowly escaped the obviously disproportionate three years' imprisonment initially called for by the prosecution. How can such an absurd trial possibly have gone ahead, in the face of considerable protest from the international community? The answer is perhaps that where a fragile state is dependent on the support of a strong Church, it must secure that support at any price, even the right to freedom of expression.

Alexander Kosolapov (1943–),
***Icon Caviar,* 1995–2005,**
print on canvas, 142 × 120 cm, collection of the
Tsukanov Family Foundation, London

A BLOW FOR ARTISTIC FREEDOM

Although he was ill, Pope John Paul II was still at the head of the Vatican in 1999. Cattelan, however, had no qualms about showing him on the ground, his back broken, struck down by a meteorite. The outcry his provocative piece caused helped make it one the most famous and highly prized of the Italian artist's works.

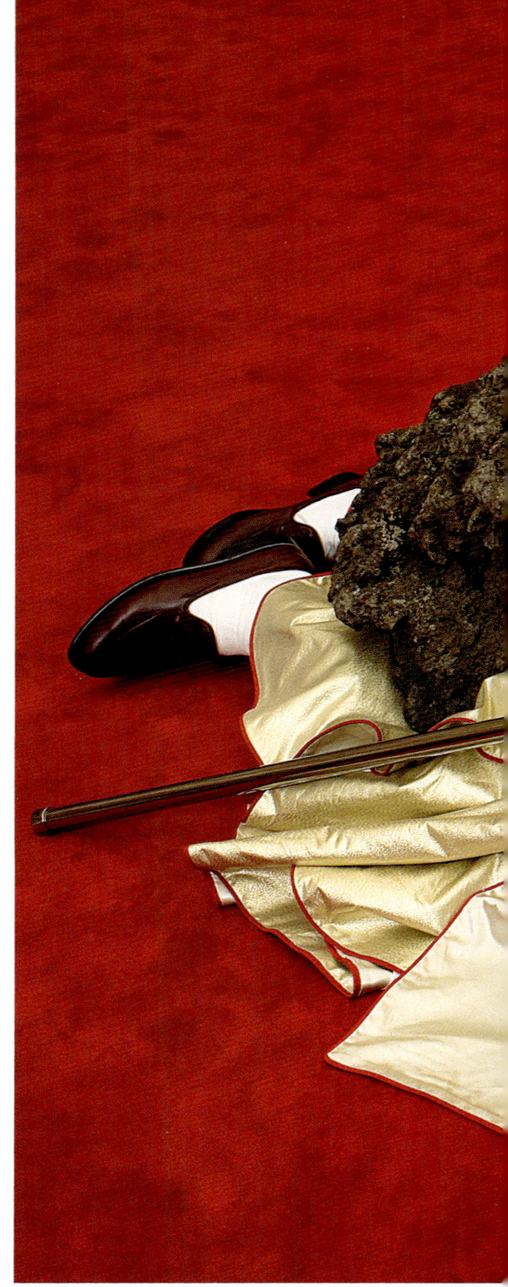

Poor pope! What can the real pope have felt on seeing himself struck down by a bolt from the blue? There is a cruel irony here. This perfect likeness of Karol Wojtyla, otherwise known as John Paul II, was the work of a troublemaker of an artist, and this hyperrealist provocation was not his first. In this particular case, however, the reaction it provoked went beyond simple displeasure to physical hostility. The piece prompted several critical responses in Warsaw in 2000. A television host known for his conservative ideas was one of the first to respond, by covering the pope with a sheet. He was followed by two extremist nationalist politicians, who took it into their heads to take away the meteorite and stand the holy father upright. They only made the pontiff's situation worse, poor thing, because he was parted from his legs in the process.

Following these two episodes and complaints from dozens of Polish members of parliament, the director of the Zacheta Gallery was forced to resign.

Why should an installation featuring a wax figure of the kind that can be seen in every waxwork museum the world over prompt such a violent reaction? Believers were appalled to see the pope suffer under the weight of sorrow, like an ordinary human being. It made him look feeble, weakened – unfit, finally, to fulfill his onerous office.

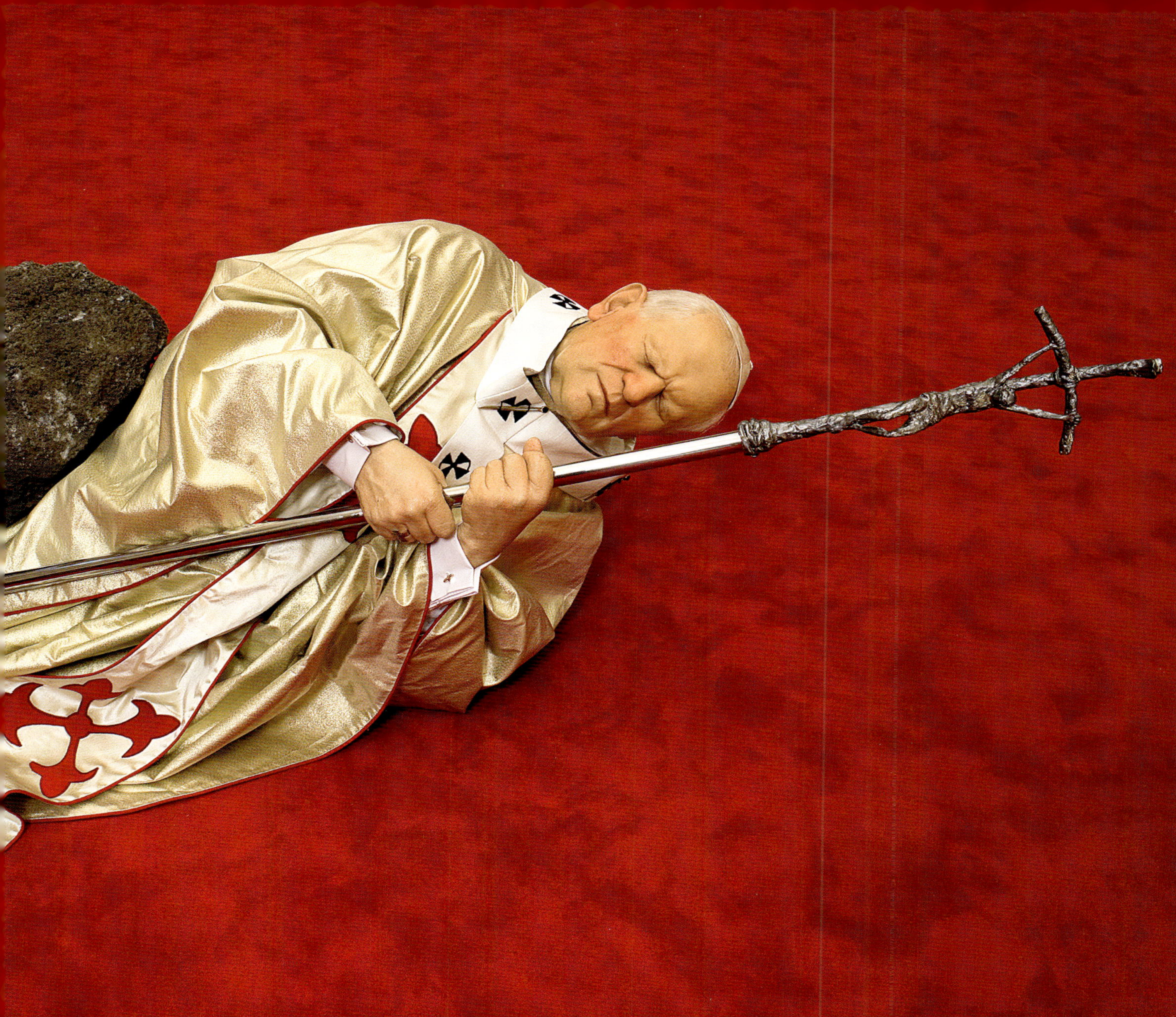

For all that, the outcry did nothing to lessen Cattelan's stock: on the contrary, the piece went up and up in price. He clearly recognized the value attached to scandal in the contemporary art market and understood that using provocation as a key element is a sure way to ensure extraordinary success.

Maurizio Cattelan, *La Nona Ora,* **1999,**
polyester resin, human hair, fabric, clothes, accessories, stone, carpet, dimensions vary, view of the exhibition entitled *Contro le idéologie* held from 24 September to 24 October 2010 at the Palazzo Reale (Sala de le Cariatidi), Milan, photograph by Zeno Zotti, courtesy of Maurizio Cattelan archive

A NEW BROOM

Mounir fatmi is used to seeing his works banned. He has had his work censored several times in recent years, notably in France and Dubai, and has been forced either to withdraw or alter it.

The subversive Tangerian artist who claims he is "never profane" has sparked controversy on several occasions recently. In September 2012, he provoked the wrath of Muslims in Toulouse with his video installation *Technologia.* The installation caused incidents when people began walking on the images of texts from the Koran projected onto the ground. One woman was even slapped in the face by an incensed fundamentalist when she failed to walk round the video images. The piece was immediately removed. Shortly afterwards, a second video, showing Salman Rushdie asleep and entitled *Sleep–Al Naim,* was withdrawn from the *Twenty-Five Years of Arab Creativity* exhibition at the Institut du Monde Arabe in Paris.

At the contemporary art fair Art Dubai in March 2011 he showed *Lost Springs,* a row of 22 flags, those of the Arab League, hung from a wall; two of them,

those of Tunisia and Egypt, whose governments were swept from power by the people in 2011 during the so-called Arab Spring, have brooms stood under them, a clear reference to the fall of Zine El Abidine Ben Ali and Hosni Mubarak. The piece suggests that other governments will soon follow suit and be swept away in turn. It was a suggestion that seriously displeased the fair's censorship committee. After extensive discussion with the gallery representing mounir fatmi, they finally agreed that it could remain on show if the brooms were removed. What people got to see for several days, then, was a truncated, incomplete and therefore meaningless piece. In his manifesto, mounir fatmi stated that he wanted a "transparent flag" and he fully understood where the problems with his piece lay: "The installation suggests an evolving process, and this is probably what the organizers did not like."

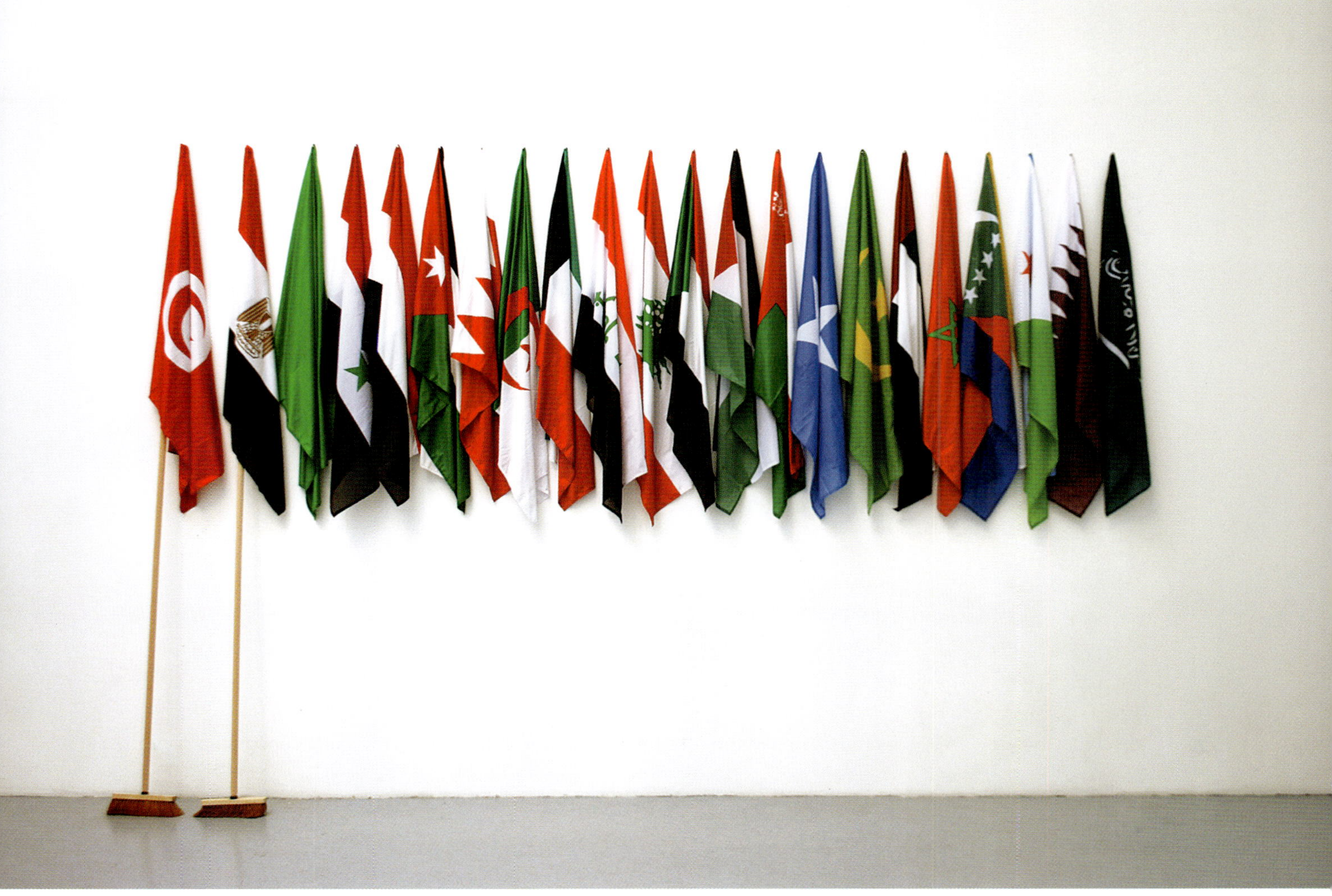

mounir fatmi (1970–), *Lost Springs,* **April 2011,**
two 3-meter high brooms, 22 Arab League flags,
Hussenot Gallery, Paris

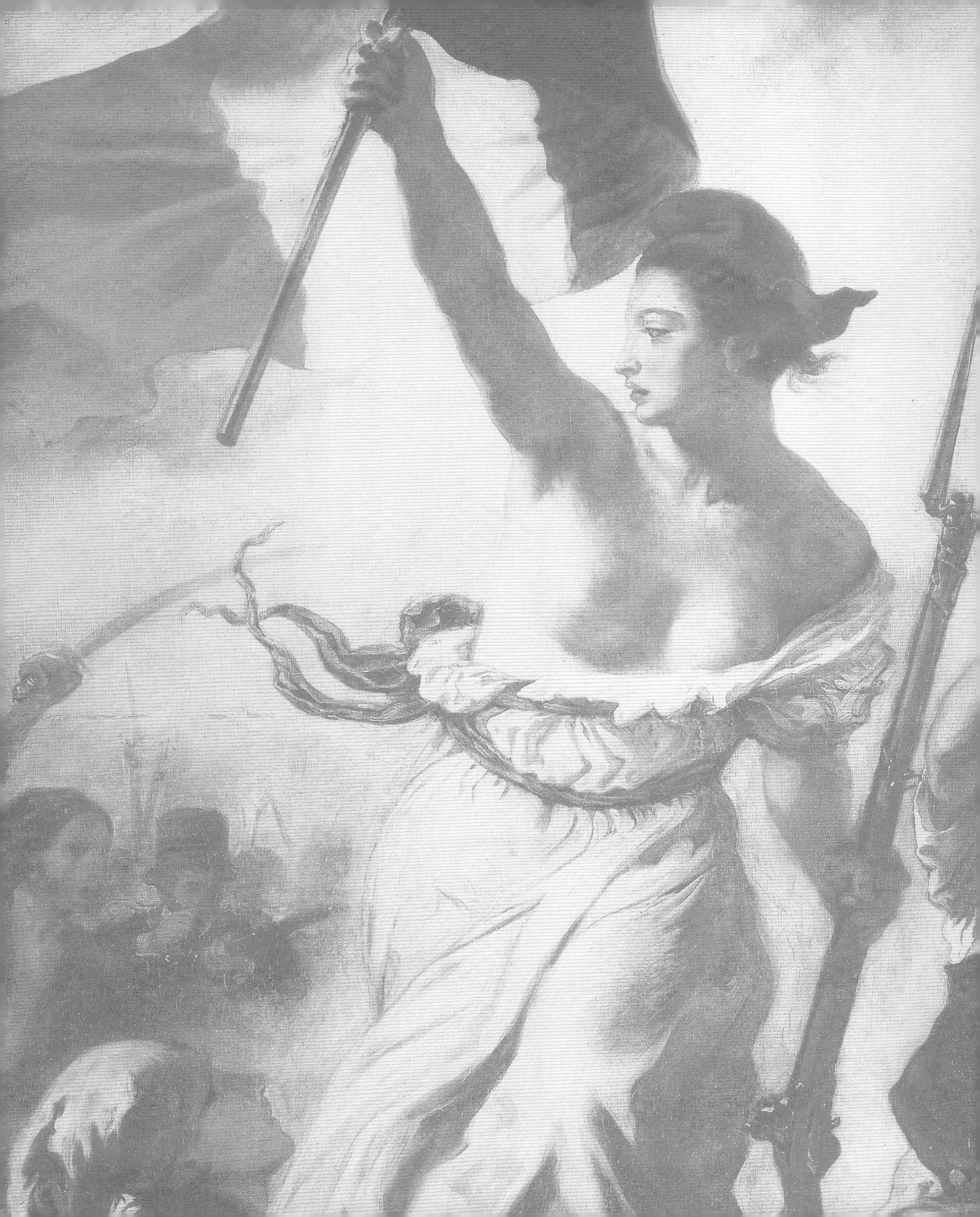

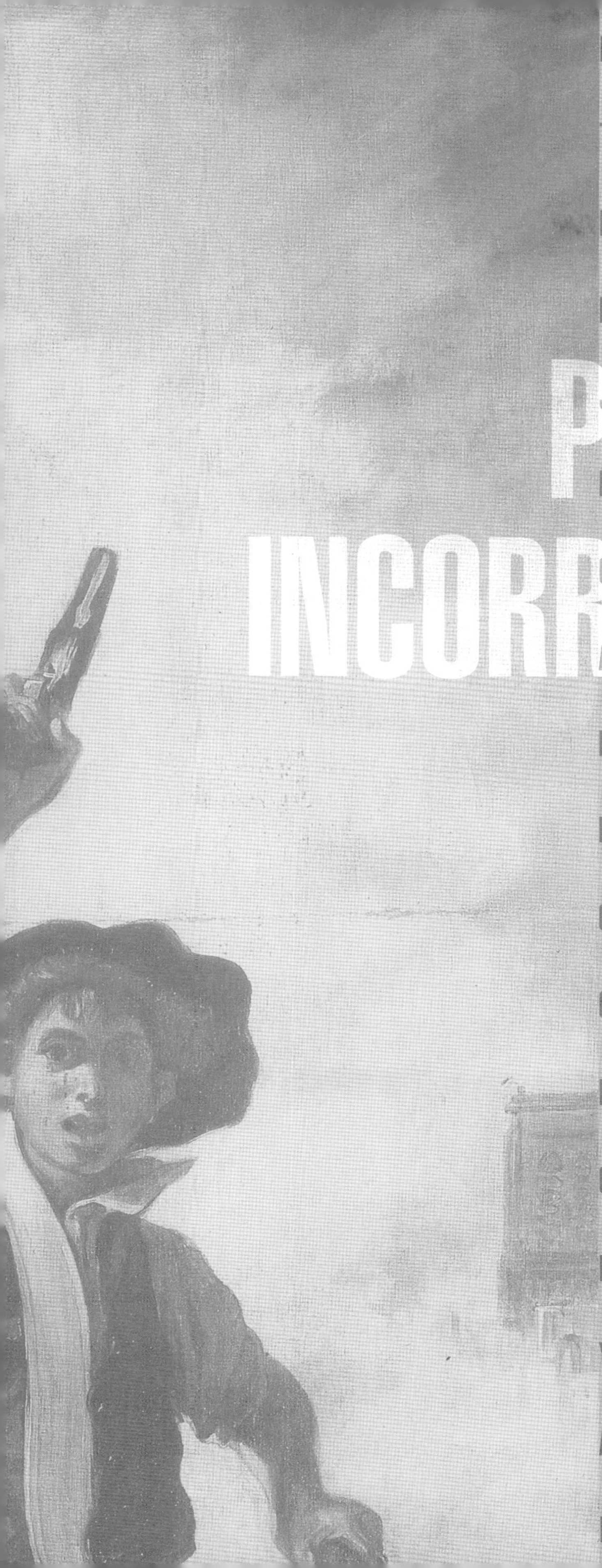

POLITICAL INCORRECTNESS

FRANCISCO GOYA

THÉODORE GÉRICAULT

EUGÈNE DELACROIX

HONORÉ DAUMIER

JEAN-FRANÇOIS MILLET

ÉDOUARD MANET

GUSTAVE CAILLEBOTTE

AUGUSTE RODIN

KAZIMIR MALEVICH

ERNST LUDWIG KIRCHNER

CHRISTOPHER RICHARD WYNNE NEVINSON

OTTO DIX

MARC CHAGALL

GENPEI AKASEGAWA

MAURIZIO CATTELAN

YINKA SHONIBARE MBE

AI WEIWEI

BLU

Artists need patrons and the state has long played this role to perfection. For centuries, art depended almost entirely on the munificence of those in power; who, in turn, derived tangible benefit from art by appropriating art for their own purposes, commissioning aggrandizing portraits or paintings celebrating their achievements or power. Politics and art do not always make easy bedfellows, however, and relations between them are often poisoned by mistrust or even contempt.

Consciously or not, artists inevitably communicate a way of looking at the world, creating images that are often universally easy to understand but that can nevertheless carry another message. Works of art can become political tools for they reflect the prejudices and hopes, the hidden desires and fears of their time.

As greater realism gradually crept into art over the centuries, it sent ripples of alarm through those in power, for this development increased the importance and influence of the artist. It was because it did so that the bourgeoisie in the nineteenth century responded with such dismay to works by artists trying to convey a more accurate picture of the world. They could allow an uncompromising picture of war if it involved some distant, exotic culture; they could not if it was set in their own country. By the same token, it seems, Delacroix's turbaned men slaughtering beautiful brown tawny-skinned women (*The Massacre at Chios,* 1824) were acceptable, while Nevinson's ghastly vision of the trenches in the First World War was not.

Authorities usually justify imposing censorship by claiming that it is "for the common good." For several decades, however, countries that clamp down on artistic freedom have been severely criticized by international bodies that campaign for freedom and human rights. But where it was once more generally the province of the state, censorship now tends to be the concern of small groups of private individuals who take it upon themselves to decide what can and cannot enter the public realm. Religious and family groups take a keen interest in what is happening in art, ready to complain at the slightest departure from what they perceive as acceptable or decent.

Sadly, there are still a number of authoritarian regimes in which artists are censored the moment they depart from the norms imposed on them by the state. These include Russia, where whole groups of artists are banned, and China, home to an indomitable few who persist in their artistic resistance in the face of repeated intimidation. It is not easy to be a dissident artist in a country where the government has no qualms about inflicting harsh punishment on anyone who fails to conform. On the other hand, a benevolent state can be inhibiting in its own way: it can encourage artists to slip into a cozy, risk-free life that is hardly conducive to real creativity.

A BITTER PILL

It was not always easy being a man of the court and an artist at the same time in Spain at the end of the eighteenth century, especially if, like Goya, your natural bent was to satirize, and it was one you found hard to curb.

From 1797 to 1799, Francisco Goya produced a group of eighty bitingly ironic prints depicting Spanish society. Significantly, Goya chose not to sell these through the usual channels of distribution of the day (by subscription, for instance). He opted instead to offer them for sale in the pharmacy on the ground floor of the house in which he lived in the aptly called Calle del Desengaño (Disenchantment Street) in Madrid, and it was there, among the bottles and pomades, the perfumes, sweets and multi-colored powders that the public were invited to buy *Los Caprichos*. Why did Goya elect to adopt such an usual sales approach? The most likely answer is that he wanted to be able to oversee their distribution himself and so be in a position to deal promptly with the scandal he expected. And he was probably right. When he put an advertisement in the local paper announcing the sale of *Los Caprichos*, he did not have to wait long for buyers to respond. Twenty-seven of the three hundred sets of prints he produced sold within a few days. Controversy erupted soon after. Beneath the apparently fantastical surface of the prints, critics quickly detected a barely veiled satire of Spanish society. Wary of the Inquisition, Goya quickly withdrew the prints from sale.

But what was it that people saw in the prints that so upset them? With his sharp powers of observation and his surreal imagination, in this series Goya brilliantly exposed the vices of his day and his country. He exposes the obscurantism of the Church, the corruption of those in power and office, as well as the failings of the ordinary people, in a series of prints by turn critical, enigmatic, and sometimes fantastical, peopled not only by beggars, prostitutes, drunkards and lechers, but also by ecclesiastics, lovers, hags, and gluttons.

In 1803 Goya gave the copper plates and 240 unsold sets of prints of *Los Caprichos* to the King of Spain, Charles IV, thereby securing his protection.

Francisco Goya (1746–1828), *Los Caprichos*, plate 23, "Aquellos polbos" (Those specks of dust), 1799,
etching, aquatint, drypoint and burin, 21.9 x 15 cm,
private collection

A prisoner in a tall pointed hat listens to a member of the Church deliver his sentence. The title alludes to the popular saying "Aquellos polbos ... trajeron estos lodos" (These specks of dust brought this mud along with them). The Inquisition fe t targeted by the inscription.

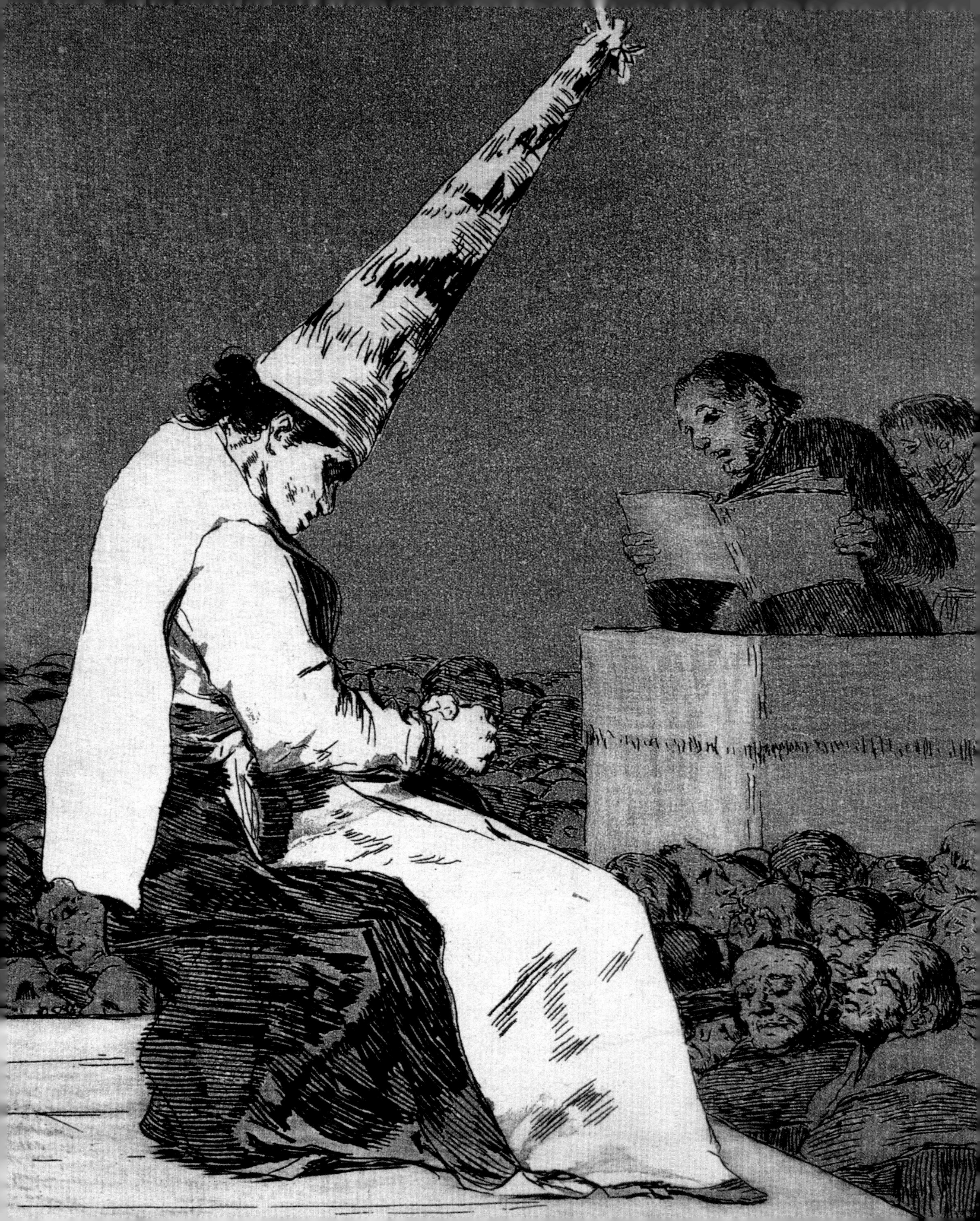

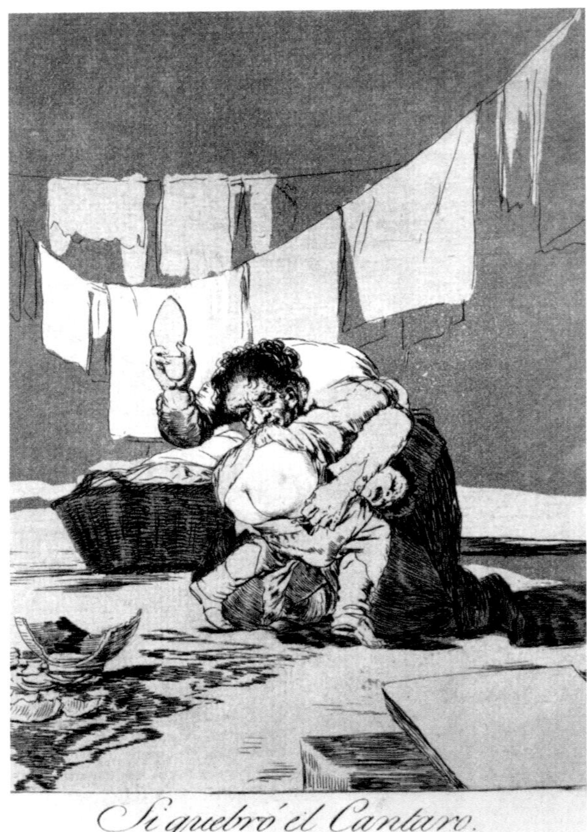

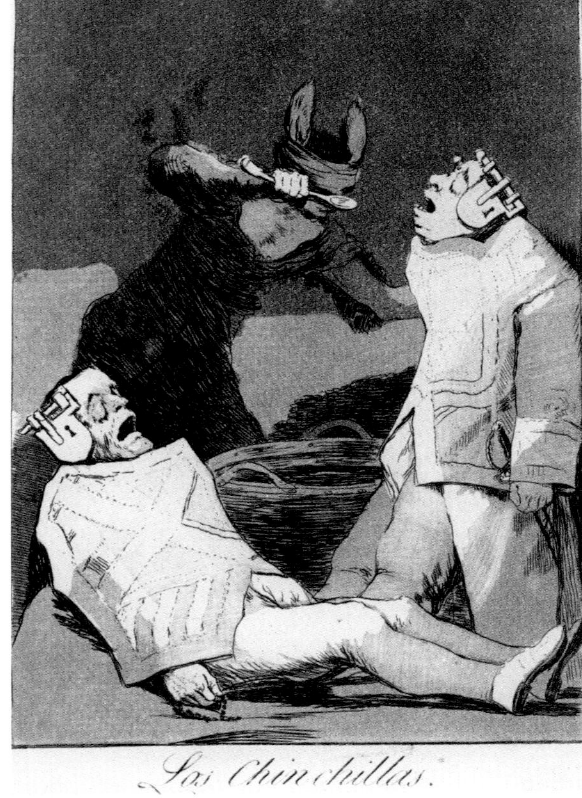

Francisco Goya (1746–1828), *Los Caprichos*, **plate 25,**
"Si quebró el cántaro" (Yes, he broke the pitcher), 1799,
etching, aquatint, drypoint and burin, 20.9 x 15.2 cm,
private collection
The violent mother with her bestial features exposes
the violence to which children were often exposed.

Francisco Goya (1746–1828), *Los Caprichos*, **plate 50,**
"Los Chinchillas" (The Chinchillas), 1799,
etching, aquatint, drypoint and burin, 20.9 x 15.2 cm,
private collection
Two noblemen are spoon-fed by a man with the head of an ass.
They allow themselves to be stuffed like chinchillas. The padlocks
on the sides of their heads symbolize their closed minds.

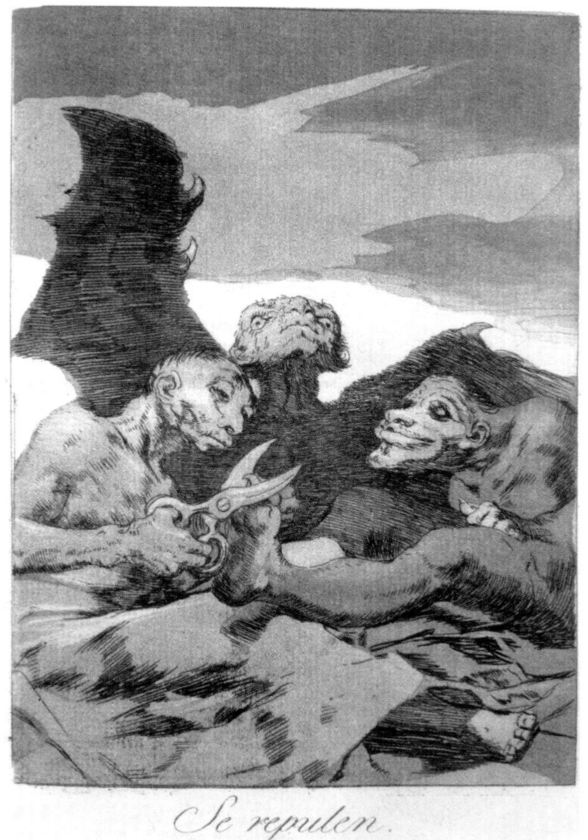

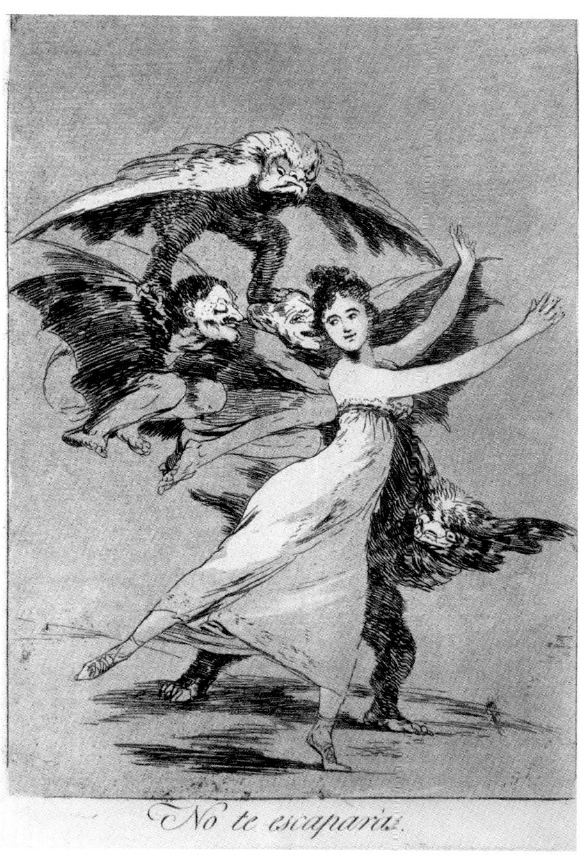

Francisco Goya (1746–1828), *Los Caprichos,* **plate 51,**
"Se repulen" (They spruce themselves up), 1799,
etching, aquatint, drypoint and burin, 21.4 x 14.9 cm,
private collection
A warlock cuts another's talon-like nails, screened by the wing
of a third phantasmagorical creature, as if they hope to get away
without being seen. Goya is probably making a reference here
to the legend that witches could be identified by their big claws,
exposing what he called "harmful common beliefs."

Francisco de Goya (1746–1828), *Los Caprichos,* **plate 72,**
"No te escaparàs" (You will not escape), 1799,
etching, aquatint, drypoint and burin, 21.7 x 15.2 cm,
private collection
This young girl is chased by lecherous monsters. It was intended
perhaps as a warning against the pleasures of the flesh, or as
a denunciation of marriages of convenience.

A PAINTING THAT MADE WAVES

Théodore Géricault made a practice of taking inspiration for his paintings from items in the news and caused a considerable stir when he chose to portray the terrible story of the raft of *The Medusa*. People with uneasy consciences read his depiction of the distress of the victims of the shipwreck as a veiled criticism of the abuse of power, negligence, and racism, and felt the picture was aimed at them.

In July 1816 the French frigate *The Medusa* sank off the coast of Africa and everyone had to abandon ship. There were not enough lifeboats, however, and one hundred and fifty members of the crew had to pile onto a makeshift raft. The poor victims of the shipwreck had to endure a living hell for seventeen days; only fifteen came out of the ordeal alive.

Géricault chose to depict the moment when the survivors see the boat that has come to rescue them. They mass into a human pyramid on top of the bodies of the dead. The topmost figure waving a flag of hope is black. The picture was exhibited at the Salon of 1831, some twenty-nine years after the abolition of slavery in France. Géricault made his stand on the subject clear by having the composition dominated by a Tahitian (there were three on board when *The Medusa* sank). The main cause of controversy, however, was the violence of the painting. While the drawing and modeling of the figures may have followed classical tradition, the subject matter and its treatment were disturbingly innovative and crude, with no hint of redeeming heroism to justify the horror. The bodies of the dead and living are intertwined, hinting at the cannibalism to which the survivors resorted. To capture the quality of dead flesh, Géricault worked from real cadavers and was inevitably harshly criticized for this hideous

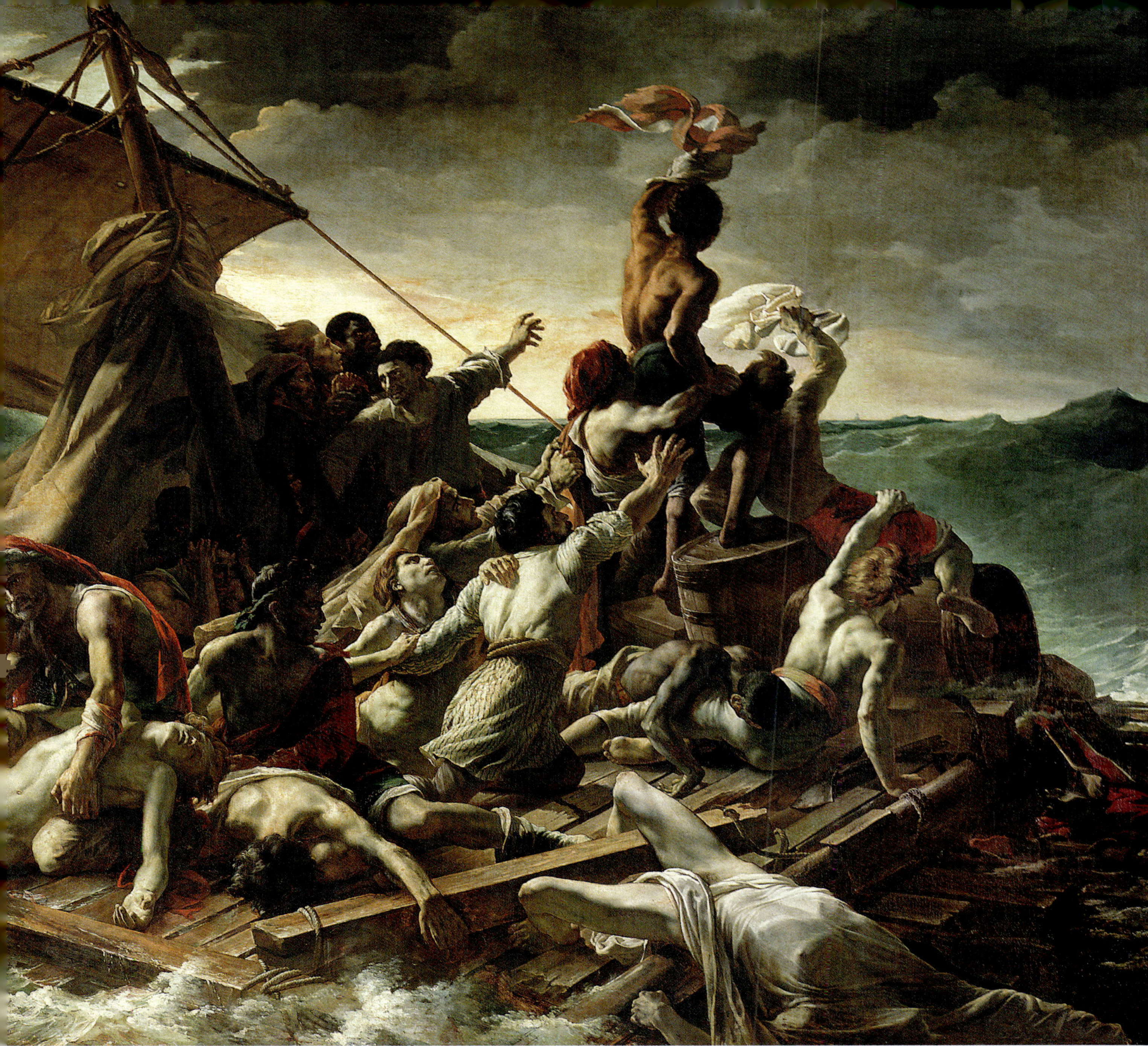

pursuit of realism. People began to ask if it was really necessary to display such atrocity in a public place, all the more because they could detect in it an element of censure – of the government for its negligence, and of the rich and powerful for monopolizing all the life-boats. There was nothing here that the newspapers had not already reported, but people were apparently simply not ready to see the event depicted in all its sordid detail in a work of art.

Théodore Géricault (1791–1824), *The Raft of the Medusa*, **1819,**
oil on canvas, 491 x 716 cm, Musée du Louvre, Paris

TO THE BARRICADES!

The nineteenth century was a time of political upheaval, and it is difficult to say where precisely Delacroix's political sympathies lay. He certainly had liberal leanings, but could hardly be called a revolutionary. Yet this is the reputation he acquired through his highly controversial painting *Liberty Leading the People*.

If Delacroix expressed hostility in this painting, it was primarily aimed at academicism. Instead of adhering to strict rules of drawing and composition, he preferred to give his Romantic fervor full rein through color and spontaneity. It earned him an enduring reputation as a rebellious, even seditious, artist, in spite of the fact that he exhibited regularly in the Salons with obvious success. He undoubtedly had some sympathy for the values of the Revolution, which come through loud and clear in this painting. It is easy to imagine the fury this revolutionary allegory provoked in viewers barely recovered from the political upheavals of their day when they were confronted with it in the Salon of 1831. The bourgeoisie did not want to be reminded of the events of the all too recent past: the Phrygian cap on the woman's head, the stripped corpses, the smoke, the violence – all sent shudders down their spines. If that was not bad enough, people saw the choice of subject and its treatment as tantamount to an incitement to riot. The combination of the surly looking man of the people, the bourgeois figure in rumpled clothes, the pistol-wielding young boy, and the robust, immodest figure of Liberty were deeply disturbing to the staid visitors to the Salon.

The picture became a matter of state, with the king, Louis-Philippe, endeavoring to calm people down and suppress scandal at all costs. The painting had been intended to hang in the throne room, but there was no longer any question of that. It hung for a while in the Palace museum where it won admiration from some but continued nevertheless to provoke debate. It was therefore removed and placed in store before eventually being returned to Delacroix. History was to have the last laugh, however: the painting that critics wanted to relegate to outer darkness is now considered a key work in French culture.

Eugène Delacroix (1798–1863),
***Liberty Leading the People (28 July 1830)*, 1830,**
oil on canvas, 260 x 325 cm, Musée du Louvre, Paris

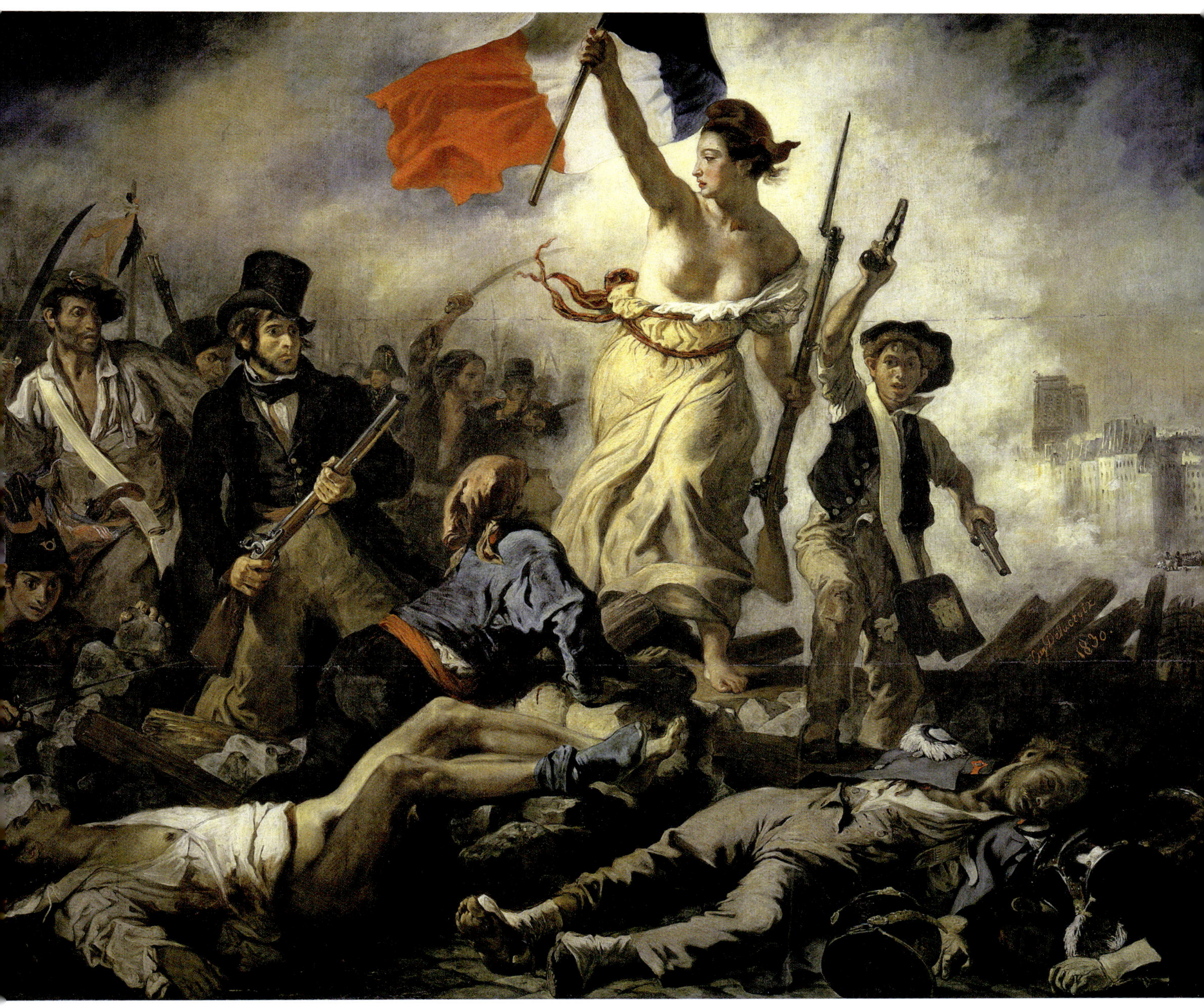

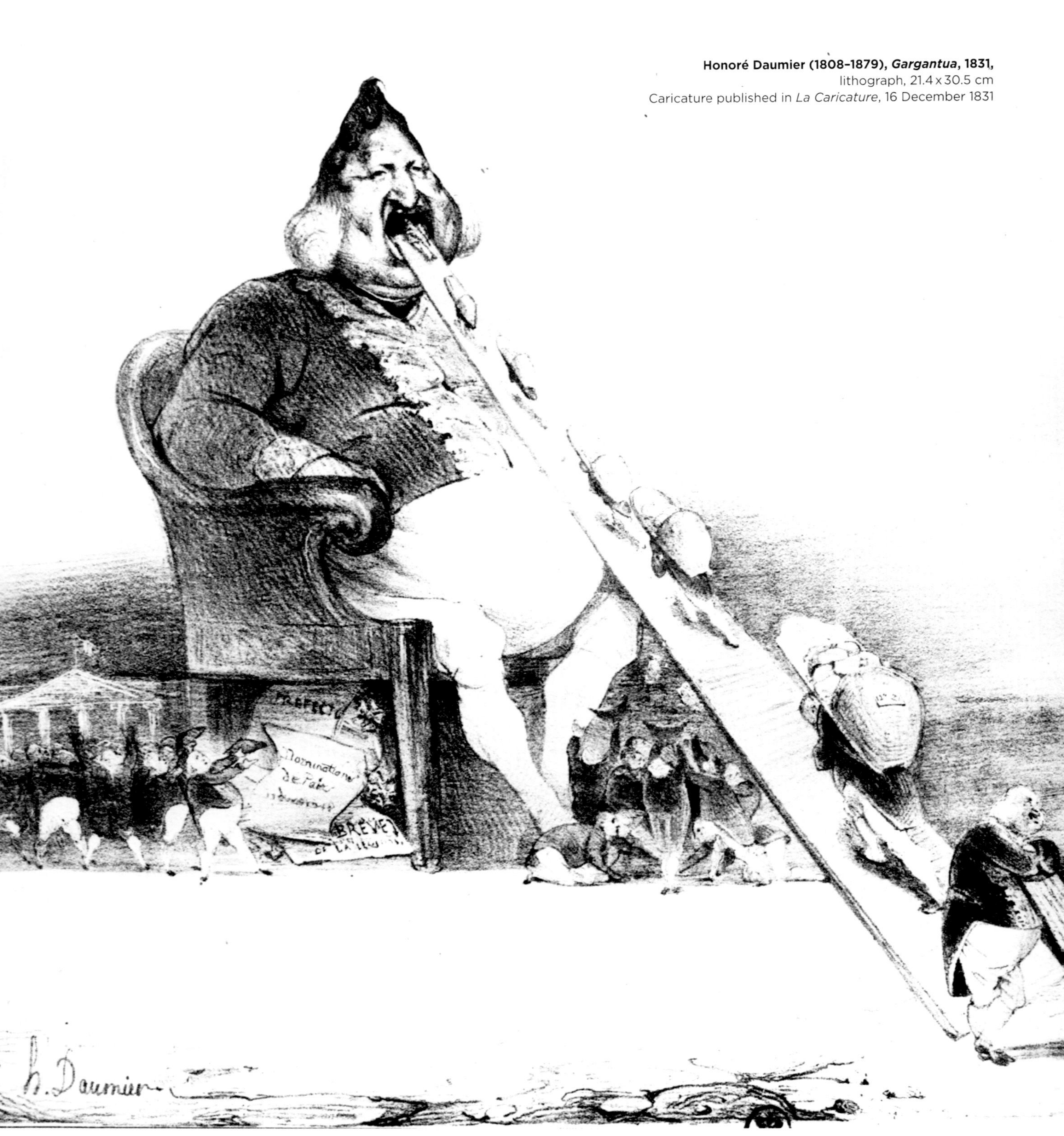

Honoré Daumier (1808–1879), *Gargantua*, 1831,
lithograph, 21.4 x 30.5 cm
Caricature published in *La Caricature*, 16 December 1831

GOING PEAR SHAPED

Honoré Daumier was famous in the nineteenth century for causing trouble with his scathing caricatures. He meted out judgment fearlessly, sparing no one, least of all the great. His own origins were modest and he accused those in power of squeezing the people dry. He even refused the Legion of Honor.

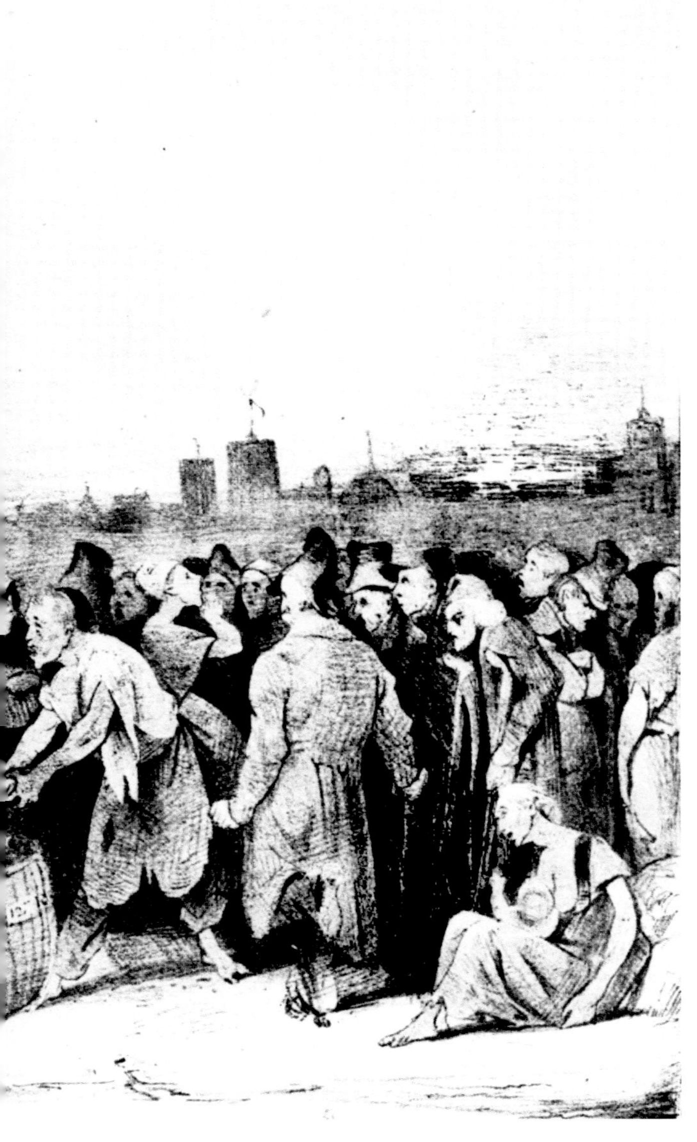

Daumier revealed a talent for drawing as a child. He later trained as an artist, avidly copying the works of great painters and sculptors. His own inclinations led him towards a different sort of art, however. The caricaturist Charles Philipon took him under his wing. It was Philipon who first lit upon the idea of turning King Louis Philippe's face into a pear, and, inspired by him, Daumier found fame with *Gargantua.* This shows a bloated king greedily swallowing up all the money of the emaciated, poverty-stricken people. The digested gold is discharged from under his chair in the form of decorations and appointments, which go only to the richest, who are all podgy like him. For this flagrant insult, Daumier was given a six-month prison sentence and a fine. Humor was not enough to keep him safe from censorship and he was gagged by an act of 1831, prohibited from publishing his prints. He refused to admit defeat, however, and was quick to develop new skills to meet the circumstances, turning his caricatures into sculptures, painting, and illustrations for the works of Balzac, whose social criticism chimed perfectly with his own. Such were the political ups and downs of that turbulent century that Daumier was able eventually to return to drawing caricatures. While many people were undoubtedly angered by his work, Daumier also had many supporters, including Charles Baudelaire, who praised the artist's ability to speak directly to viewers.

A GENTLE REVOLUTION

The early part of Millet's career was uneventful. With the revolution of 1848 and the renewed victory it brought the people, however, the focus of his work changed: rural scenes became such a dominant feature of his work that he was nicknamed the "peasant painter." While we may see nothing untoward in these peaceful country scenes, Millet's contemporaries sensed the shadow of revolution playing over them.

Millet had begun to make a name for himself before he caused a stir, and first exhibited at the Salon of 1840. He grew up in the country, which he readily depicted in all its bucolic, and unreal, charm. Everyone liked the inoffensive view he conjured up images, which were perfectly in tune with a still prevalent neo-classical taste for tender naiads and refined shepherds. When he decided to adopt a more realistic approach, however, his admirers took fright. His paintings seem to offer an incarnation of social history, reminding the public of the uprising of 1848 and the misery of the country people who marched on the towns during the Second Empire. There is extraordinary gentleness in his paintings, however. But he proceeded cautiously. There is no direct criticism in the work somewhat evasively called *The Gleaners*. The color is not dazzling, the gestures seem heavy, made more ponderous by the warm light of the sun. At first sight it is as if we have stumbled onto a scene of everyday rural life, but there is nothing chance about this painting. The drawing and the composition are so masterfully controlled that they are all but invisible behind the impression of peaceful equilibrium they create. The solemnity of this picture lends dignity to the women. Indistinguishable from each other in their poor clothes and physical attitudes, they seem to stand for all workers forced to break their backs to make the bourgeoisie richer, and so convey a vague and faceless sense of menace. Millet may have troubled people in his lifetime, but he was appreciated and celebrated after his death. His work evokes a nostalgic memory of an ancestral countryside before the destruction wrought by industrialization.

Jean-François Millet (1814–1875), *The Gleaners*, 1857, oil on canvas, 83.6 x 111 cm, Musée d'Orsay, Paris

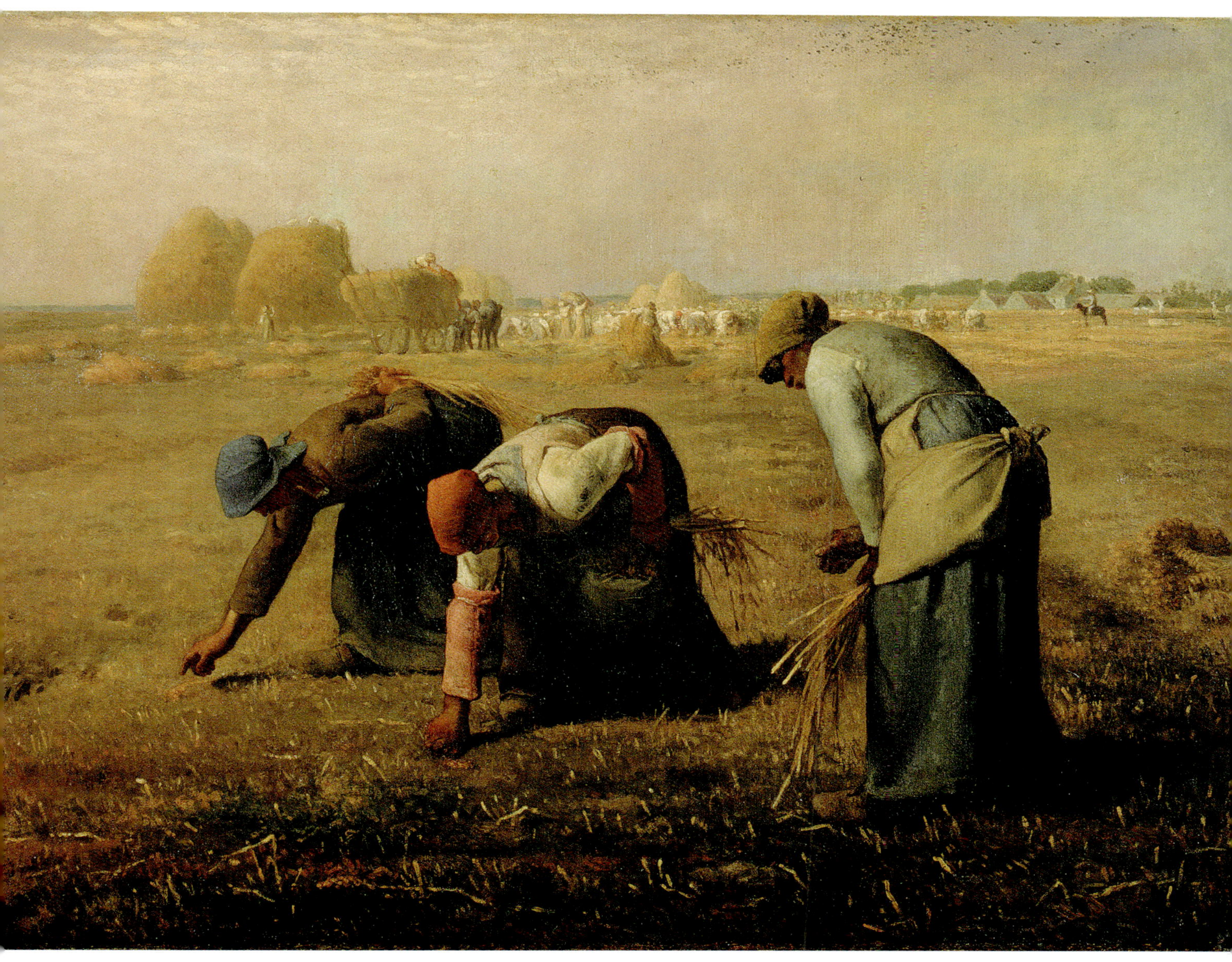

MANET WITH ALL GUNS BLAZING

Used as he was to scandal, Manet had never before been subject to the unrelenting censorship occasioned by *The Execution of Emperor Maximilian*. It has to be said that the painting illustrates what remains without doubt one of the greatest political blunders of Napoleon III, which brought him widespread condemnation both on the international stage and in his own country.

Some history is needed here in order to understand the impact this violent work had. In June 1867, Emperor Maximilian of Mexico was executed by the Mexican people over whom he was supposed to reign. This was entirely due to the actions of Napoleon III, who had not only uprooted this hapless member of the great house of Habsburg from his peaceful existence and set him on the throne of Mexico without consulting the local people, but had then withdrawn his troops, leaving the poor puppet emperor to be massacred without any support. Fierce republican that he was, Manet could not let such an episode go unchallenged. Armed with his brushes, he painted a forceful denunciation of the execution Napoleon had allowed to happen.

In the painting, a dignified Maximilian calmly watches as his two faithful generals are put to death and equally nobly awaits his turn. Manet initially gave one of the men firing a sombrero. To drive his point home, he painted it out and replaced it with a kepi and uniform reminiscent of those of the French army.

Manet's political commitment did not stop there: he made a lithograph of the painting so that he could circulate the image more widely. He did all this without worrying about how it might be viewed by a touchy and eagle-eyed government. The reaction was not long in coming: the work was banned from the Salon, without the jury having a say in the matter. This was followed in 1869 by a letter summoning Manet to retrieve his original lithograph and banning him from publishing it. The ban was not lifted until after his death, seventeen years later. In the interim, Émile Zola, then a young journalist, went into action to try and help his friend. He wrote a piece sharply criticizing the government in *La Tribune* of 4 February 1869, but to no avail: Manet had dared launch an attack on a political subject that was far too sensitive to allow it to be tolerated.

Édouard Manet (1832–1883),
***The Execution of Emperor Maximilian*, 1867,**
oil on canvas, 252 x 305 cm, Städtische Kunsthalle, Mannheim

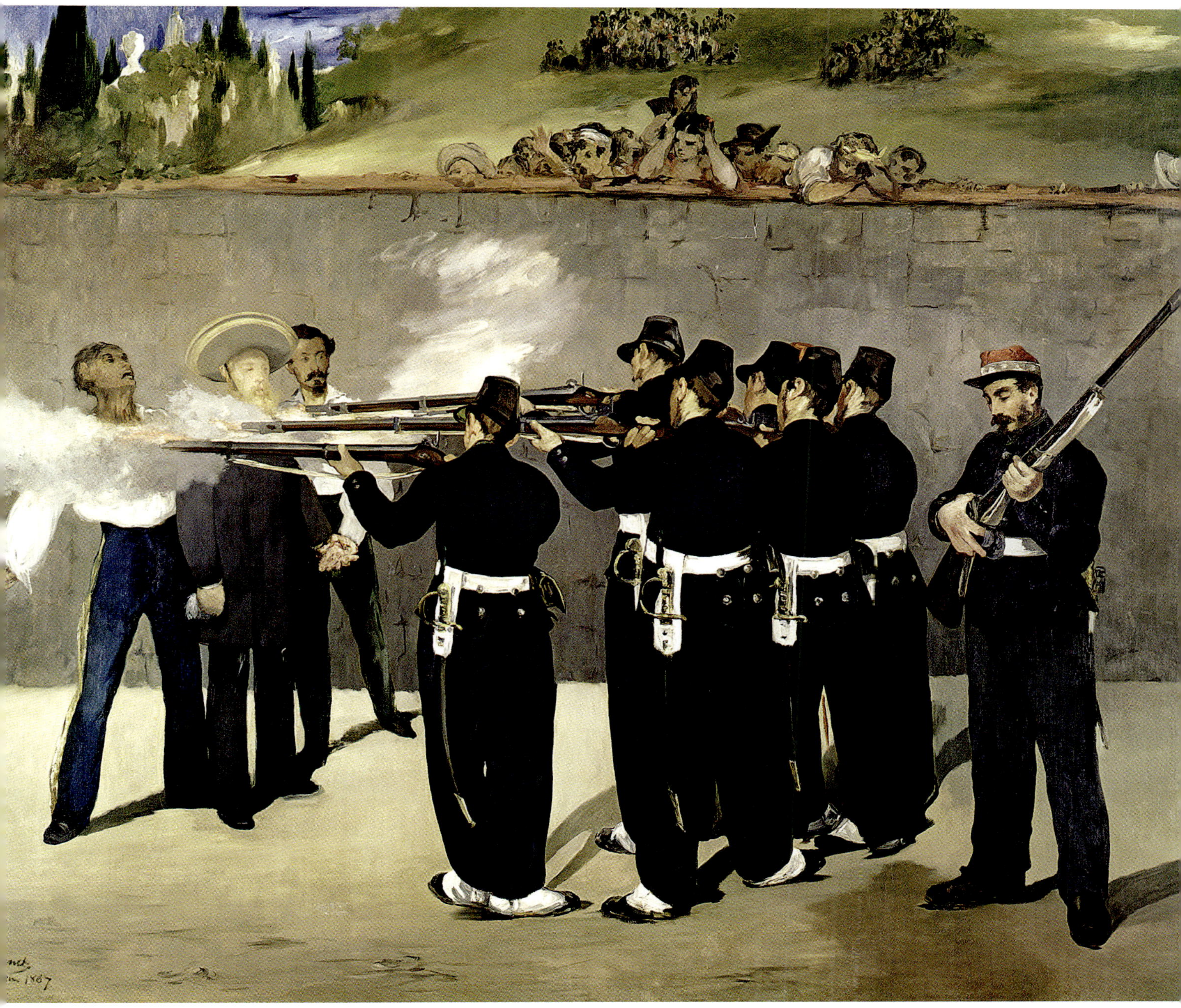

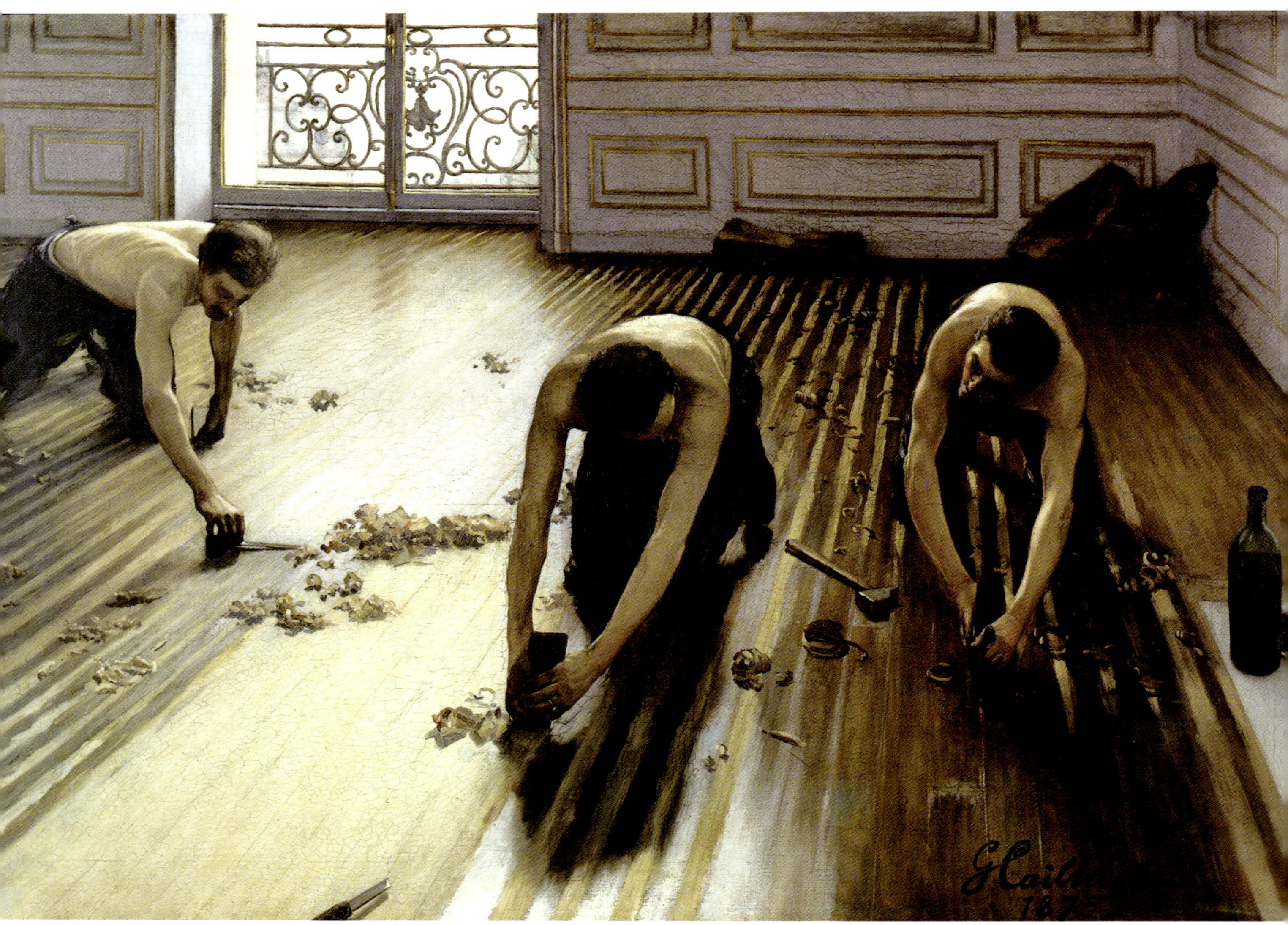

Gustave Caillebotte (1848–1894), *The Floor Scrapers*, **1875,**
oil on canvas, 102 x 146.5 cm, Musée d'Orsay, Paris

A DISPUTED LEGACY

Gustave Caillebotte's own paintings may have displeased the bourgeoisie, but the bequest he made in his will caused a greater stir. He left sixty-five Impressionist paintings from his own collection to the nation – and the nation refused them. The paintings were widely regarded as decadent, and the very thought of them alarmed the government and inflamed public opinion: there were provocative articles, debates, and passionate declarations by leading political figures.

Caillebotte's own paintings did not get a very good press. *The Floor Scrapers* portrays laborers at work with a realism that was considered vulgar. In the same way that Millet's peasants did (see p. 58), the workers here reminded people of a reality that they found disquieting in these times of social unrest. The painting was rejected by the Salon of 1875. Caillebotte showed it instead at the second Impressionist exhibition in 1876. He was to stand by this group of artists from then on. He was wealthy and acted as a generous patron, supporting his friends by buying their paintings.

When he died in 1894, Caillebotte left a will in which he donated his collection to the nation, with specific instructions that it should go first to the Luxembourg Palace and then to the Louvre. There was an outcry: although the furor caused by Impressionists scandal had died down a little in the ensuing twenty years, the authorities and bourgeoisie rejected the bequest by a majority. There was no way paintings like that were going to be allowed into the hallowed temple of culture. These days, exhibitions of Impressionist works draw record crowds, but in the late nineteenth century the state had no time for such works and turned them down.

Negotiators sought a compromise. Eventually some works were exhibited in the Luxembourg Palace, in an annex on their own. This did nothing to placate either his supporters or critics. Caillebotte's executors deplored the fact that his last wishes were not being respected, while detractors of the movement remained as outraged as ever. Journalists got out their sharpest quills, eighteen members of the Académie des Beaux-Arts made a formal protest to the Minister of Public Instruction, and the concerned bourgeoisie wailed. But the arrangement remained unchanged.

CAST IN THE SAME MOLD AS DREYFUS

When it came to describing Rodin's plaster model of Balzac, the imagination of critics knew no bounds: it was a snowman, a block of salt dissolving in the rain, a stalactite formed by limestone … Rodin was criticized for not delivering the sculpture when he had spent six years struggling to complete it. The most unbelievable part of this scandal, however, was that he found himself caught up in the infamous Dreyfus affair.

Half a century after Balzac's death, the respected Société des Gens de Lettres decided to commission a statue in his memory. Émile Zola suggested the celebrated Rodin, and he was accepted. Rodin took the subject very much to heart; he found out all he could about the author of *La Comédie humaine* and debated long and hard about the clothes, the pose, the face. He was late with the commission and when it was shown at the Salon of 1898, the already seething members of the Société exploded with fury at what they considered a crude and ugly figure. They refused to accept that it was a statue of Balzac and rejected it outright. What had been intended as a homage seemed to them to have become an insult. Critics were divided: Rodin was already well known and recognized as a master, but that did not stop *Balzac* from being slated. Rodin's friends rushed to his aid and organized a subscription to have the figure cast in bronze and exhibited in a public space. The idea was taken up by others, but this caused yet more division. A great many important people con-tributed to the fund, and it turned out that most of them were supporters of Dreyfus. These were people who had stood up in defense of a young captain of Jewish descent falsely accused of spying in a case that revealed deeply rooted anti-Semitism in French society. The affair created social and political rifts that rocked France and led to violent clashes. The rifts thus extended into the field of sculpture, with one camp supporting Rodin's sculpture and the other, anti-Dreyfus, camp rejecting it. Rodin was put in a very awkward position by this turn of events. Absurdly, he found himself on the side of those who despised his *Balzac*, for he himself was a member of the anti-Dreyfus camp. In the end he did his best to diffuse the situation by returning the money he had been paid and taking the sculpture back. He firmly refused all offers to buy it.

Auguste Rodin (1840–1917), *Balzac*, 1897,
plaster, 275 x 121 x 132 cm, Musée d'Orsay, Paris

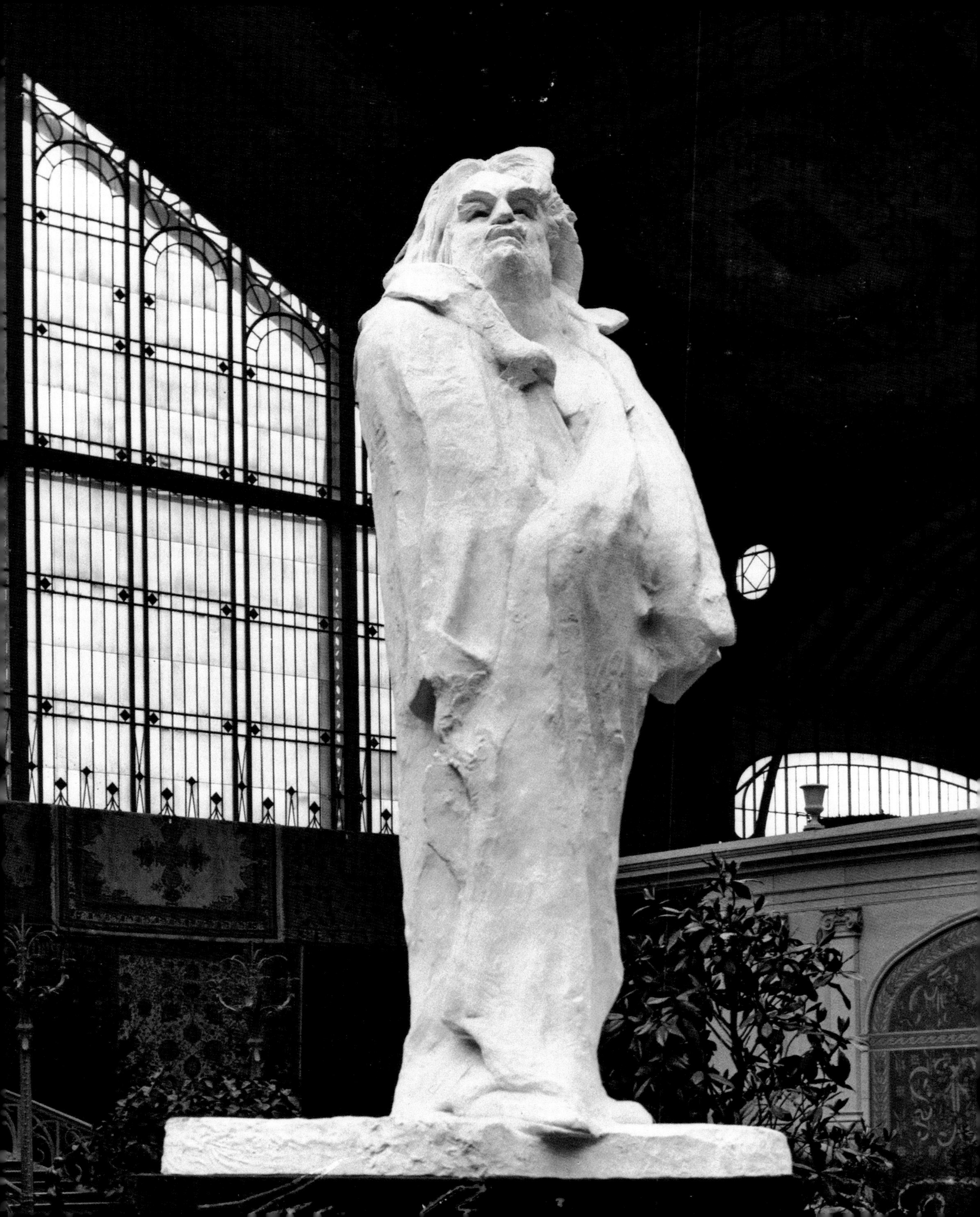

REVOLUTIONARY ART VS. REVOLUTIONARY POLITICS

Born in the Ukraine, Kazimir Malevich became an emblematic figure of the Russian avant-garde. He turned to radical abstraction in his art after experimenting with the major movements in Western art such as Impressionism and Futurism. Although he supported the Bolsheviks, Malevich experienced severe repression at their hands and learned to his cost that political revolution and artistic revolution do not necessarily go hand in hand.

At the *0.10* exhibition in Petrograd (now Saint Petersburg) in 1915, Malevich showed nothing but squares and rectangles of color, marking a first in art history. Suprematism, which focuses on the ultimate expression of pure form, was born. *Black Square* dominated the show from a corner of the gallery. With *Black Circle* and *Black Cross* it made up a sort of triptych that became an emblem of the Suprematist movement.

In 1917 the Tsarist regime fell and Malevich aligned himself with the Bolsheviks. They imposed an artistic conservatism, however, which was completely at odds with Suprematism. Because it was not materialist, abstract art was deemed useless to the cause. Malevich was the victim of repression from 1919 onwards and was first interrogated by police in 1921. He succumbed to severe depression and paralysis of his right hand as he continued to be harassed and intimidated by the police. He effectively signed the warrant for his own arrest in 1927 when he referred in a newspaper to the "cultural difficulties" in the Soviet Union. From then on he was disgraced and degraded by the government and no longer took part in any publication or exhibition. He was arrested and sent to the political prison in Leningrad (formerly Petrograd, now St Petersburg) in 1930. While he was in prison his studio was ransacked and his sketchbooks were destroyed by the authorities.

In 1932, Socialist Realism was imposed as state policy and all other forms of artistic expression were suppressed. With Stalin's rise to power in 1934, sanctions hardened. In a bid to keep on the right side of the secret police, who were watching his every move, ready to pounce on and condemn the slightest suggestion of abstraction, Malevich turned once more to figurative art. But his efforts were in vain, for the authorities refused to let him travel to France, where the cancer that was eating away at him might have been treated. Although Malevich's work had achieved international renown by the time he died in 1935, it continued to be ignored by the Soviet government.

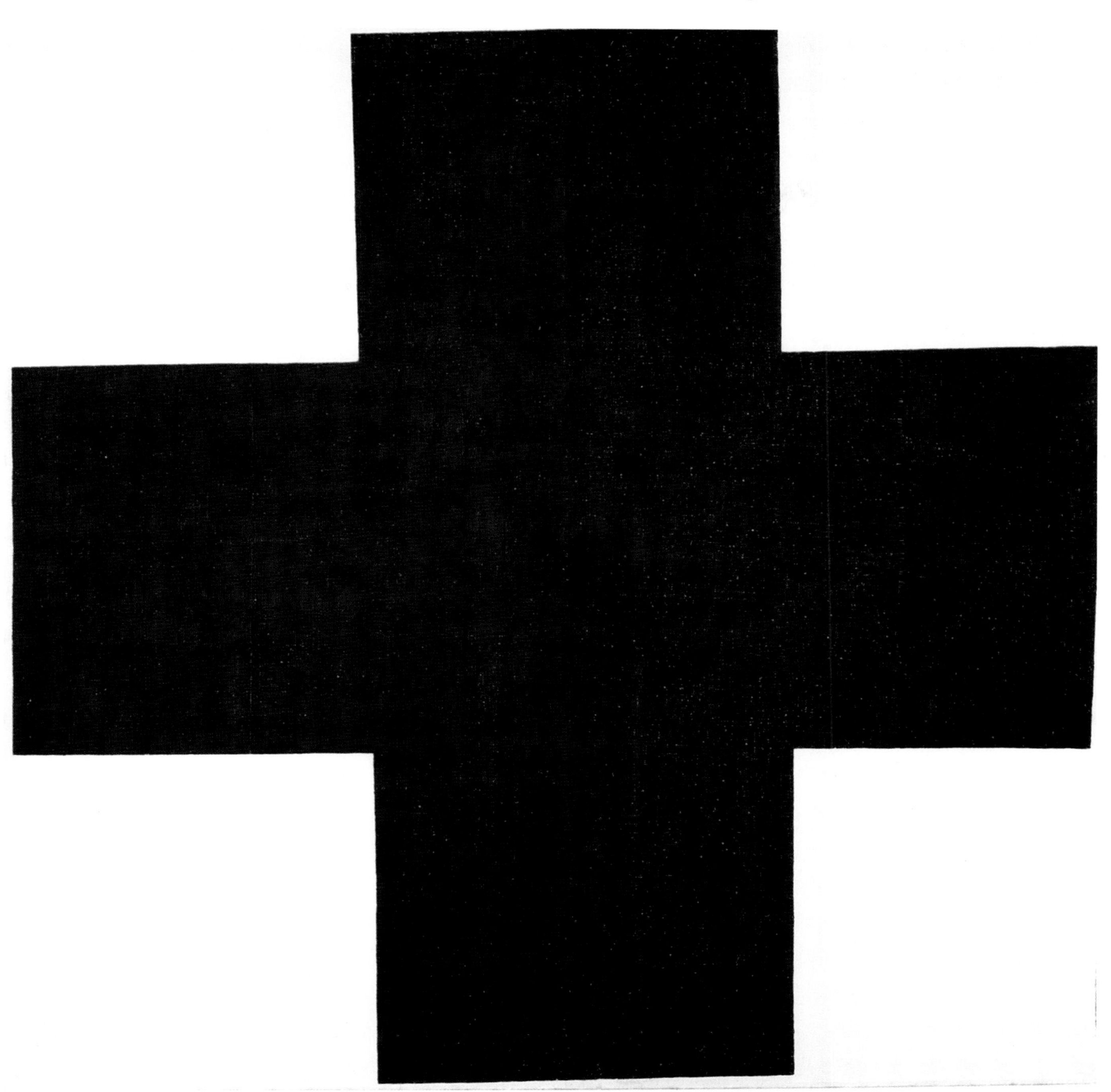

Kazimir Malevich (1878–1935), *Black Cross*, **1923–1929,**
oil on canvas, 106.4 x 106.4 cm,
State Russian Museum, Saint Petersburg

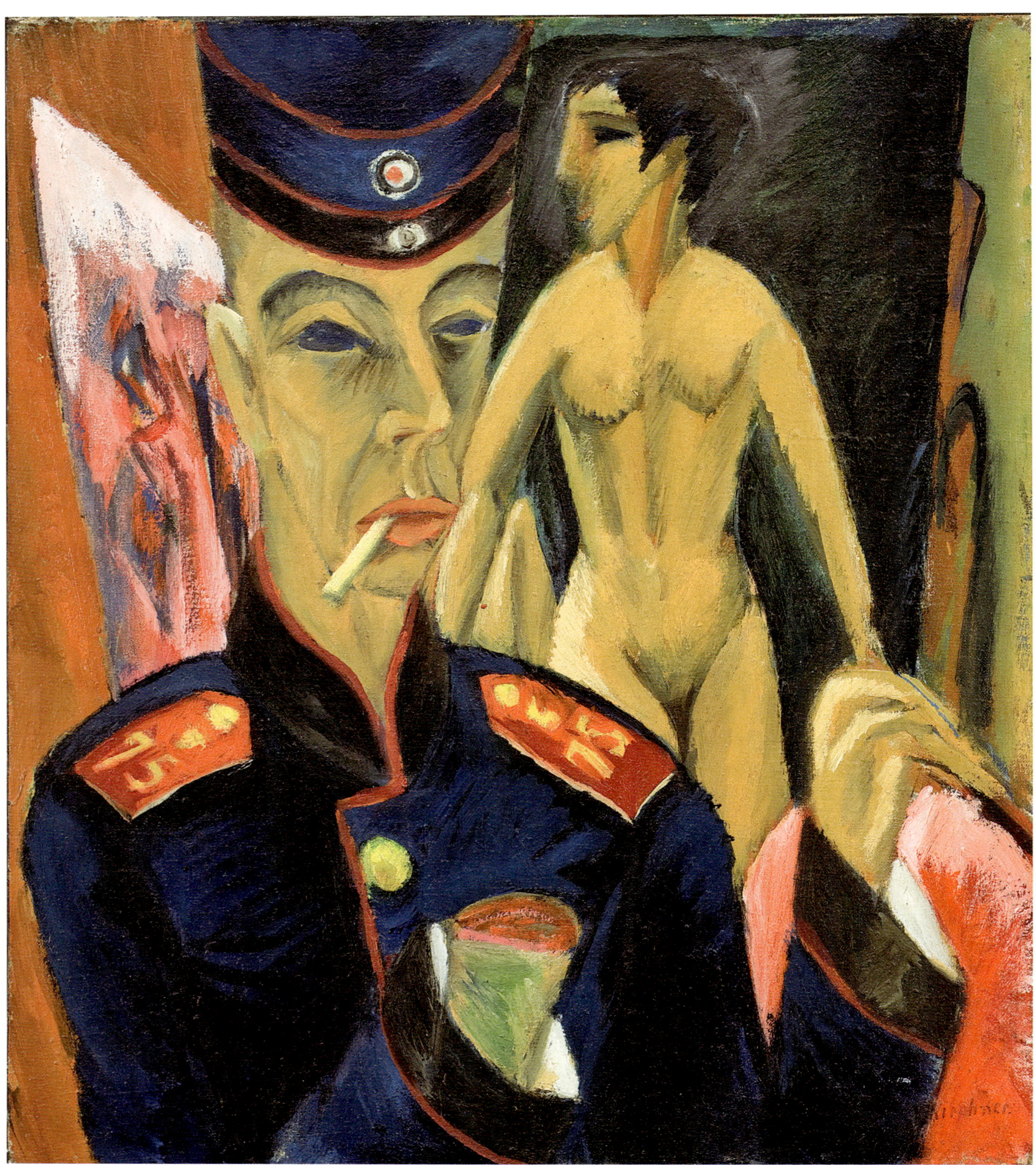

A "DEGENERATE" ARTIST

Ernst Ludwig Kirchner was one of the founders of the Die Brücke (The Bridge) movement. This group of German Expressionist artists renounced conventions in favor of subjectivity. They were among the first painters to be censored by the Nazis when they "purged" the museums. Mentally unstable, Kirchner suffered greatly from these attacks, and ultimately took his own life.

After the declaration of war in 1914, Kirchner enlisted as a "volunteer in spite of himself" and was called up in the spring of 1915. Several months later, he was exempted when his nervous condition was judged to be alarming. The short period he spent at the Front had a profound effect on him and he had great difficulties in recovering his health. His *Self-Portrait as a Soldier* bears witness to this. The blood-drenched stump of his arm symbolizes the brutality of war that shatters the individual – physically and mentally – while the naked silhouette represents the exhausted painter, who has lost his creative powers.

In 1937 the Nazis launched a campaign against modernism in favor of "pure" – meaning heroic – art. Kirchner saw 639 of his works, including the *Self-Portrait as a Soldier*, seized and removed from German museums. Thirty-two paintings were singled out to be part of the traveling exhibition *Entartete Kunst* (Degenerate Art), which presented avant-garde works alongside those of the mentally ill, the aim being to stigmatize modern art among the population. The *Self-Portrait* was intentionally renamed *Soldier with Whore* and, in this way, suggested that the painter only felt contempt for the heroism of soldiers. The same year, Kirchner was expelled from the Prussian Academy of Arts. Although he had an established international reputation, he was severely affected by these events. His depressive state and the political situation in Germany led to his suicide by gunshot on 15 June 1938.

Ernst Ludwig Kirchner (1880–1938),
***Self-Portrait as a Soldier*, 1915,**
oil on canvas, 69.2 x 61 cm,
Allen Memorial Art Museum, Oberlin College, Oberlin, Ohio

DEMORALIZING THE TROOPS IS STRICTLY FORBIDDEN

Richard Nevinson worked as a volunteer ambulance driver during the First World War. On his return from the Front in 1917, in the grips of full-blown depression, he painted *Paths of Glory*, which, almost photographic in its realism, represents a major departure from his usual Cubo-Futurist style.

Nevinson painted this picture while officially employed as a war artist by the British government. The disillusioned view of the conflict it projects, devoid of action and heroism, met with strong disapproval. The painting shows the bodies of two Tommies, as British soldiers were nicknamed, lying abandoned face down in the mud, their bodies swollen. They look doomed to remain there in front of the barbed wire, slowly decomposing, alone and unknown. Nevinson presents a reality which is disturbing: in the First World War huge numbers of soldiers died like this, utterly disregarded and unattended, their bodies left to lie where they fell, unburied.

In 1917, however, the war was still in full swing and British troops were becoming demoralized. There was no way an official war artist could be allowed to demonstrate such pessimism. Three months before Nevinson's solo show was due to open at the Leicester Galleries in March 1918, the officer in charge of overseeing the work of war artists banned the painting from going on public show. Nevinson retorted by hanging the painting on the wall on the night of the private view, with a strip of paper across it with the word "Censored" on it. The War Office, the ministry responsible for British land forces, was furious. Not only had Nevinson dared to put on display a work that had been banned, but he had contrived to draw attention in the most provocative way to the censorship that had wanted him gagged. The media were quick to make the most of the scandal and thus guarantee the artist's fame.

In 1957, the American film director Stanley Kubrick used the title *Paths of Glory* for his film denouncing the repression of mutiny and mutineers in the Great War. Ironically, his film also fell foul of the censors, just as Nevinson's painting had done, and under government pressure it was not released in France for many years.

Christopher Richard Wynne Nevinson (1889–1946),
***Paths of Glory*, 1917,**
oil on canvas, 45.7 x 61 cm, Imperial War Museum, London

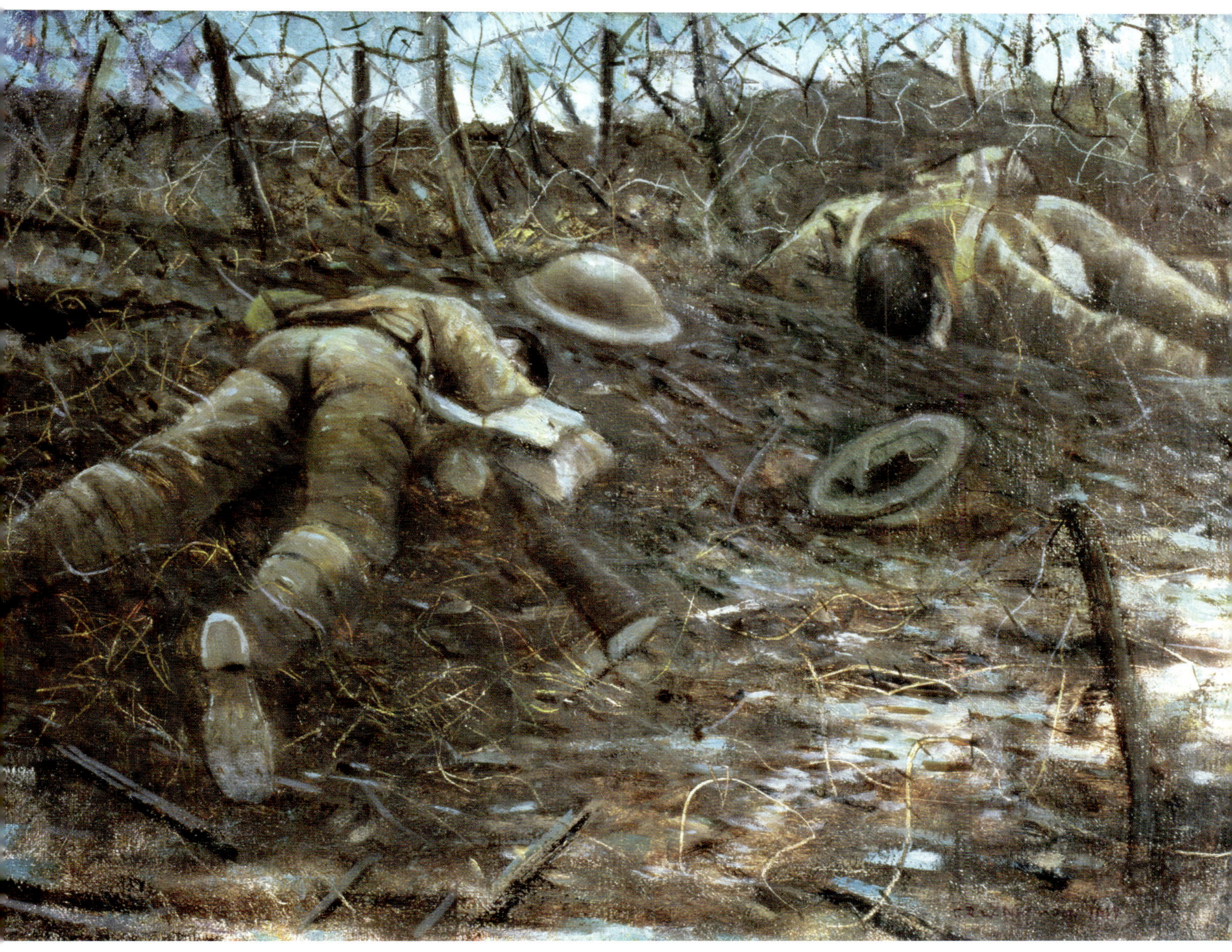

A VICTIM OF THE NAZIS

A brave and patriotic German citizen, Otto Dix signed up as a volunteer at the start of the First World War. He returned not only physically wounded but, most of all, emotionally devastated. He then used drawing and painting as outlets for his efforts to come to terms with the horrors he had seen. That did not appeal to Hitler's taste and, when he came into power in 1933, he denounced Dix's art as being degenerate and did his utmost to suppress it.

Dix brought back terrible memories from the Front. His works created after 1914–1918, each one darker than the other, vividly record the trauma he had experienced. Mass graves, abandoned corpses, dismembered bodies, eviscerated torsos, eyeless faces … He depicted the cruelty and inhumanity of conflict as no other. Even more, he drew back the curtain on the harsh reality of the post-war years: people living on the fringe of society, the poverty and violence of everyday life in the city.

However, these paintings and drawings, which made it possible for Dix to exorcise his personal demons, also brought him court cases for spreading images that were obscene and posed a "threat to public decency." But the worst was still to come. Starting in 1933, Germany's National Socialist Party, with Hitler as its leader, decided to "purify" artistic production. Modern art, which was considered corrupt, was hunted down and sometimes destroyed. Dix's work was completely the opposite the regime's official taste and the artist had to pay a high price. After the Nazis had taken power, he was deprived of his teaching position in Dresden and more than 260 of his works, including *The Trench*, were confiscated. Uncompromisingly, and with bitter directness, this canvas depicted the disaster caused by a bombardment. It was shown at the exhibition of "degenerate art" in 1937 and subsequently disappeared, probably destroyed by the regime, as was the case with thousands of other art works. Although we only have a photograph of *The Trench*, we can still see something of its power in the central panel of the triptych *The War*, which he painted ten years later and that survived the censorship of the Third Reich.

Otto Dix (1891–1969), *The Trench*, 1920–1923,
oil on canvas, 227 x 250 cm, photography of the painting
(now lost) taken in 1937 at the *Entartete Kunst* (Degenerate Art)
exhibition in Munich, Zentralarchiv, Staatliche Museen, Berlin

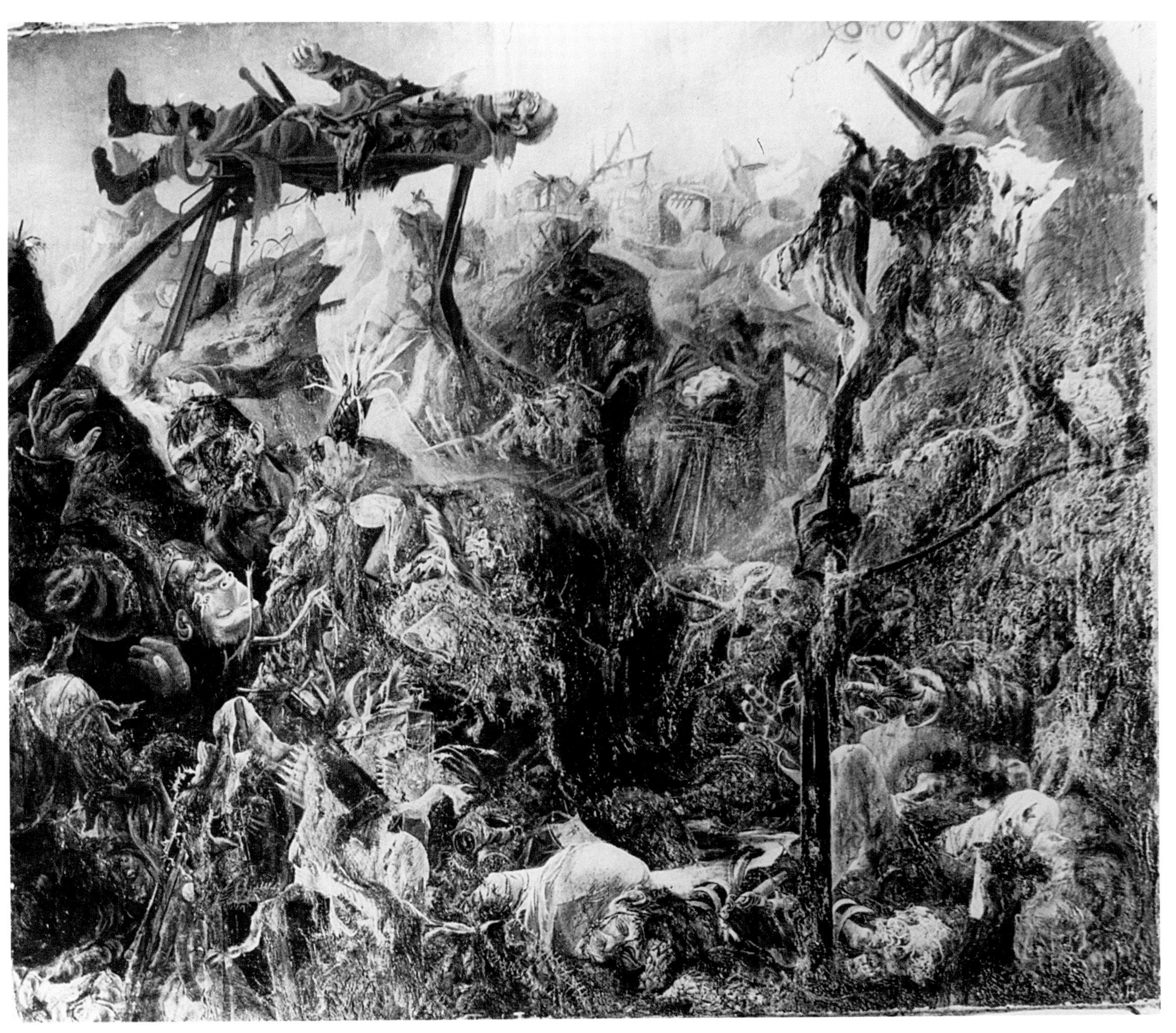

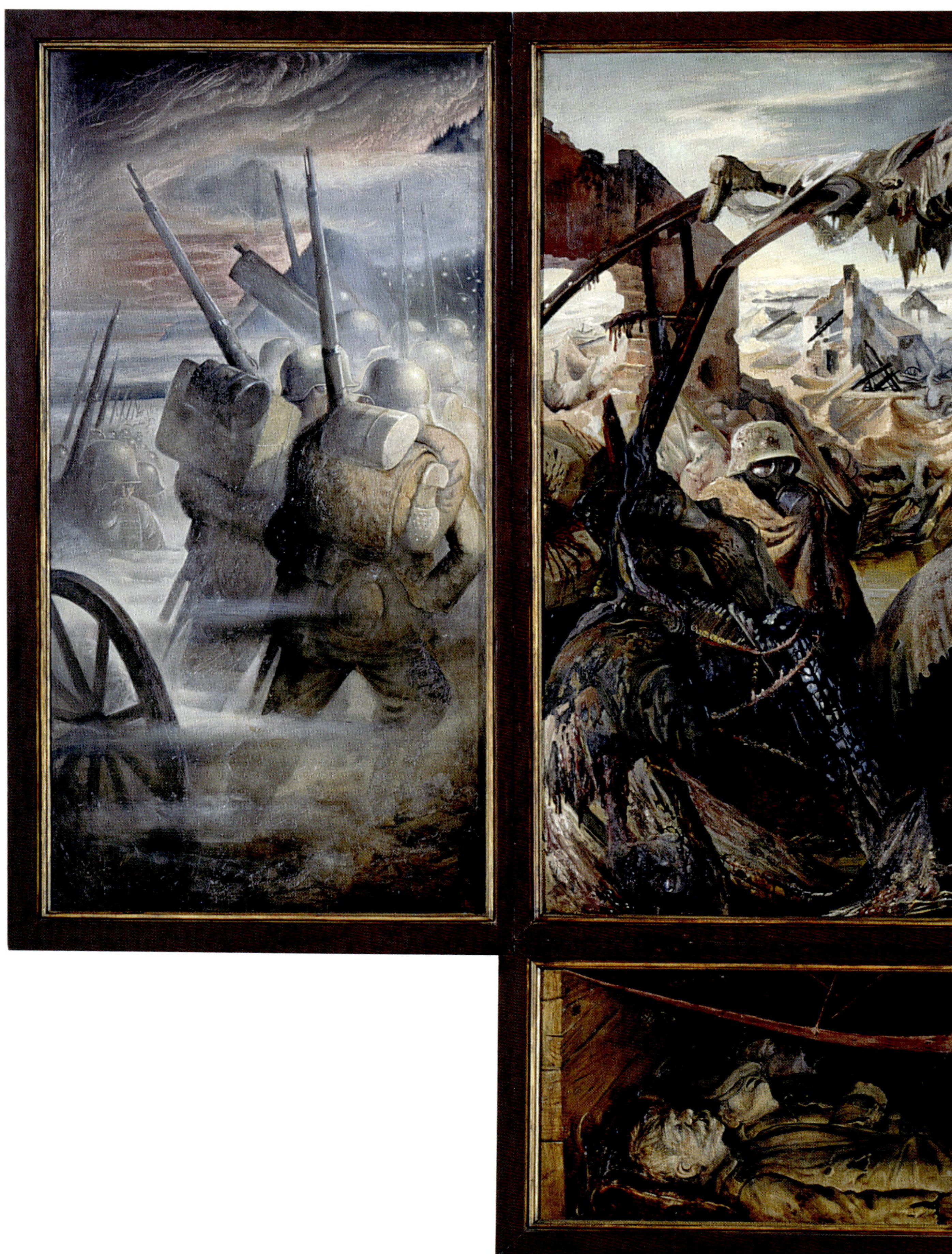

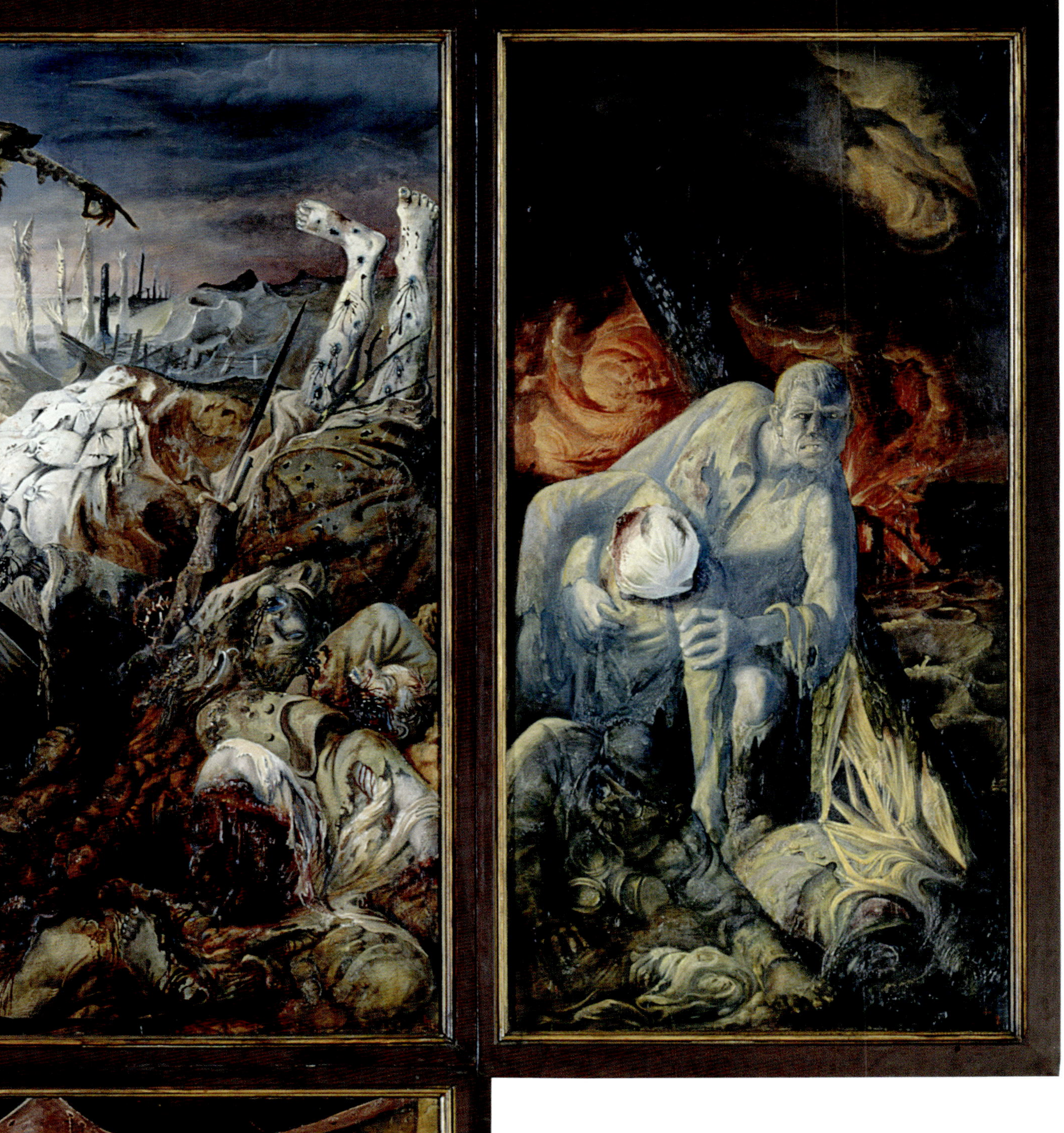

Otto Dix (1891–1969, *The War* (triptych), 1929–1932,
tempera on wood, central panel: 204×204 cm, side panels:
204×102 cm (each), predella: 60×204 cm,
Gemäldegalerie Neue Meister, Dresden
Dix included many of the elements of *The Trench* in the
central panel of this later triptych.

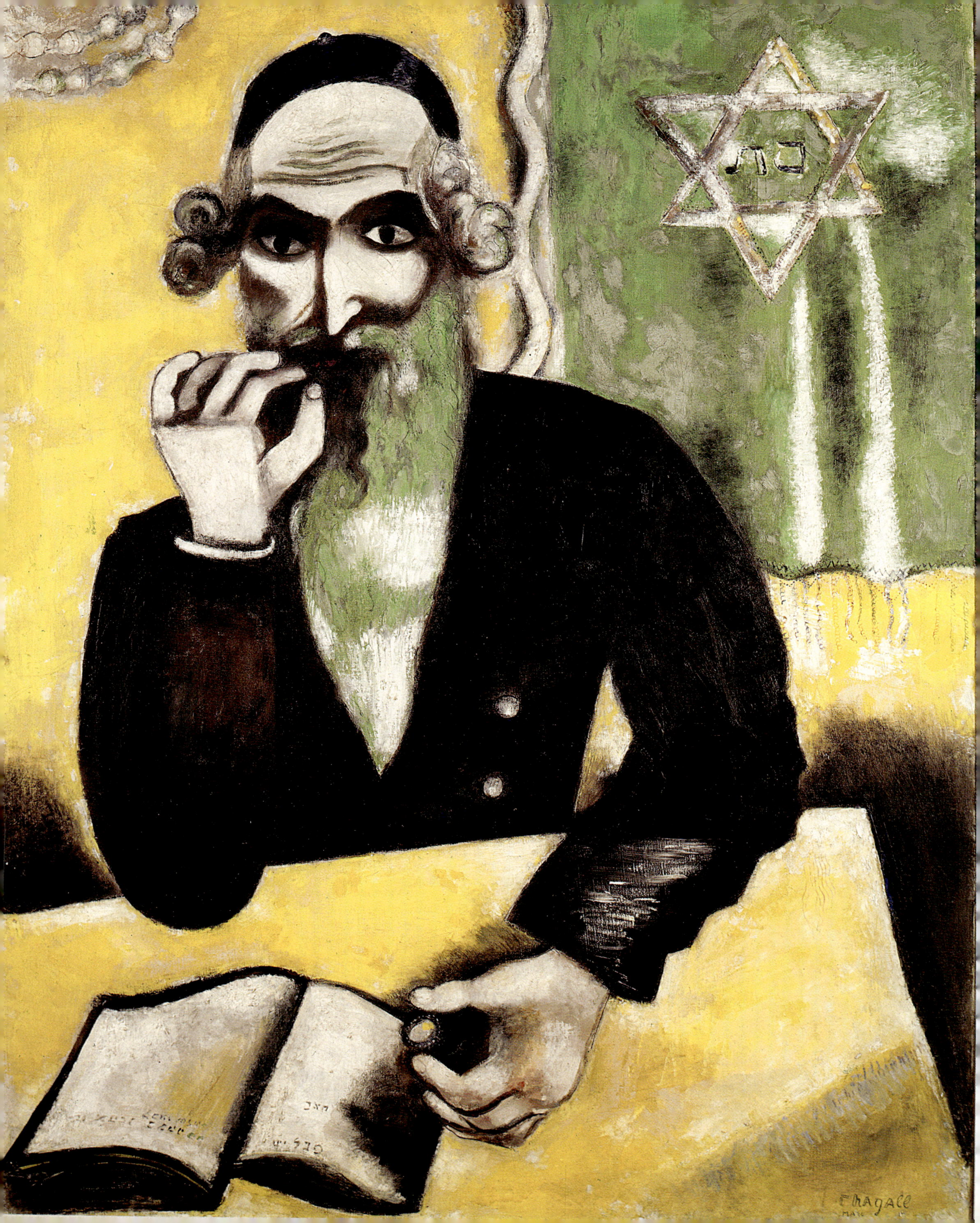
Chagall

FOREIGN, JEWISH, AND A COMMUNIST

Chagall was yet another modern artist to be attacked by the Nazis. With their expressive colors and naïve, unrealistic figures, his paintings epitomized what the Nazis condemned as "degenerate art." Moreover, Chagall was Jewish and often painted scenes of everyday Jewish life, which only incensed the Nazis all the more.

Chagall began a promising career in his native Russia, where a patron enabled him to go to Paris. He was welcomed with open arms by the artistic community there, who admired his poetic evocation of folk culture. Chagall exhibited in Germany in 1913 and 1914, and many of his works remained there when he returned to his native Russia, where he was appointed commissar of arts in his province. His future seemed rosy – until the rise of Nazism. In 1933, the Nazi propaganda minister Joseph Goebbels organized an exhibition of "degenerate art." Not only did he include a number of Chagall's paintings, he destroyed three of them.

A *Pinch of Snuff* embodies everything the Third Reich despised. In it a rabbi wearing a yarmulke (skull cap) takes a pinch of snuff in a synagogue ornamented with Jewish symbols: a Star of David, a seyfer (religious text), and a menorah (seven-branched candelabrum) in the top left corner. Its Expressionist style was the opposite of what was officially approved in art. There is nothing ideal about the rabbi's face, his beard is green, his hands are unrealistic. To cap it all, Chagall was Jewish foreigner who had been a member of the Communist Party.

At this point, however much he may have lamented the loss of some of his works, Chagall, who had moved to Paris and had acquired French nationality, was still not unduly worried. While the damning *Entartete Kunst* (Degenerate Art) exhibition was going on, a far more flattering retrospective of Chagall's work was taking place in Basel. In 1941, however, Chagall was arrested in Marseille. He was rescued by the American journalist Varian Fry, who helped many artists to escape the Nazis, and he took refuge in the United States, then the last bastion against the anti-Semitism that posed such a threat to both his work and his life.

Marc Chagall (1887–1985),
***A Pinch of Snuff (The Rabbi),* 1923–1926,**
oil on canvas, 117 x 89.5 cm, Musée des Beaux-Arts, Basel

COUNTERFEITER IN SPITE OF HIMSELF

Genpei Akasegawa is a Japanese conceptual artist and writer who delights in using ordinary objects in a novel way. Alongside the Japanese Anti-Art group, he questions a form of everyday life that mass culture has made bland and lacking in surprises. In the 1960s, a court case engulfed him: though he had a good defense, he was found guilty of having forged banknotes.

In 1963, the young avant-garde artist mailed several close friends an invitation to his next exhibition of collages in Tokyo. The card showed a reproduction of a 1,000-yen note on the front, with information on the opening on the back. In the following months, Genpei Akasegawa duplicated this image of a banknote and used it in performances, and for creating various works, without being bothered in any way. However, on 8 January 1964, the police knocked on his door to question him. When the authorities got wind of the affair, they decided to start an investigation. They based their accusations that he had made imitations of banknotes on a dubious old edict dating from the year 1894 forbidding the production of objects "that could be confused with currency." This was followed by a sensational court case that was avidly reported in the Japanese media. The artist insisted that he had never intended that his "notes" should be taken for real ones; it was only art! But in June 1967 he was found guilty and give a three-months suspended prison sentence and one year on parole. He appealed twice but in 1970 a tribunal upheld the conviction.

Nobody – not even the judges – believed that Genpei Akasegawa was guilty. Nevertheless, to make simulacra of banknotes is to interfere with the function of a major instrument of the state. This modern-day crime of *lèse-majesté* had not gone unnoticed by the authorities, who celebrated a triumph. Be that as it may, with this affair Genpei Akasegawa became extremely well known in his native country – which was doubtlessly not the result the judges had hoped for!

Genpei Akasegawa (1937–),
***One-Thousand-Yen Note Trial Impound Object: Mask,* 1963,**
imitation one-thousand-Yen sheets, plaster mask, string, wire, paper tags, overall 37 x 25 x 19 cm, © Collection Walker Art Center, Minneapolis, T.B. Walker Acquisition Fund, 2009. Courtesy: SCAI THE BATHHOUSE

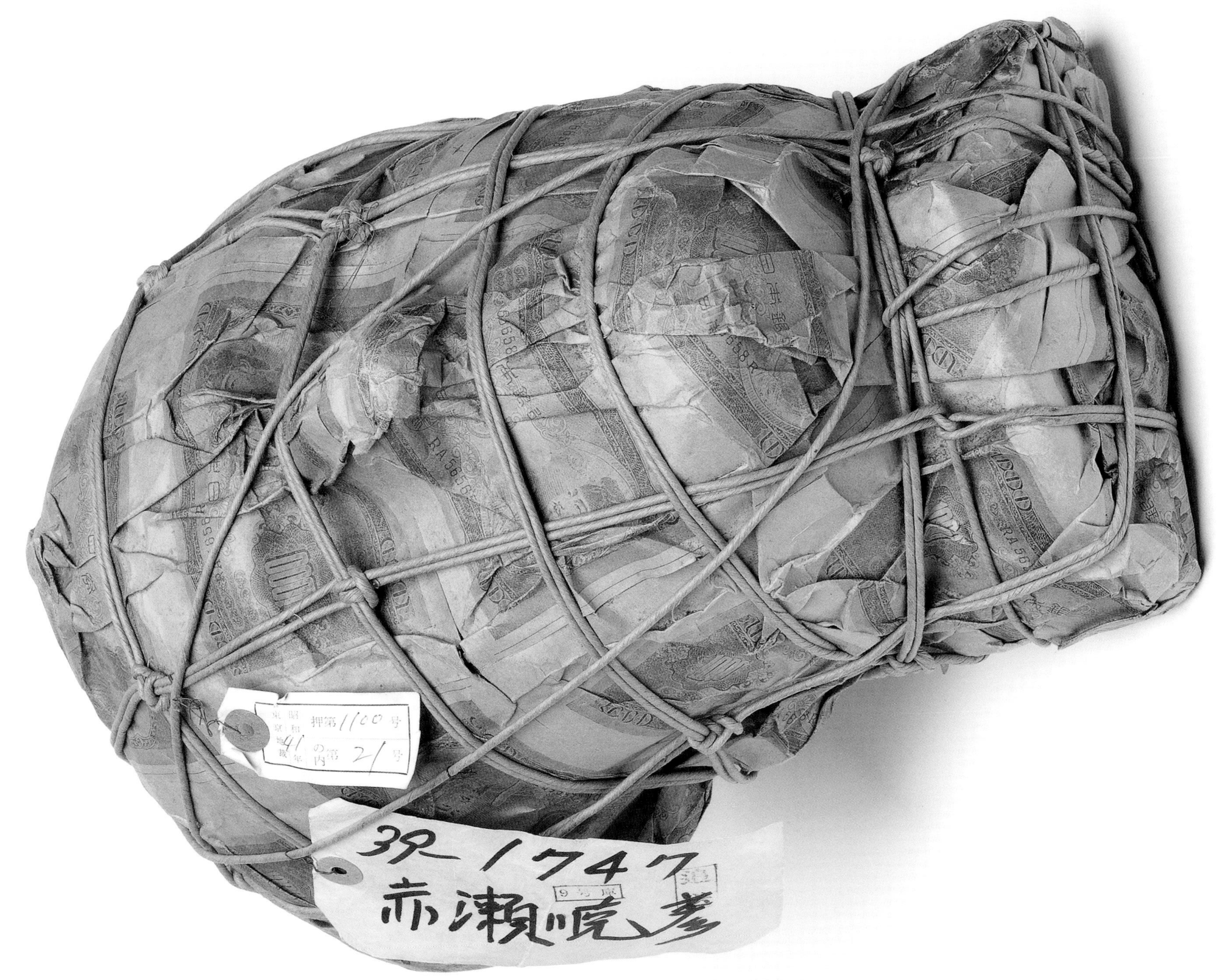

東京地裁 昭和41年 押第1100号 の内第21号
39-1747
赤瀬川原平

EVIL INCARNATE

Is it possible to show a Hitler kneeling in prayer in the old Warsaw Ghetto? According to some Jewish organizations, it is a line that should not be crossed.

As shown by his sculpture of Pope John Paul II (see p. 40), Maurizio Cattelan likes to depict recognizable historical figures, including political and religious authorities, as well as the great masters of modern art such as Pablo Picasso. This attraction to so-called "icons" results from his questioning of our excessive consumption of images in everyday life. Cattelan also understands how to represent these famous personalities: it is an opportunity to seize their power of communication and use it to breathe life into his art.

Created in 2001, *Him* is an installation that was displayed on several occasions without giving rise to any real controversy. Until recently, that is, when at the end of 2012 several Jewish organizations condemned it vehemently. More than the work itself, the place where it was shown became the subject of discussion. It was in the very heart of the Polish capital city, where thousands of Jews were persecuted by the Nazis during the Second World War, that a retrospective of the Italian artist's oeuvre had been organized under the title of *Amen*. For the Simon Wiesenthal Centre, a non-governmental organization devoted to preserving the memory of the Holocaust, this was "an insane provocation that insulted the memory of the Nazis' Jewish victims."

What is so terrifying about Cattelan's sculpture? Though hyperrealistic, this Hitler is slightly smaller than life size, as if to show his vulnerability. That is where one again discovers the despair that is part of Cattelan's oeuvre. Miniaturization certainly, but humanization above all. Because this dictator, far from being demonized by the artist, is shown kneeling as if asking for forgiveness or in prayer. Even worse, seen from a distance, one could almost say he resembles a child repenting for having done something naughty. And in this way, it reminded certain people that it was actually a human being, like the rest of us, who was behind the greatest slaughter of modern times.

Maurizio Cattelan (1960–), *Him*, 2001
wax, human hair, uniform, polyester resin, 101 x 41 x 53 cm, photo
Paolo Pellion di Persano, courtesy of: Maurizio Cattelan's Archive

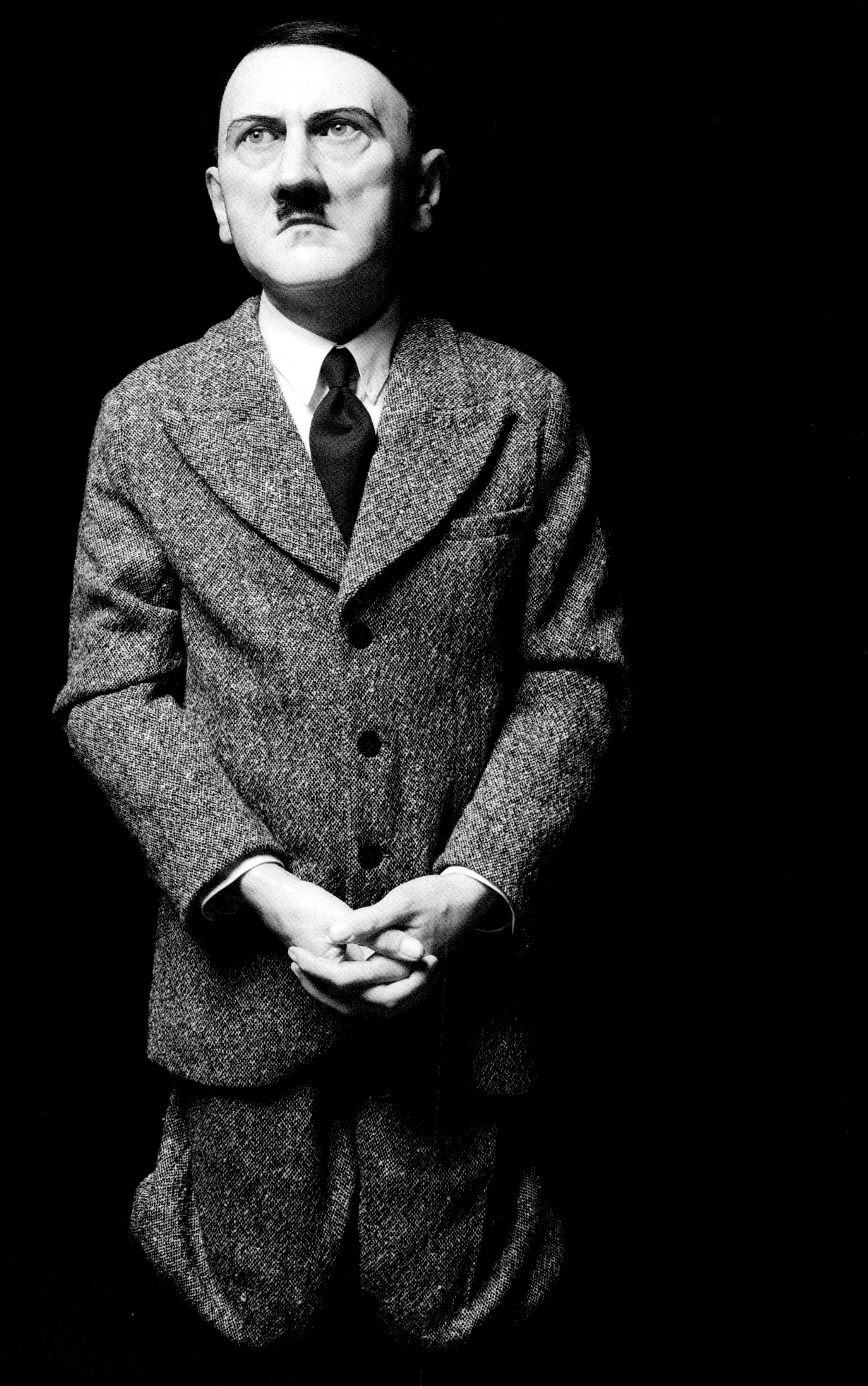

LOSING ONE'S HEAD

Yinka Shonibare MBE is a dissenter, a rebel. In his unsettling works, he explores racial stereotypes, the mixing of cultures, and the permanent rift between the West and the Developing World – subjects that embarrass those who would prefer to ignore the problems of the "rest of the world."

Shonibare is an artist with a mixed, mainly British and Nigerian, heritage. When he became a member of the prestigious honorary Order of the British Empire, he added the MBE (Member of the Most Excellent Order of the British Empire) sign to his name to underline the contradiction between this distinction and his own origins. He recalls having always immersed himself in several cultures, mixing languages, customs, and clothing styles. He is famous for his headless mannequins dressed sumptuously in the English fashions of the eighteenth century but with one peculiarity: the fabric used comes from a different age and from another continent. It is "wax," an African fabric with patterns printed through the use of wax. However, as Shonibare discovered, the costumes are hiding their secrets well. This "African" fabric was actually produced by the Dutch in the nineteenth century. They themselves were inspired by batik cloth that originated in Java. They then did business with Africa where the wax fabric became extremely successful and developed into the "traditional" way of decorating clothes!

Shonibare's works can appear amusing at first sight, but there is a feeling of uneasiness hovering above them. After initially entertaining us, these acephalous mannequins pose questions about cultural, racial, and national identities. As a metaphor for contemporary society, they are Europeans sumptuously dress in African wax cloth. It suggests that the luxury we enjoy is due to others who are much less fortunate. Can one be happy amid some much poverty? Shonibare warns us: if we do not rapidly regulate the problem of the distribution of wealth in the world, some will lose their heads.

Yinka Shonibare MBE (1962–),
How to Blow up Two Heads at Once (Ladies), **2006,**
two mannequins, two pistols, Dutch wax-printed cotton,
shoes, leather riding boots, plinth, 160 x 245 x 122 cm,
Photo: Stephen White

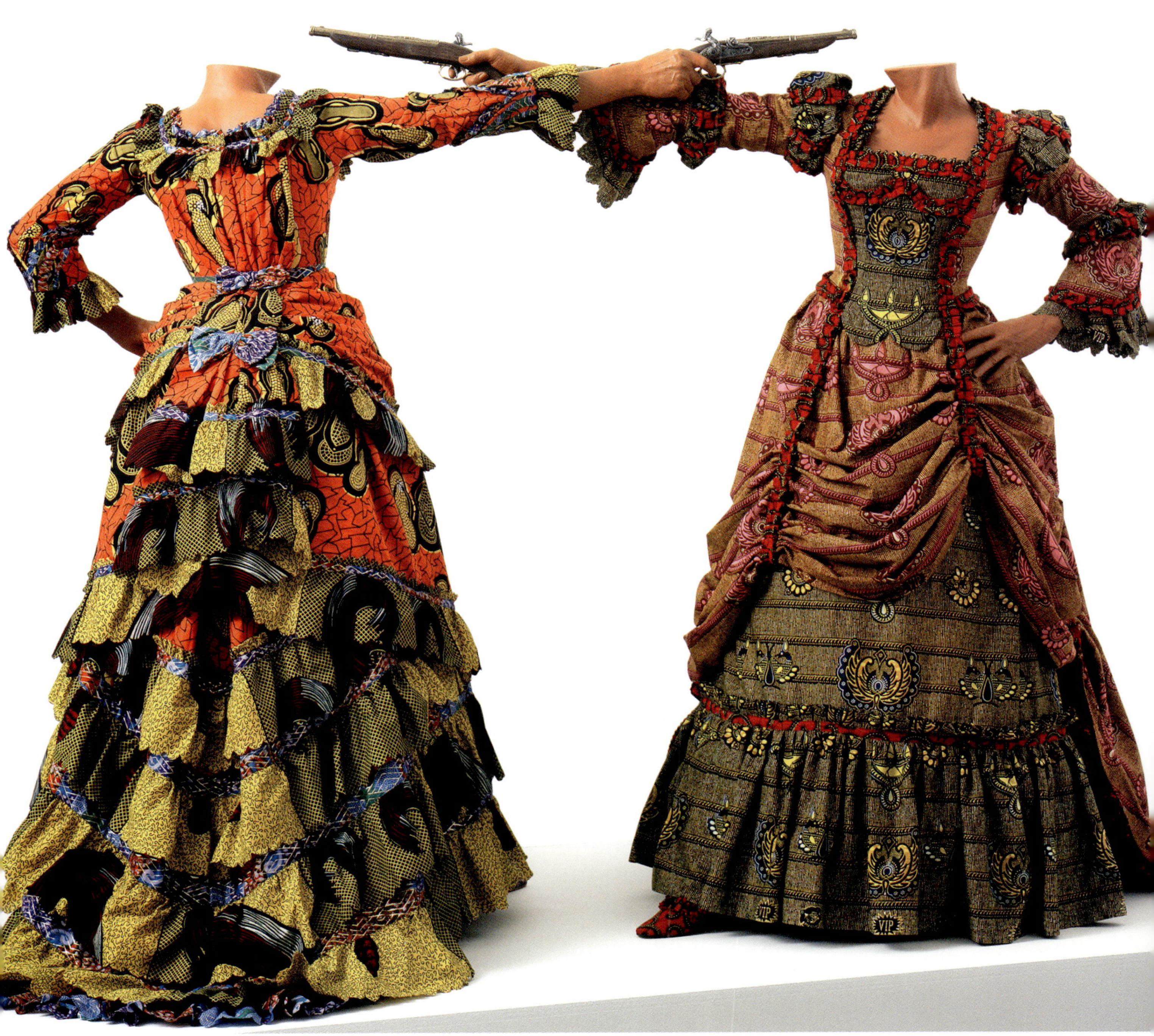

PROTEST AS ART

At the start of his career, Ai Weiwei initially found favor with the Chinese authorities. But rather than revel in the comfortable role of state-approved artist, this extraordinary anti-establishment figure has used his work and the Internet brilliantly to broadcast his opinions. Despite being harried by the Chinese government, he has carried on his artistic, social, and political fight.

In *June 1994*, Ai Weiwei's wife, Lu Qing, stands in front of Tiananmen Square and lifts her skirt, flashing her underwear while underlining the famous picture of Mao with the line of her hem. In the middle ground behind her, two soldiers patrol the square, highlighting the risk the couple are taking by committing such an affront in a place so symbolic of authoritarian power. The photograph marked the fifth anniversary of the Tiananmen Square massacre, the bloody suppression of a student demonstration, which remains a taboo subject in China.

While studying in America, Ai Weiwei discovered Marcel Duchamp. He was fascinated by Duchamp's notion of merging art and life and on his return to China took up the idea avidly, making dissidence his guiding principle and inspiration. He set himself the task, among others, of exposing the corruption that had brought about the collapse of a school that killed numerous children. He drew up a list detailing every single victim and created a memorial, while the authorities did their best to cover up the event. In 1995, he produced the first in his famous *Study of Perspective* series, photographing Tiananmen Square behind his rudely stuck up middle finger. Over the years he has repeated the gesture in front of famous landmarks all over the world. In this way he has continued to defy censorship and expose his country's faults and is particularly active in his blog and on social media. He posts texts as well as protest photographs that attract a considerable and growing following.

Ai Weiwei refuses to bow in the face of the censorship that the authorities have attempted to impose on him. In January 2011, his studio was destroyed and following this he disappeared from 3 April to 22 June: he was imprisoned and subsequently released under caution.

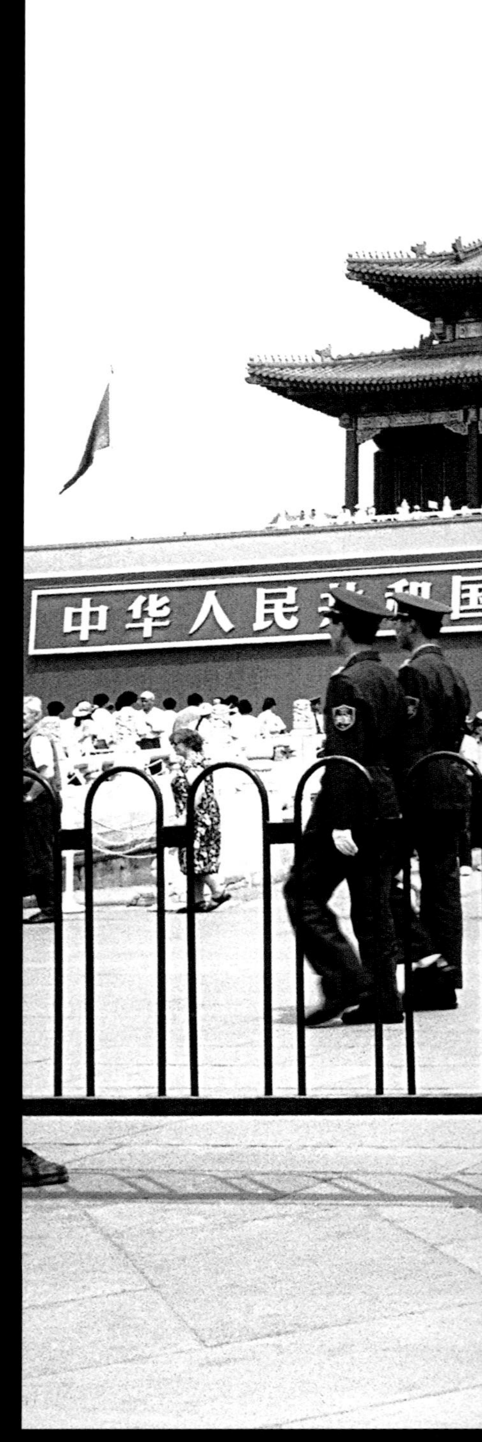

 Ai Weiwei (1957–), *June 1994,* **1994,** black-and-white photograph

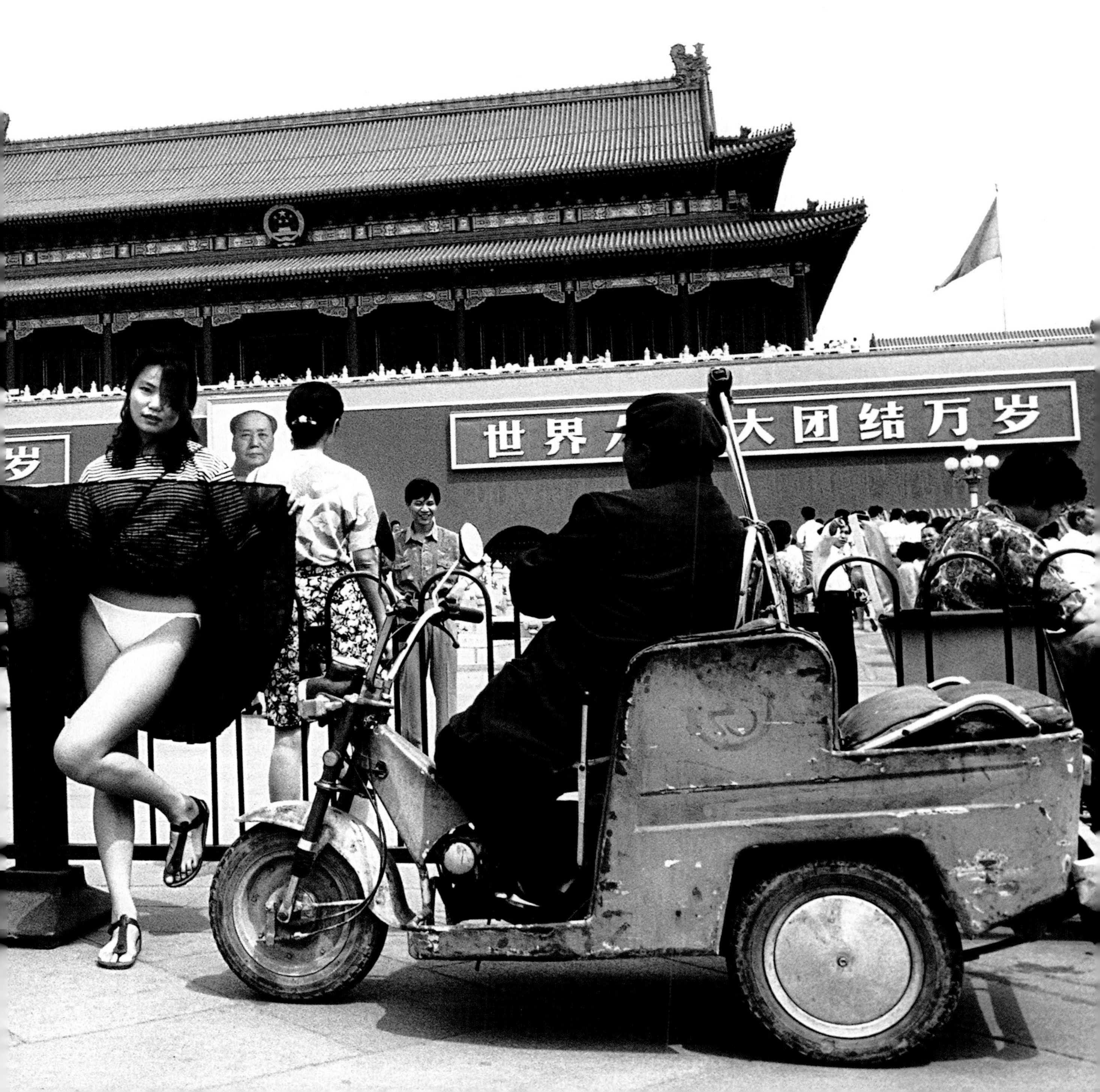
世界人民大团结万岁

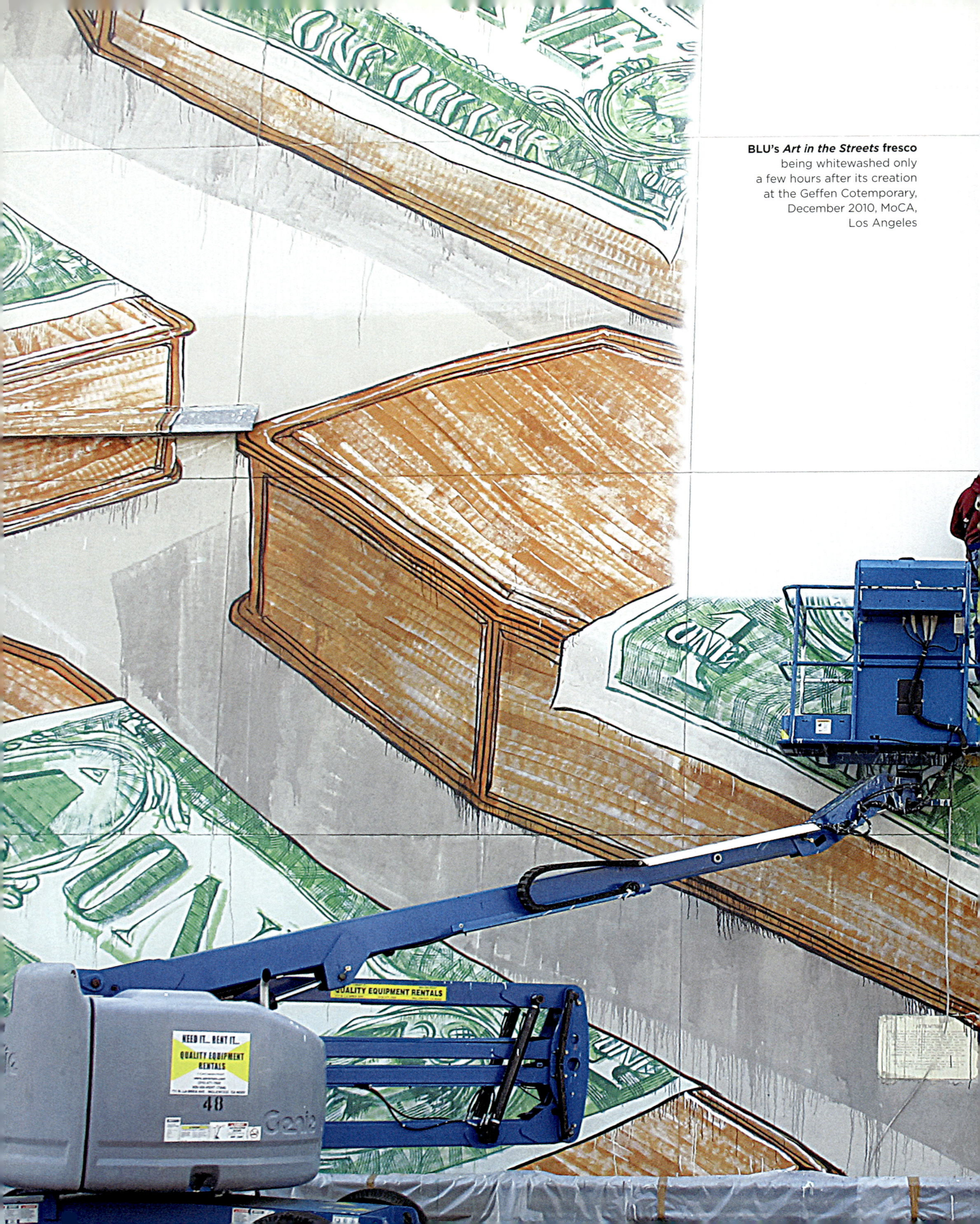

BLU's *Art in the Streets* fresco being whitewashed only a few hours after its creation at the Geffen Cotemporary, December 2010, MoCA, Los Angeles

DEATH IS ALWAYS WRONG

In 2011 the Museum of Contemporary Art (MoCA) in Los Angeles played host to the *Art in the Streets* exhibition that traced the evolution of graffiti and street art. The event was organized by Jeffrey Deitch, the Director of the MoCA, who supported many street artists. What could have happened to make him censor a fresco that he himself had commissioned?

In December 2011 the Italian graffiti artist and film-maker known under the pseudonym of BLU received a commission for the *Art in the Streets* exhibition in Los Angeles. He was charged with realizing a painting on the northern outer wall of the Geffen Contemporary, a wing of the MoCA. The artist erected a huge amount of scaffolding to tackle the task and delivered a surprising image: rows of coffins covered by one-dollar bills in place of the traditional Stars and Stripes. Censorship followed immediately: Jeffrey Deitch had the fresco covered over with white paint. The work had existed for less than 24 hours, a record even in the sphere of street art, in which creations are usually destined to disappear.

The director of the museum indicated that he did not wish to offend the local community. What was there to be afraid of? The Geffen Contemporary is located – could it be by coincidence? – next to a veterans' hospital and war memorial. But more than one person found this political justification somewhat dubious. On the one hand, it is unlikely that Jeffrey Deitch was not aware, from the very beginning, of the artist's project for an exhibition of this caliber and, on the other, the veterans themselves seemed to appreciate this artistic initiative. Some of them even participated in a demonstration supporting BLU on the Geffens parking lot!

One wonders if the director of the MoCA, an art dealer at heart, might not have felt compromised by the significance of the coffins: going beyond being an anti-war statement, were they not also the symbol of street art itself, dead under the weight of the process of commercialization in which Deitch is one of the main actors?

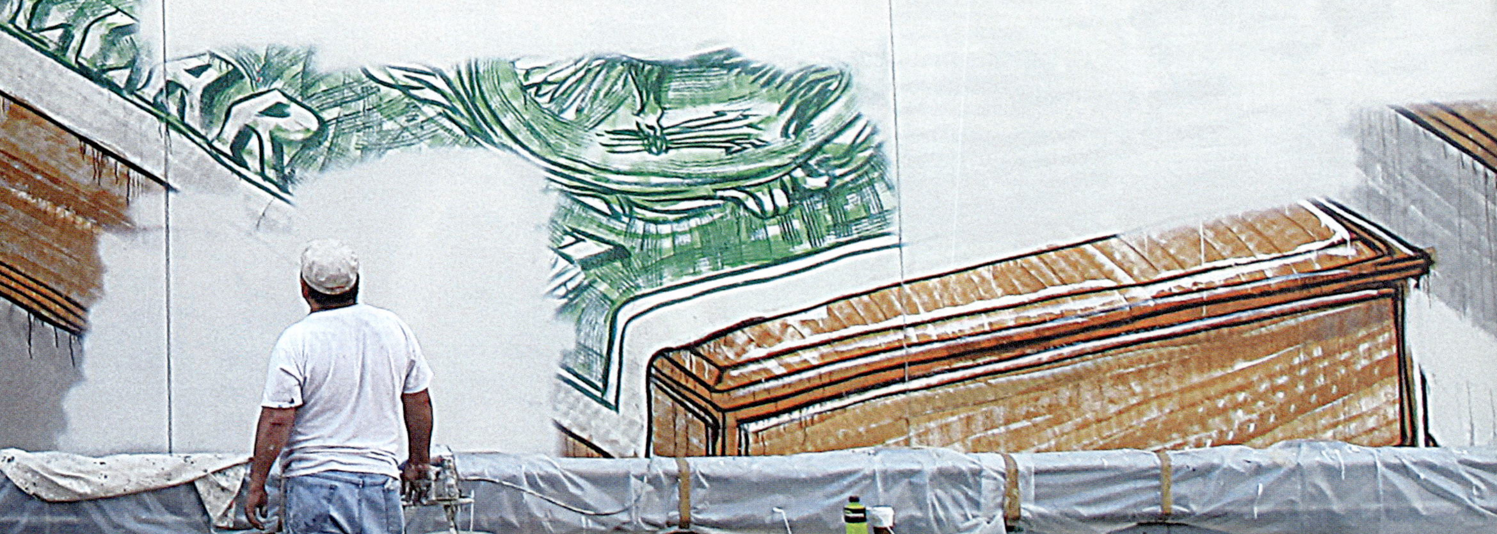

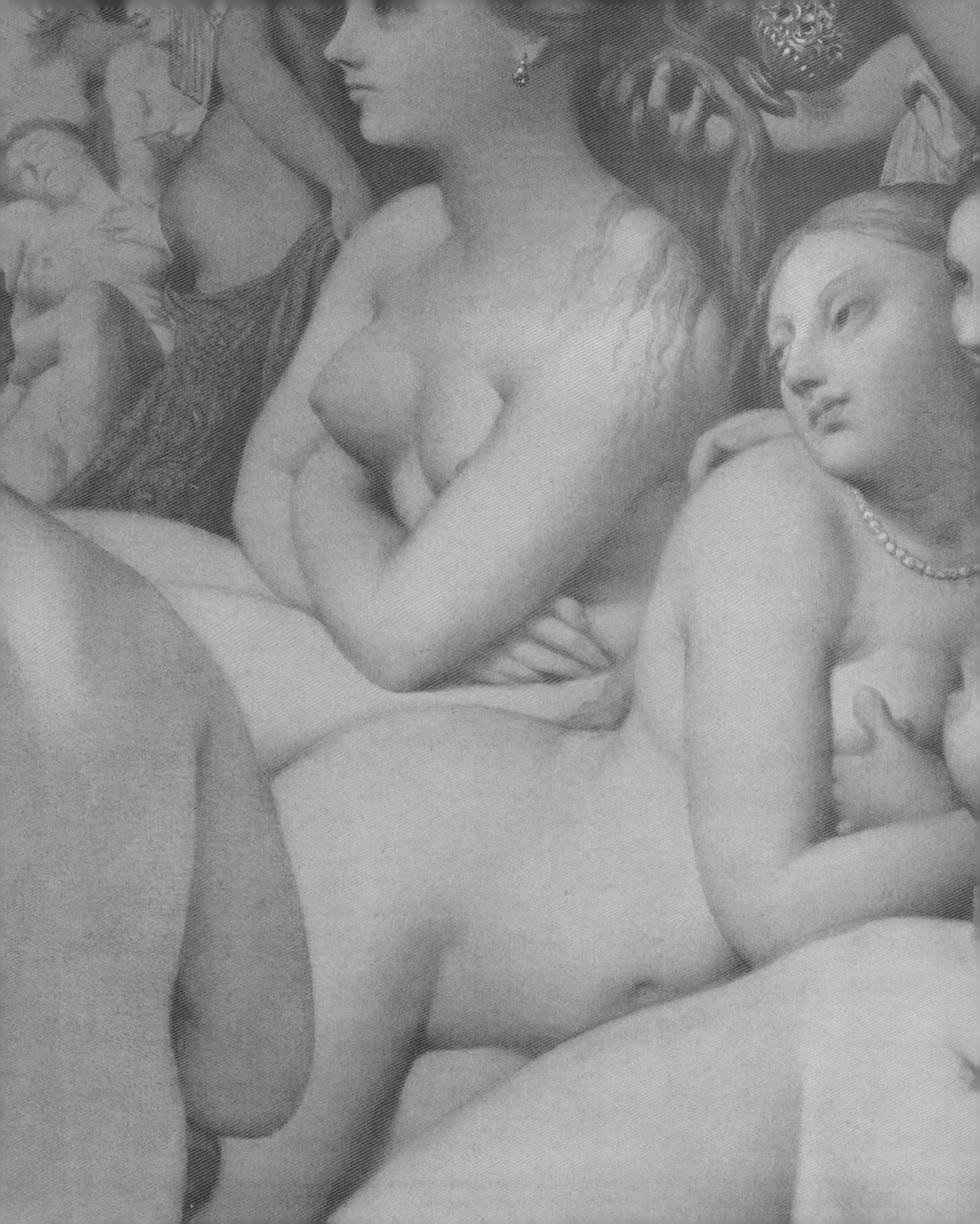

SEXUAL SCANDALS

ARTEMISIA GENTILESCHI

FRANCISCO GOYA

KATSUSHIKA HOKUSAI

JEAN-AUGUSTE-DOMINIQUE INGRES

ÉDOUARD MANET

GUSTAVE COURBET

JEAN-BAPTISTE CARPEAUX

EGON SCHIELE

CONSTANTIN BRANCUSI

AMEDEO MODIGLIANI

TAMARA DE LEMPICKA

HANS BELLMER

BALTHUS

OTTO MUEHL

OLEG KULIK

ROBERT MAPPLETHORPE

NAN GOLDIN

BLUE NOSES

ART AS REVENGE

Being a woman and a painter was already a scandal on its own in the seventeenth century. But for that woman loudly and strongly to accuse the man who raped her was more than contemporary Roman society could stand. Firm and determined despite the pressures she was put under, Artemisia Gentileschi continued to fight to obtain justice. She was to secure her lasting revenge through her work.

Artemisia Gentileschi learned how to paint as an apprentice to Agostini Tassi, who worked with her father. The close links between the two men did not stop Tassi from raping Gentileschi's nineteen-year-old daughter. The case was brought before the courts. As the victim, Artemisia Gentileschi was subjected to humiliating gynecological examination. If that were not bad enough, she was put through torture sessions to check that her accusations were not false. In spite of all this, she continued to proclaim that she was telling the truth. Tassi was found guilty but got off with a few months in prison and then carried on working with Gentileschi's father. Artemisia Gentileschi seems to have found a way of exacting ultimate revenge through her paintings of the biblical story of Judith and Holofernes, in which a young Jewish woman saves her people by pretending to give herself to a tyrant and then beheading him. Artemisia Gentileschi first painted the scene not long after the rape, during the course of the trial. The version illustrated here was painted several years later, but the memory of the events was clearly still searing for Gentileschi. Tassi is recognizable in the features of the decapitated Holofernes, while Judith is a self-portrait of the artist. The blood in the picture makes us think of the blood the rape would have produced: it spurts out onto the woman and onto the white sheets, and spreads out over the bed, where it is echoed by the red cloth covering the man's genitals, linking it directly to the rapist.

In Caravaggio's depiction of the scene, painted in 1599, Judith comes across as weak and squeamish. In Gentileschi's version she is the opposite: strong, focused, and satisfied. She grasps the tyrant's hair, just as Gentileschi said she did to fend off Tassi, and has firm hold of the sword that she thrusts straight down like a cross.

The painting was something of an embarrassment to a male chauvinist society that did not take kindly to sexual scandals being revealed, and it was to be kept hidden from public view by its prudent owners for a very long time.

Artemisia Gentileschi (1597– c. 1651),
***Judith and Holofernes*, c. 1620,**
oil on canvas, 199 × 162.5 cm, Uffizi Gallery, Florence

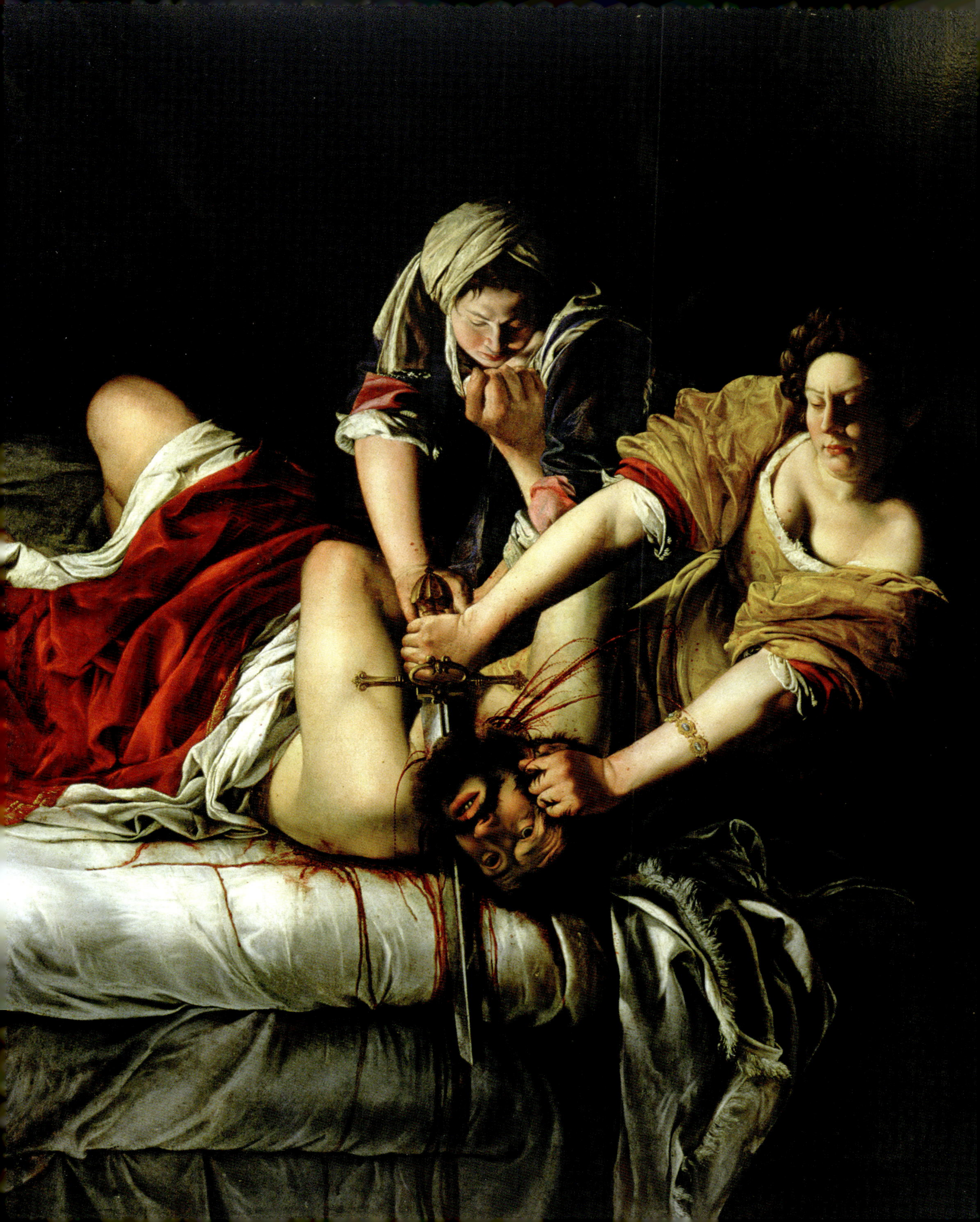

UNDRESSING THE SUBJECT

The eroticism of a nude is obvious enough, but a clothed woman can be equally titillating and sensual, as Manuel de Godoy, prime minister of Spain under Charles V, clearly understood, since he commissioned first the undressed version of the *Maja* and then its clothed twin.

In her diaphanous dress drawn in at the waist, revealing white stockinged feet in pointed shoes, Goya's *Clothed Maja* is provocative in her own right, but is even more so when seen alongside her naked counterpart. This is why the man who commissioned the paintings kept them firmly out of sight in his private collection. Side by side, the two chart a story both of the woman herself, who has either just taken off her clothes or just put them back on; and also of our prurience as viewers eager to see what hides beneath her dress. We do not know precisely who the subject of Goya's painting was, but there are all sorts of hypotheses: that she was the Duchess of Albi with whom Goya was besotted, for instance, or else Godoy's mistress.

While the *Nude Maja* looks brazenly out at the viewer with a shameless air, her clothed counterpart comes across as altogether calmer, a faint smile playing on her lips, and seems to exchanges a knowing look with the viewer. The heightened color on her rosy cheeks and her slightly disheveled hair suggest that she has just got dressed again after a sexual interlude that has taken place in the interval between the two paintings. Doubtless wanting to add another dimension to this erotic tale, Godoy hung the two paintings next to Velázquez's *Rokeby Venus* (c. 1647–1651, National Gallery, London). With its back view of a nude, it would have given viewers a chance to enjoy yet more delights of the female form.

The Inquisition got wind of the paintings after the prime minister's death and roundly condemned them, demanding to know their background. Goya was

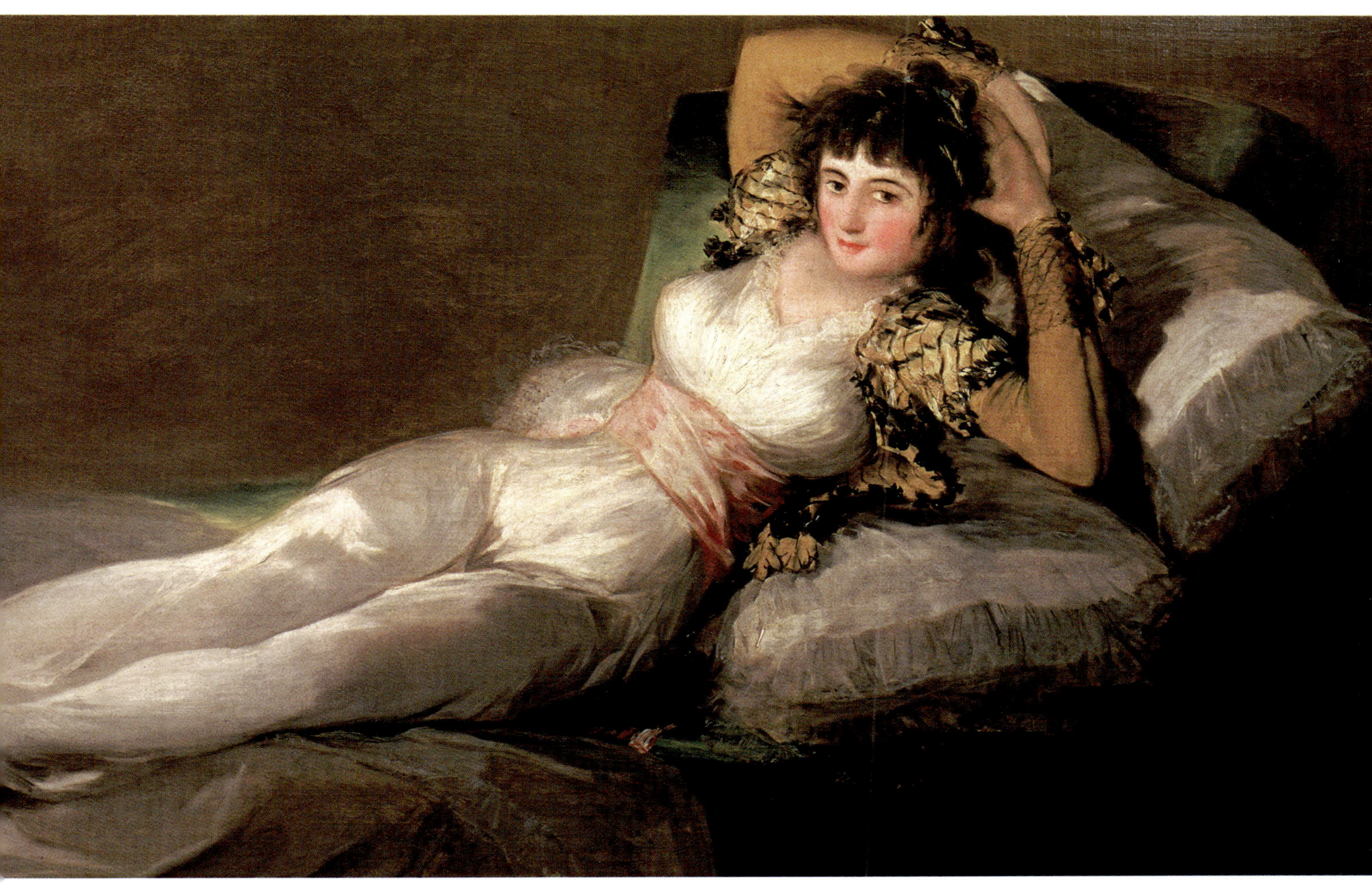

used to incurring the disapprobation of the inquisitors he caricatured in his *Caprichos* (see. p. 48), but
they never gave him undue cause for concern. This
was almost certainly because of the position he com-
manded as court painter.

Francisco Goya (1746–1828), *The Nude Maja***, 1800,**
oil on canvas, 95 x 190 cm, Museo del Prado, Madrid

Following pages:
Francisco Goya (1746–1828), *The Clothed Maja***, 1800,**
oil on canvas, 98 x 191 cm, Museo del Prado, Madrid

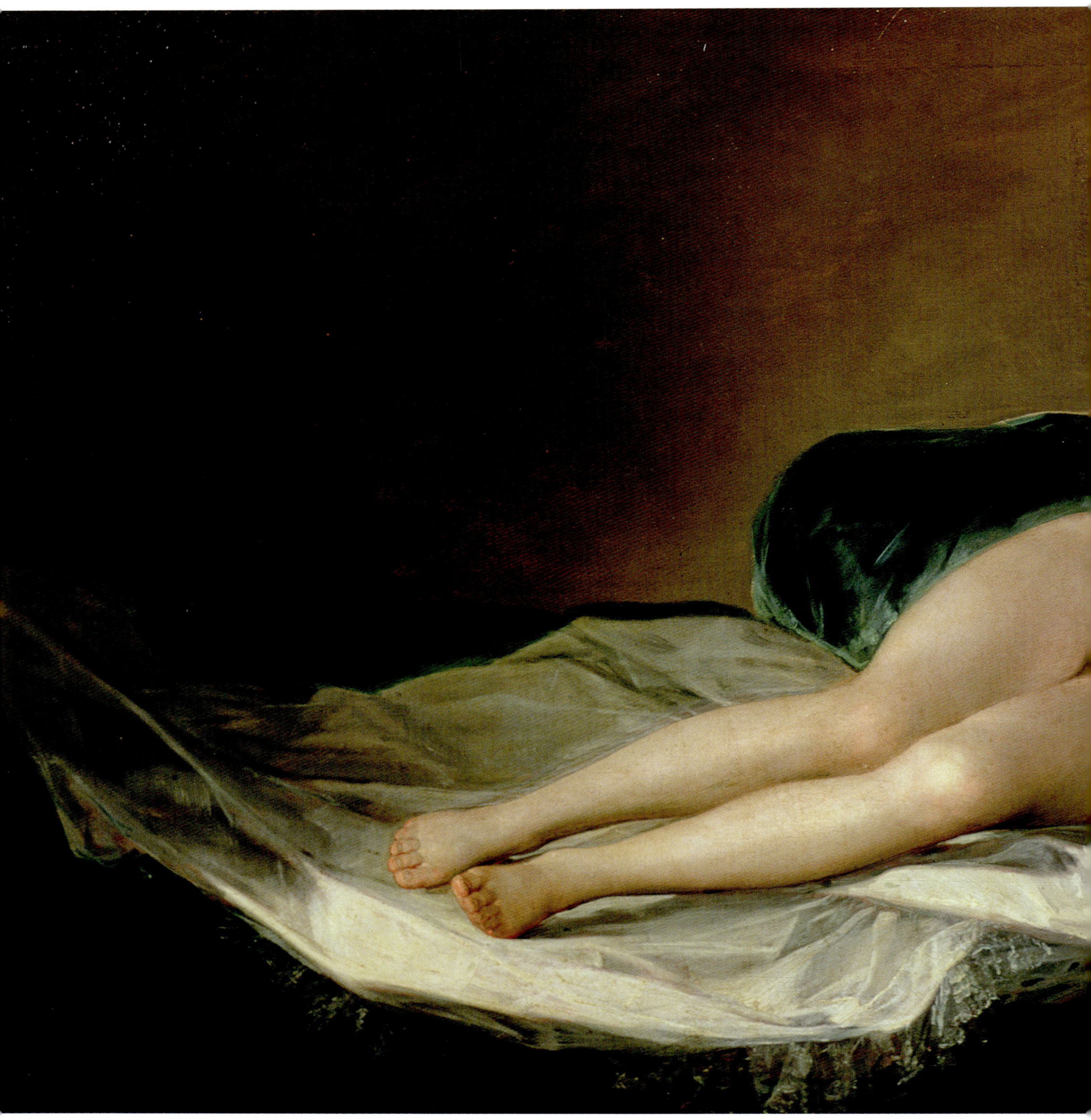

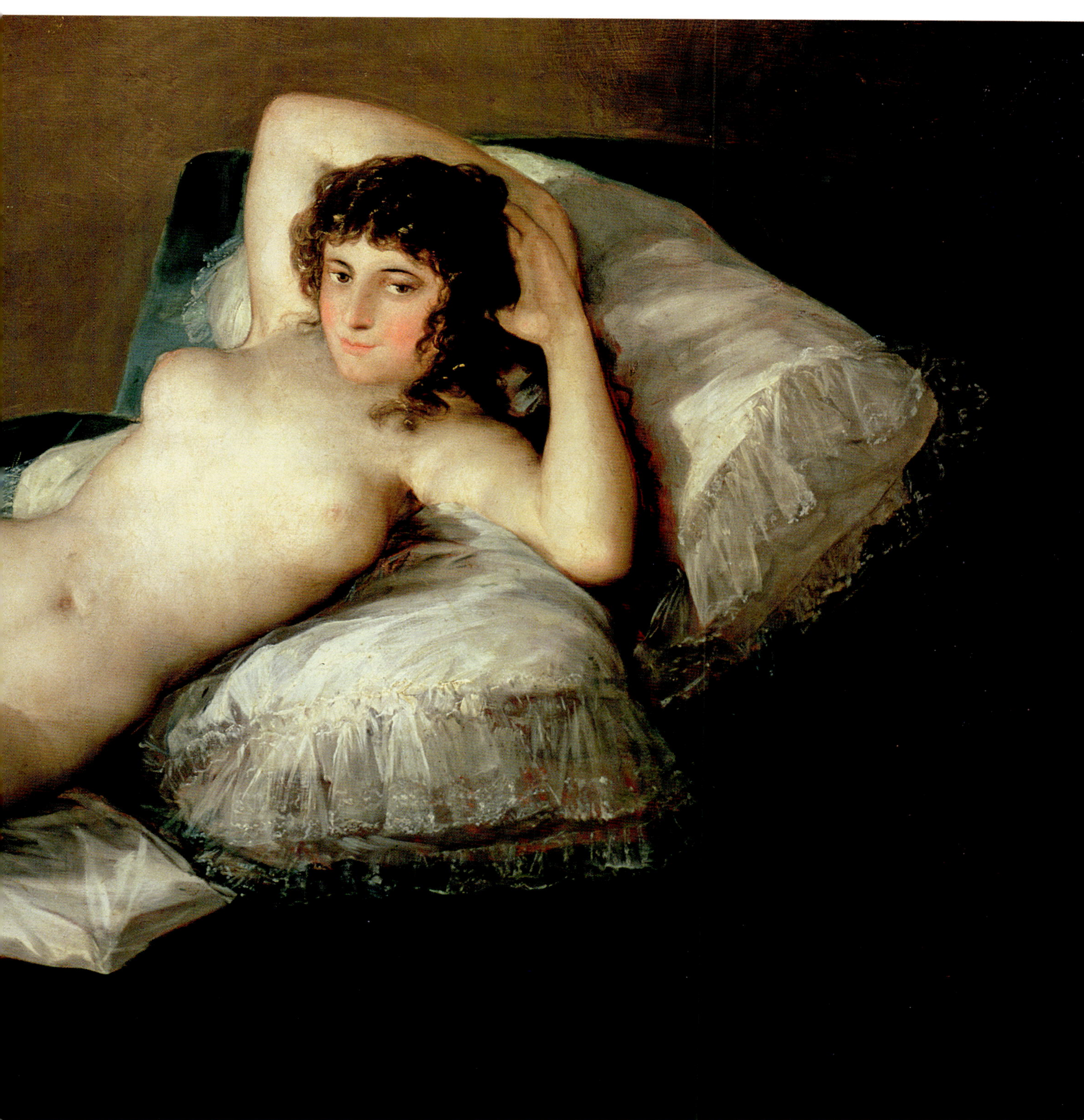

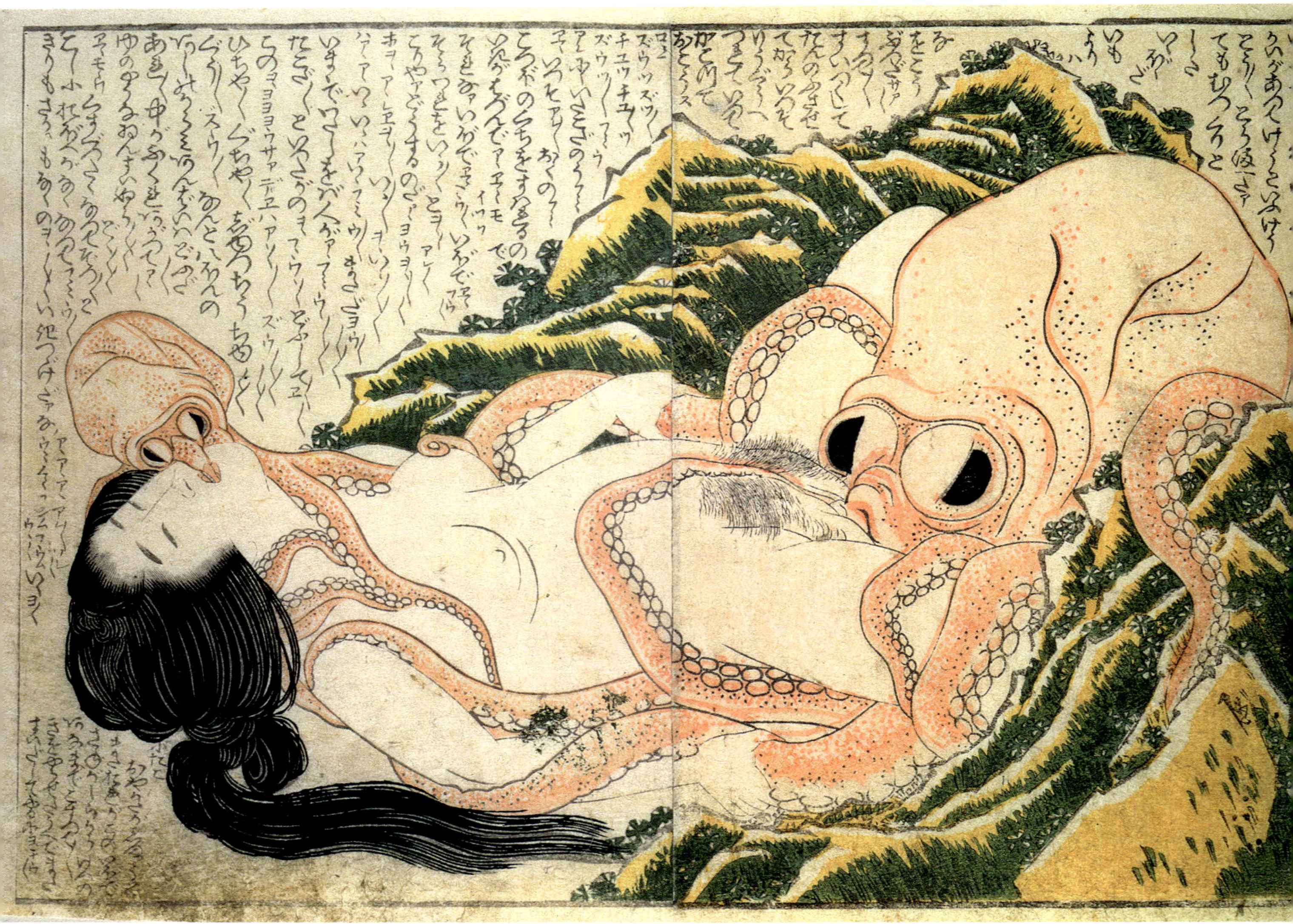

THE TENTACLES OF LOVE

Katsushika Hokusai was a prolific and multi-talented artist famous not only for painting and prints but even for writing novels. In the course of his long career, he produced at least 30,000 designs for prints. He is considered the father of Manga (comics), and like all Japanese masters of the period he went in for the illicit practice of producing erotic prints.

During the Tempo period (1830–1843) Hokusai produced a great many *shunga*. Literally translated as "pictures of spring," these were hugely popular prints depicting all kinds of sexual acts and incorporating people from all levels of society, from geishas to peasant girls and celebrated kabuki actors, the stars of the age. One of their most notable features was the disproportionate size they made the sexual organs, without any attempt at anatomical accuracy. The reason for this was that as well as having an obviously powerful erotic value, *shunga* were designed to serve an educational and social purpose. They were used to teach young couples, and bound collections of them were presented to newlyweds and courtesans.

The Dream of the Fisherman's Wife is one of a series of zoophilic drawings of women in the clasps of octopuses. In this scene a woman drunk with pleasure abandons herself to the expert tentacles of two lecherous octopuses. The first sucks hungrily at her vulva while the other kisses her greedily and pinches a nipple. It has all the classic elements of a *shunga*: unrestrained imagination, but humor too, and refinement.

Like his fellow artists, Hokusai circulated these drawings in secret. The government tried repeatedly to stop them being broadcast. In 1661, an edict was issued banning erotic books, among other things; a much stricter edict followed in 1772, banning all new work unless it had been approved in advance by a censorship committee. This forced *shunga* underground but in no way halted their production. Ironically, it was not censorship that eventually put a stop to them, but serious competition in the shape of erotic photography.

Katsushika Hokusai (1760–1849),
***The Dream of the Fisherman's Wife*, 1814,**
woodblock print, 1814, 18.9 x 26.6 cm, opening from the illustrated book *Kinoe no Komatsu* ("Young pines bursting with sap"), British Museum, London

"LIKE MAGGOTS ON A PIECE OF CAKE"

Paul Claudel

This painting by Ingres is widely considered to be his most erotic and remained hidden away from public view for a long time. It took fifty years from the time it was painted, and a good deal of hesitation by the Louvre, before it was acquired for the nation. The mass of nude bodies, their indecent poses and gestures, were too immodest for late nineteenth-century society.

At the age of eighty-two, Ingres had a fine career behind him. Decried and admired in turn, he was famous enough for Prince Napoleon to commission a painting from him. Ingres chose an exotic Oriental theme of the kind then in vogue.

So much for the subject. For the figures and the composition, Ingres drew on the many female nudes he had drawn and painted in the course of his long career. The woman playing the stringed instrument in the foreground, for instance, is clearly based on *The Bather of Valpinçon* (1808, Louvre, Paris). Her figure is distorted and her pose impossible to hold: it is not physically possible for so much of her left breast to be visible under her arm, or for her neck to be twisted in such a way that her face can be seen in profile. Ingres was regularly derided for the way he abused anatomy, but it is precisely his voluptuous distortion of anatomy that lends his figures their sensuality. He conjures up an idealized image of woman by accentuating the rounded forms of the female body in sinuous curves with his brush. He even extends the curve motif to the format of the painting, making it a tondo to create the sense that we are intruding voyeuristically into the scene, as if we were looking at it through a keyhole. The women dance, sit about, caress one another's breasts, completely oblivious to our presence as spectators.

The painting was returned to the painter, Prince Napoleon's wife finding it impossible to accept such indecency. It was eventually bought by the Turkish emissary Khalil Bey, who collected erotic art and commissioned *The Origin of the World* from Courbet (see p. 104).

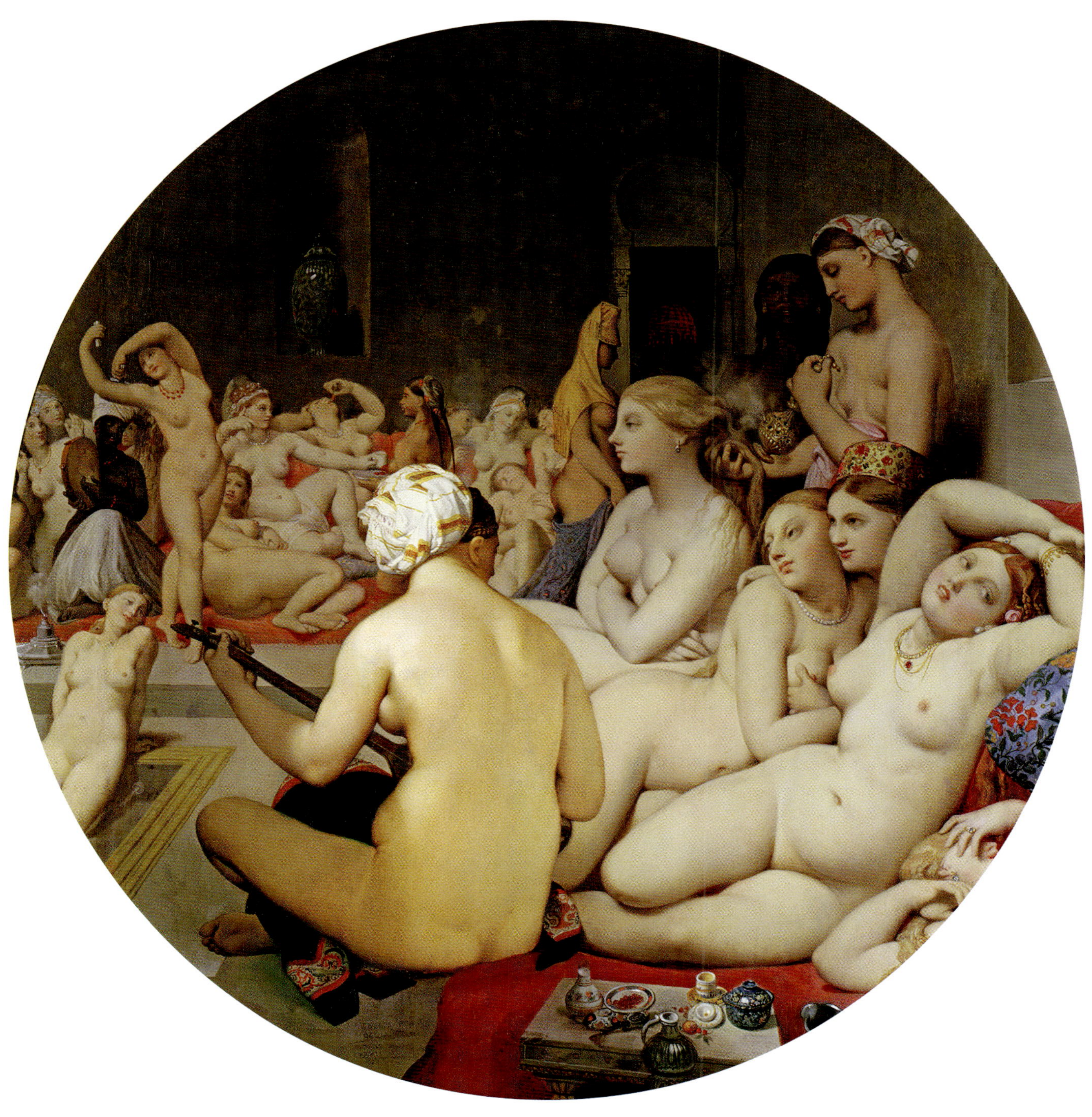

Jean-Auguste-Dominique Ingres (1780–1867),
The Turkish Bath, **1862,**
oil on wood, 108 x 110 cm, Musée du Louvre, Paris

SUCCÈS DE SCANDALE

In 1863, Manet's *Olympia* was exhibited at the official Salon in Paris. This female nude stirred up an immense uproar that is considered the most notorious in the history of art. The picture itself had to be protected and was hung higher – many outraged visitors had actually threatened to destroy it.

The academic art world and the decent citizens of the period did not take up arms against a simple nude. Nudity was considered appropriate if it was idealized in a mythological or allegorical scene. But in this case, the canonical Venus with her immaculate rosy skin was shown as an everyday, common prostitute. Far from trying to disguise this outrage against decorum, Manet provided many indications of this woman's social position. The black cat caused a commotion; the public recognized it as a symbol of scandalous lust. Far from its apparent innocence, the bouquet of flowers also contributed to the scandal – it is definitely a lover's present that the servant is bringing to her mistress. As for the woman, she shows no modesty, no embarrassment, no shame. She looks us up and down, sure of herself, provocative. A hand placed on her thigh hides her genitals as if to challenge the desire of the person contemplating her. The scene is made even more unsettling by the play of glances: the (presumed male) spectator becomes a voyeur and the dark, cold glance of the prostitute follows him wherever he goes. The pub-lic was enraged at the audacity of the subject but also made fun of the way it was treated. Manet did not respect the academic rules and it was believed that he did not know how to paint. However, that was a deliberate choice on the part of the painter. He wanted to depict reality as he saw it and not as it was interpreted by art; he wanted to renew artistic expression. Therefore not perfection, but a woman with a broad face, an unglamorized body, and skin shaded by the light and its reflections.

Manet was deeply affected by the virulence of the critics. His intention with this work was not to infuriate but to continue on his search for a realistic vision. He tried to justify himself with "I did what I saw." However, those who – like the writer Émile Zola – recognized the achievement of this painter were rare.

Édouard Manet (1832–1883), *Olympia*, 1863, oil on canvas, 130 x 190 cm, Musée d'Orsay, Paris

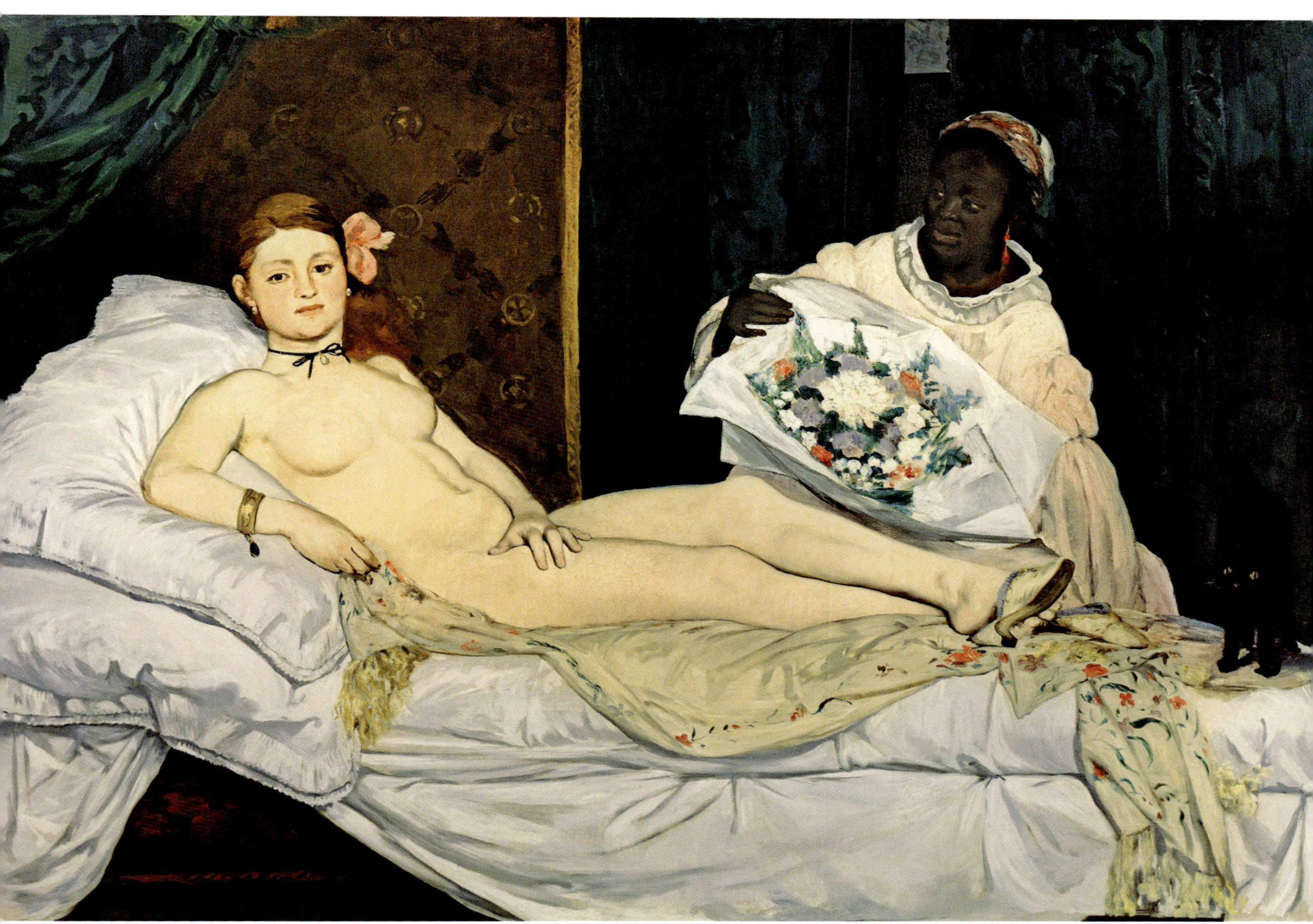

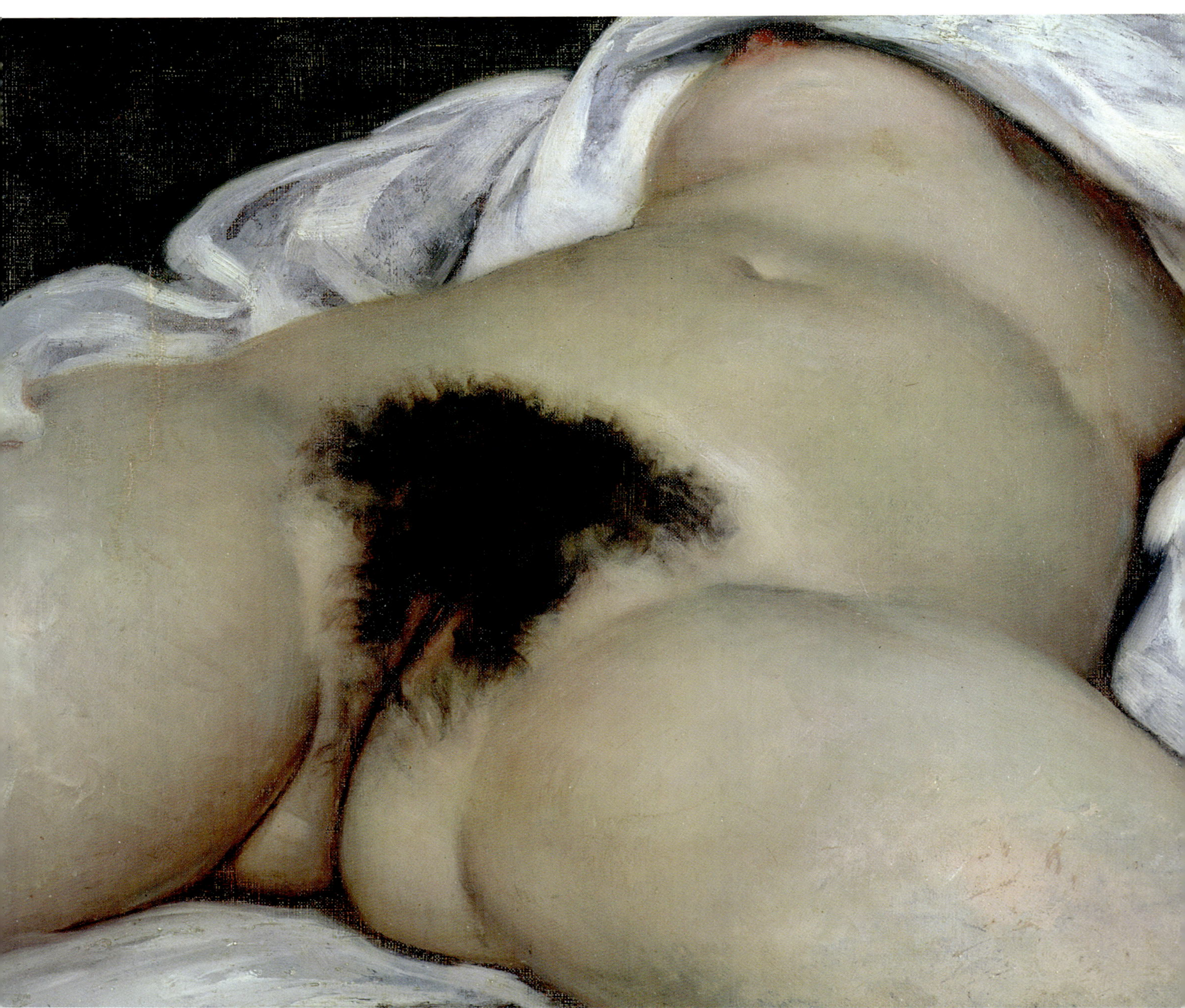

THE MYSTERY OF THE ORIGIN

Painted and delivered in secret to a Turkish diplomat who, crippled with debts, had to sell it, left behind in Budapest, confiscated by the Nazis and then the Soviets, before resurfacing in Paris in the possession of a famous French psychoanalyst … The fate of *The Origin of the World* is just as extraordinary as its subject.

It is difficult to relate the precise history of this painting, which for so long led a clandestine existence hidden from the eyes of the public and their moral judgment. Hardly inclined to keep things quiet, Courbet still did not let it be known that this incredible canvas passed directly from the artist's hand to those of the man who commissioned it, the Turkish diplomat Khalil Bey in 1866 (he also commissioned Ingres' *The Turkish Bath*, see p. 100). Around a decade later, the work was mentioned by one of the rare spectators who had been allowed to gaze upon it, the writer Maxime Du Camp, who ranted and raged in *Les Convulsions de Paris* (1878): "There is a word used to describe people capable of this kind of garbage, perfectly suited to illustrate the works of the Marquis de Sade, but I cannot utter this word in the presence of my readers because it is one that is only commonly used in butcheries." Little is known about the trials and tribulations of the painting after Khalil Bey had been forced to separate himself from his personal collection. It could have been fated for destruction at the hands of the Nazis and then saved by the Soviets, who possibly resold it. No matter what happened, *The Origin of the World* turned up again in the home of the psychoanalyst Jacques Lacan, where it was hidden behind a canvas his wife commissioned from André Masson.

Finally, the painting came into the collection of the Musée d'Orsay in 1995 under the name it is known as today. Nobody is certain of how this title actually originated; it does not seem to have come from the artist. It undoubtedly results from an attempt to minimize the pornographic impact of these genitals by investing them with a maternal significance.

In 2013 a discovery created waves of uncertainty: an art lover stated that he had found the head of *The Origin of the World*. Some experts agreed that the canvas could have been cropped and that the genitals were merely one part of the original female nude. Other specialists regard this with disdain as an eccentric claim that diminished the work's originality. Is an attempt being made to diminish the scandalous potential of this vulva by providing it with a complete body? The work has still not finished provoking strong reactions.

Gustave Courbet (1819–1877), *The Origin of the World*, 1866,
oil on canvas, 46 × 55 cm, Musée d'Orsay, Paris

A WORK THAT CAUSED A LOT OF INK TO FLOW

When commissioned by Charles Garnier to create an allegory of dance for the Paris Opéra, Carpeaux produced a sculpture that was widely considered to be immoral – a bacchanal. The extraordinary skill he had shown in capturing the grace and movement of dance did nothing to win over its many detractors.

Carpeaux worked on *La Danse* for three years in his efforts to capture the feeling of movement and energy in stone. To do this, he made sketches of the pupils of the Opéra's ballet class. When his work was installed on the façade of the majestic building in 1869, it was soon jeered at by the bourgeoisie, who judged art only by the criteria – and morals – of the official Salon. Too many figures, too much energetic movement, and above all too much sensuality – and all of this with a touch of madness. The ecstatic women around the central Spirit of Dance have let their finery fall to be better able to whirl around uninhibitedly in the frenzied dance. Their smiles are demonic, their charms shamelessly laid bare.

The reactions were not long in coming. A bottle of ink was hurled at the buttocks of one of the bacchantes. This iconoclastic act was copied and the controversy swelled up. The conservative press picked up the story of the scandal and could not find sufficient malignant epithets to qualify the artist as a pornographer and his sculpture as indecent. Tongues started to wag and pens were flourished. The writer Prosper Merimée set the tone: "He has produced a group of savages dancing the cancan in front of the door of the Opéra. It is amazing that the officers of the law have not intervened." Finally, Napoleon III stepped in. He ordered that the group be removed and demanded that Carpeaux try again – but that this time the subject should be "treated with decency." The artist refused and a new sculptor was commissioned.

But history brought about a different conclusion: the Franco-Prussian War of 1870 put an end to the debate and Carpeaux was not forced to comply: his work was allowed to stay where it was. Charles Garnier, the innovative architect, had grasped his friend's genius, something that public opinion would take years to recognize.

Jean-Baptiste Carpeaux (1827–1875), *La Danse*, 1869, marble, 420 × 298 × 145 cm, Musée d'Orsay, Paris
The sculpture that can be seen on the façade today is a copy made by Paul Belmondo.

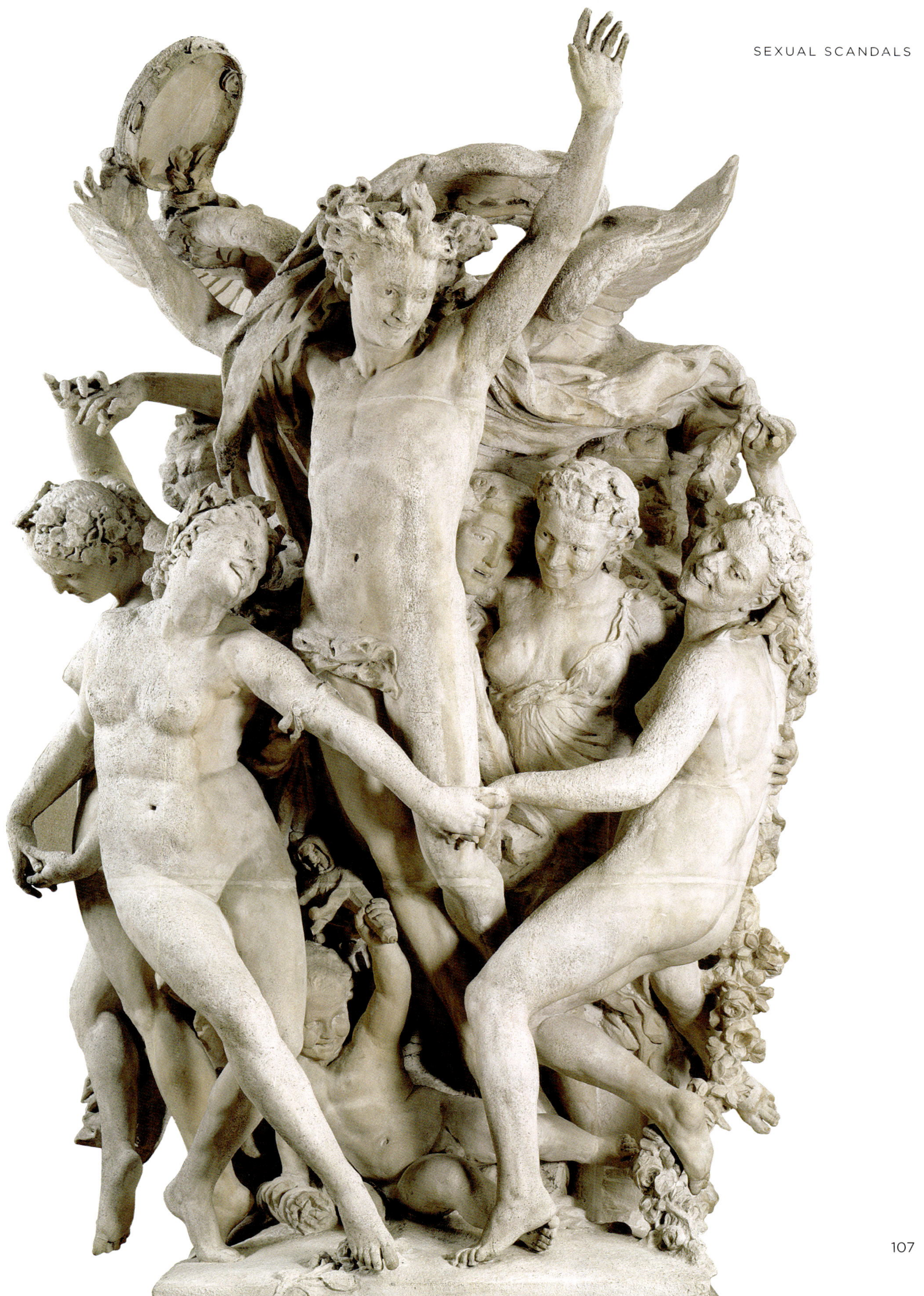

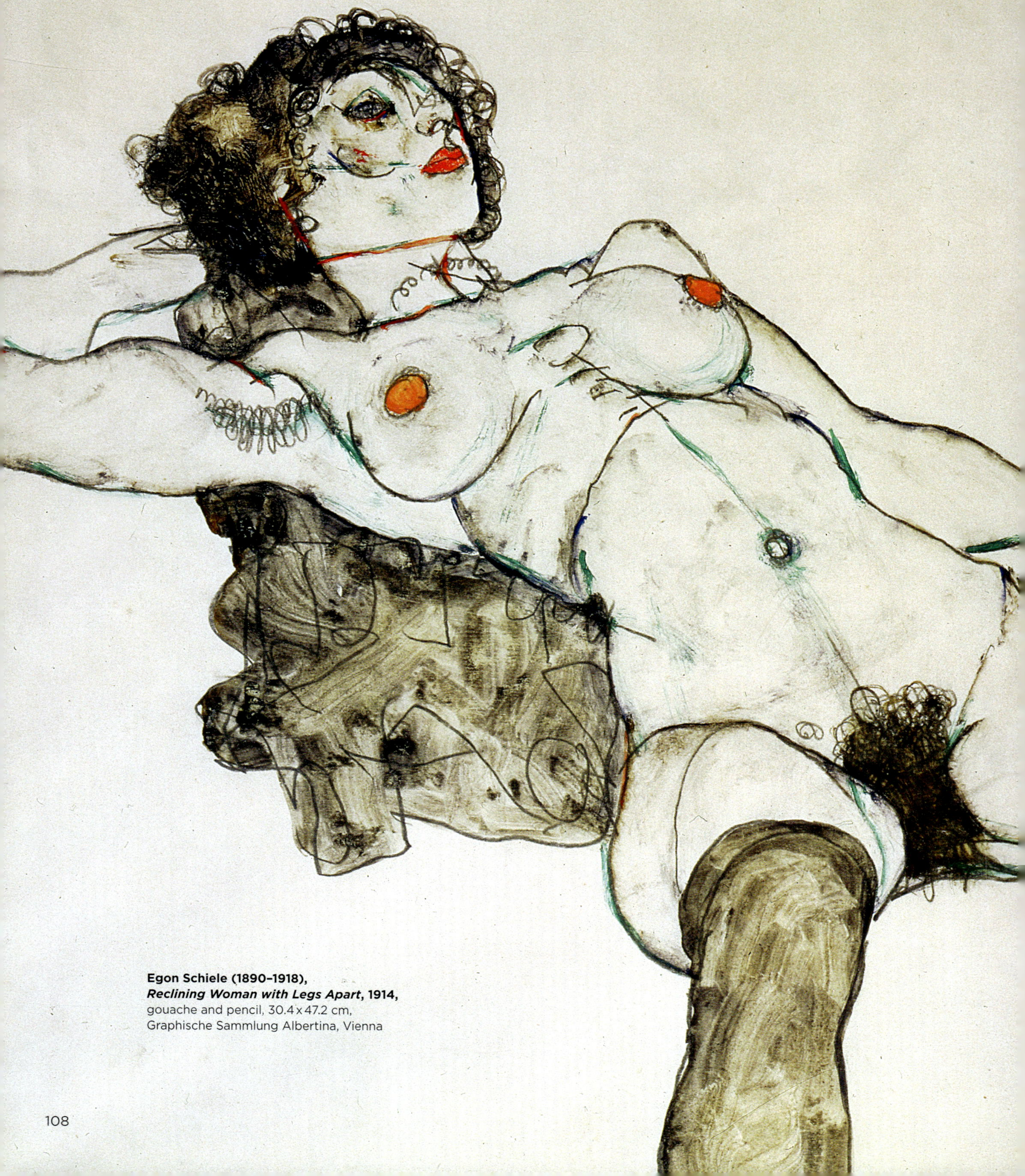

Egon Schiele (1890–1918),
Reclining Woman with Legs Apart, **1914,**
gouache and pencil, 30.4 x 47.2 cm,
Graphische Sammlung Albertina, Vienna

THE ARTIST AS MARTYR

During his short life, Egon Schiele was subjected to condemnation and injustice. He felt so persecuted that he even portrayed himself with the attributes of Saint Sebastian. His favorite subject was the human body – naked not nude. The female nudes he created at the end of his career contributed both to his success and to his arrest and traumatizing imprisonment.

There is neither grace nor harmony in Schiele's immodest portraits; only the contorted, tormented bodies of those wallowing in their despondency and cheerless solitude. Influenced by the Secessionist painters around Gustav Klimt, Schiele set out to express his inner agitation without being concerned about his style. He was not well thought of in his Viennese surroundings. His neighbors did not appreciate that their children were allowed to play freely in the painter's studio and possibly come face to face with an improper sketch or painting.

In 1912, Schiele was unjustly attacked in a sordid affair. The father of an adolescent girl accused him of abduction and rape. The painter was arrested and spent 24 days in prison. The young girl's accusations were false but it provided the opportunity for the state to take a closer interest in Egon Schiele's life. They discovered masses of erotic works in his studio and learned that he sometimes sold them illicitly. On the heels of this discovery, the court condemned him for distributing erotic drawings and for gross indecency. At the trial, Schiele had to submit to the most horrible form of humiliation: the judge publicly burned one of his drawings. Vienna became increasingly hostile towards the artist and Schiele, wounded by the dishonesty of those in power, comforted himself by taking on the role of a martyr, which he played until the very end.

In 1918, his pregnant wife was carried away by Spanish influenza; he succumbed to the same disease a few days later; he was twenty-eight.

PHALLIC FEMININITY

Brancusi explained: "Artworks are mirrors in which everybody sees what he looks like." So what do you see in this image? A phallus? There you have the scandal! However, the artist insisted that he had only wanted to represent a woman, simplified to the extreme.

The story begins with Princess Marie de Bonaparte, whom the artist showed leaning over her mirror in a sculpture which has since disappeared. Starting out from there, Brancusi attempted to simplify the form to its extreme; to reduce it to essentials. He lovingly polished his work for five years to reduce it to the essence he was obsessed with. He wanted to represent the idea of the woman per se. Forced to justify himself, Brancusi explained his approach, which was in no way obscene: "I believe that I am victorious at last, that I have conquered the material. … And my material is so beautiful, has such sinuous lines, which shine like pure gold and integrate all of the world's feminine effigies into a single archetype." The artist was not a natural troublemaker and he was severely hurt by the caustic criticism that greeted *Princess X*. The work was turned down for the first time at the Salon d'Antin organized by André Salmon in 1916. But the real scandal occurred in 1930 at the Salon des Indépendants presided over by Henri Matisse and Paul Signac. They were alarmed by the phallic shape of the sculpture, which they feared could provoke an incident. The sculpture was moved to a discrete place for the opening and visit by the minister and then completely removed by order of the chief of police. One month later, a protest signed by more than seventy artists and other leading figures was printed in *Le Journal du people* under the title of: "For the Independence of Art." Thanks to this support, *Princess X* was able to return to the exhibition, where it continued to provoke condemnation and ribald humor.

Constantin Brancusi (1876–1957), *Princess X*, **1915–1916,**
polished bronze with stone base (limestone),
61.7 × 40.5 × 22.2 cm, Musée National d'Art Moderne –
Centre Georges – Pompidou, Paris

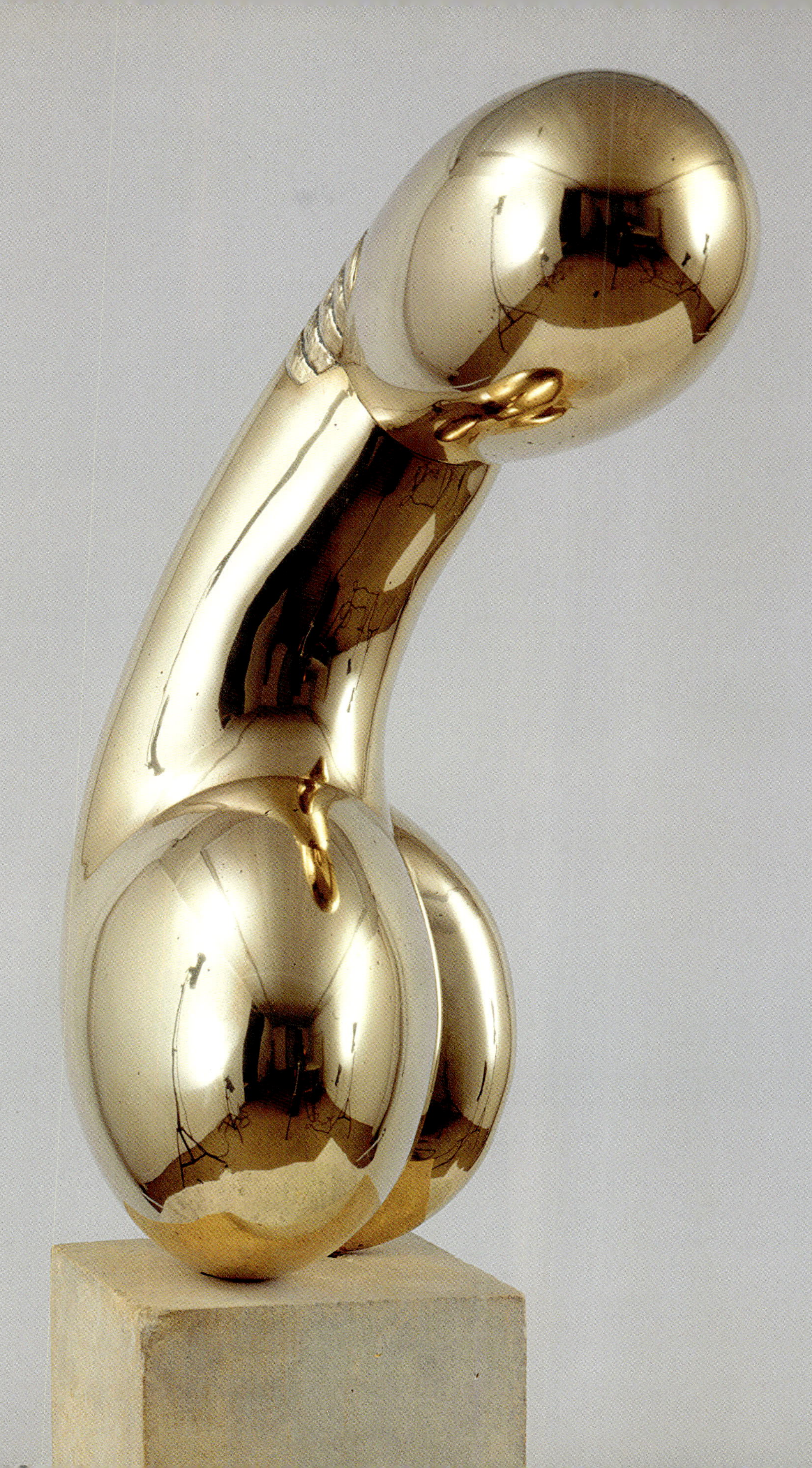

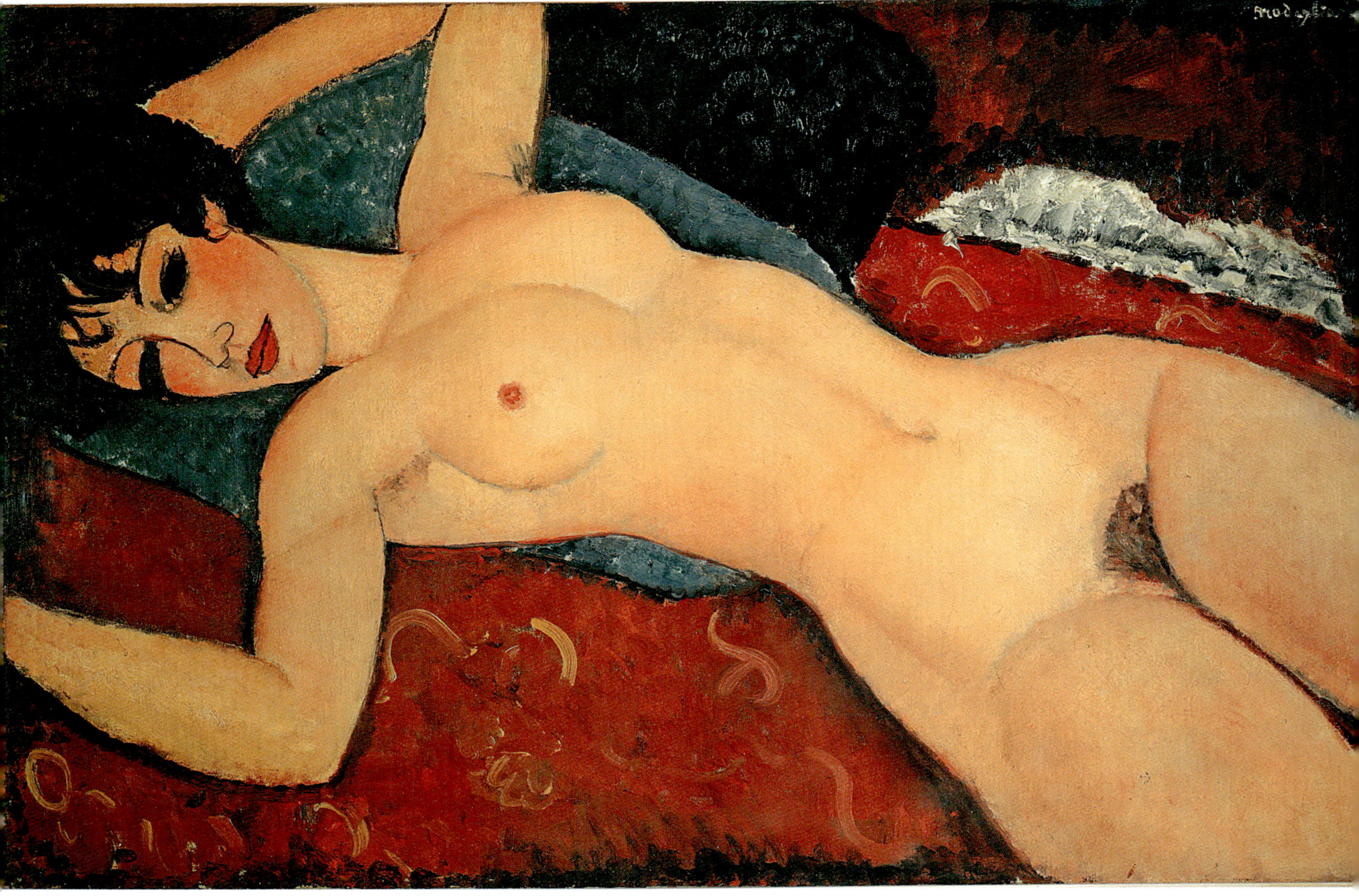

"THESE NUDES ... THEY'VE GOT HHHAIR!"

In spite of his intense production, Modigliani had sold very few works by 1917. The young Italian artist who had arrived in Paris around 1906 was eking out a meager existence at the time. But in that year, luck seemed to smile on him at last.

It was the poet Leopold Zborowski who introduced Modigliani to the famous dealer Berthe Weill, who had her gallery on Montmartre. She succumbed to the charm of his works, those "sumptuous nudes, angular figures, delicious portraits," and organized an exhibition of them at her gallery. The opening of the first solo exhibition of works by Modigliani opened there on 3 December 1917. *The Italian Woman, The Innocent, The Woman with Large Eyes ...* Thirty-two canvases including four nudes as well as some drawings were presented to a handpicked public on that evening.

Very soon a crowd of passers-by gathered like moths around a flame in front of the illuminated gallery window. The district police chief, whose offices were located across the street, became intrigued by the spectacle and wanted to see what was happening. What a calamity! One could see one of Modigliani's nude women from the street. An officer was immediately sent to order the removal of the four nudes, "that garbage," or else all of the canvas would be confiscated as offending public decency. Berthe

Weill was perplexed: "But what is the matter with these nudes?" In her memoirs, the gallery owner relates that the police chief then replied outraged and with his eyes bulging: "These nudes! ... these nudes ... they've got hhhair!"

Modigliani had dared to show the woman in all of her eroticism and animal nature and found himself punished for that. He was one of the first to have shown the hair on the pubis and armpits of his models that was usually so well hidden from the eyes of the viewers of the period. Out of modesty ... or self-censorship.

The exhibition continued without any kind of disturbance, but also without the four offending pictures. Modigliani sold only two drawings and returned to his impecunious existence. Two years later, he lost his life through tubercular meningitis at the age of thirty-six.

Amedeo Modigliani (1884–1920), *Reclining Nude*, 1917, oil on canvas, 20 x 92 cm, private collection, Milan

THE ART OF LOVE AND SUCCESS

Tamara de Lempicka was one of the great icons of the Paris of the Roaring Twenties. She made a work of art out of her life, which she fashioned just as expertly as her paintings. Liberated and carefree, she seduced men as well as women and declared that she almost always painted only those she had loved.

Of Polish origin, Lempicka went to live in Saint Petersburg, where she led an extravagant life. She set her heart on a sophisticated lawyer and showed up at a costume ball dressed as a peasant girl with a goose on a leash in order to attract the womanizer's attention. The strategy worked: at the age of nineteen, she married Tadeusz Lempicki dressed in a robe she had designed herself – the train took up the entire length of the chapel. Forced to flee from Russia after the Revolution, she escaped with her lover at the time, a Swedish diplomat, while her husband was arrested for being an agent of the tsarist police. Freed through the intervention of the diplomat, he rejoined his wife in Paris in 1918. There, Lempicka was not satisfied with leading the simple life of a refugee and, more than ever before, stepped into the limelight as a woman and artist in order to regain the wealth and fame she loved so much. She exhibited her work for the first time at the 1922 Salon d'Automne in Paris. Despite the fact that assessments were mostly negative, by 1925 her commercial success made it possible for her gradually to attain the prosperity she longed for. She was soon a doyen of Parisian high society and nightlife.

La Chemise Rose I dates from 1933. The year marked a turning point in her life; she was soon to embark on her second marriage, which turned her into Baroness Kuffner and an artist suddenly inspired by religion. However, this lascivious painting is far from being pious. A young woman with a sultry look and dazzling red lips seems to be issuing a provocative invitation. The fine chemise, the undergarment half removed, uncovers her cheeky breasts with their erect tips. The cushion the model is leaning against and the curtain in the background give the spectator the feeling of breaking in on an intimate scene. It is difficult not to imagine that this is one of the female lovers of the bisexual artist who customarily caressed her canvas with a brush inspired by her paramours.

Tamara de Lempicka (1898–1980), *La Chemise Rose I*, **1933,** oil on wooden panel, 41 x33 cm, Beatrice Levy Collection, Florida

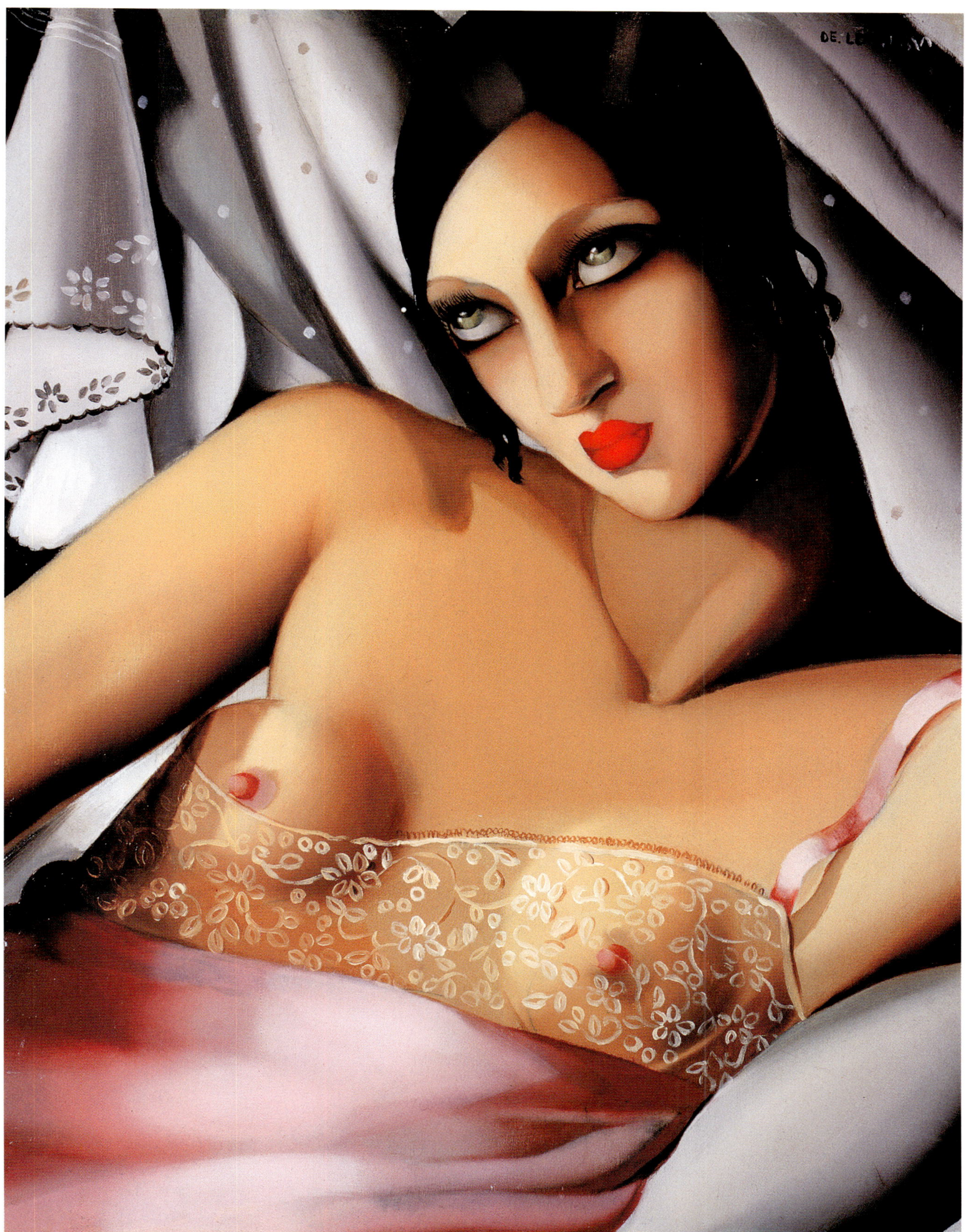

PLAYING WITH THE EROTIC

In the years 1933–1934, Hans Bellmer dreamed up a prototype for an anthropomorphic creature. This repellent, attractive, protean *Doll* was to become his fetish object – much to the dislike of the maliciously wagging tongues that saw nothing but perversity.

Bellmer rediscovered his old toys in 1932. In the same year, he attended a ballet performance of the tale *Coppelia* by E.T.A. Hoffmann, in which a doll has the main role. Excited and inspired by the play and his long-abandoned toys, he created the first version of his doll, a wooden sculpture that acted as the model for the great majority of the works that followed. This preposterous marionette symbolized his rejection of paternal and political authority. Disgusted by Nazi Germany and by his father, who had become a party member, the artist actually declared that he no longer intended to do anything that could be in any way beneficial to the state.

The doll-object also constituted a reflection on the image of the body. Like a maniac, Bellmer subjected it to whatever entered his head – he broke it, mutilated it, hung it on a tree, displayed it naked or clothed, and then photographed it. These series of images both fascinate and bewilder; they show a woman-child object at the mercy of a masculine fantasy.

In a second version of his doll, Bellmer added a mechanism that seemed almost to give life to his creature: the limbs now moved around a central "ball joint" that made all combinations and the rotations he desired possible. The most perverse and most tender obsessions (it is all a question of the point of view) now became physically possible.

In Paris, the Surrealists were overwhelmed by Bell-

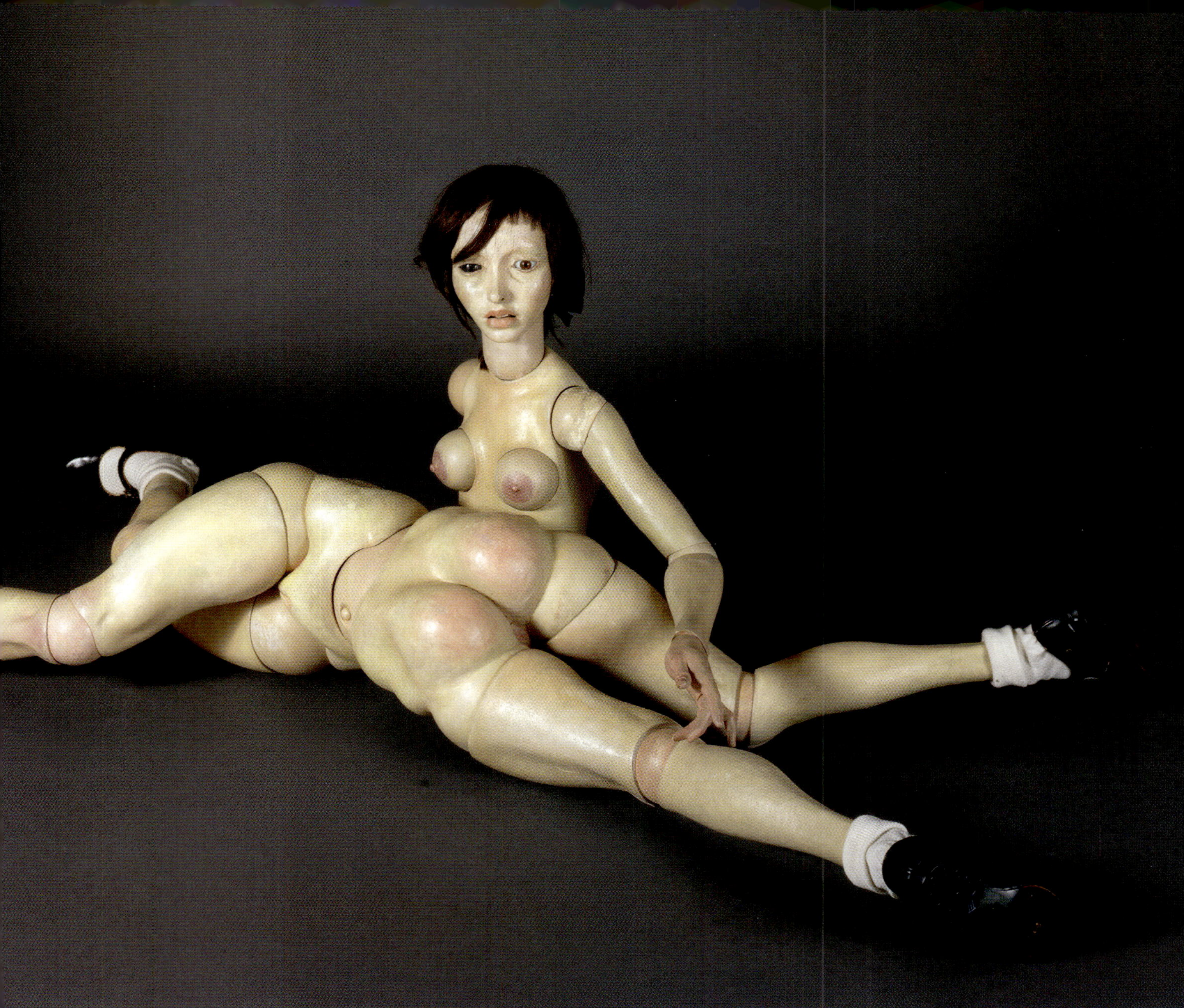

mer's doll and it was shown at the *Surrealist Exhibition of Objects* held in May 1936 at Charles Ratton's gallery. On that occasion, the object was dismembered and the individual pieces fixed to a wooden panel. Unsettled, the more sensitive souls fell into a state of shock: what kind of warped imagination could give birth to such an atrocity? The answer is simple: that of a man plagued by Nazism and the desire to make his dreams come to life ... even the craziest.

Hans Bellmer (1902–1975), *Doll*, **1935–1936,**
articulated object of painted wood, papier mâché, hair, shoes, stockings, 61 x 170 x 51 cm,
Musée National d'art Moderne – Centre Georges – Pompidou, Paris

"A DRAMA OF THE FLESH"

Balthus, the mysterious artist who was famous in his lifetime, never disguised his love of adolescent bodies. He relished painting nymphets, observed furtively, in intimate scenes. Often poorly understood, his works touch on one of the major taboos of the twentieth century: pedophilia.

An adult woman, the teacher, has a young girl lying across her lap like a guitar. Her right hand grasps a tuft of her "instrument's" hair in a sadistic gesture while the left hand delicately strokes the imaginary strings on the naked thighs of the young model only a few centimeters away from her smooth, openly presented, genitals. The lips of the adolescent are slightly open and do not clearly indicate whether she is feeling pleasure or pain. Is this a scene of rape or of consensual sex? This remains unclear but either way the scandal is there.

Balthus held critics in contempt and rejected any accusations of perversity. Fascinated by childhood, he aimed at capturing the passage to adolescence, the crucial moment when innocence become experience. Hence the recurring motif of the nymphet in his works. Hypersexualized, provocative, their legs spread, his young girls are not aware that they are being observed; the concept of modesty is still unknown to them. In 1933, Balthus wrote about *The Guitar Lesson* in a letter to Antoinette de Watteville, his future wife: "I want to bring into the open, with sincerity and emotion, all of the pulsating tragedy of this drama of the flesh, to proclaim at the top of my voice the unwavering laws of instinct." The artist ultimately confessed, however, that he had also painted this canvas to shock, his aim being to advance his career through notoriety. Subsequently, he subjected it to self-censorship and refused to show it in public. The Museum of Modern Art in New York (MoMA) acquired the painting but certain influential donors applied pressure for four years to have it disappear from the collection. It was then sold and is today part of a private collection, protected from any kind of censure.

Balthasar Kłossowski de Rola, known as Balthus (1908–2001),
***The Guitar Lesson*, 1934,**
oil on canvas, 161 x 138.5 cm, private collection

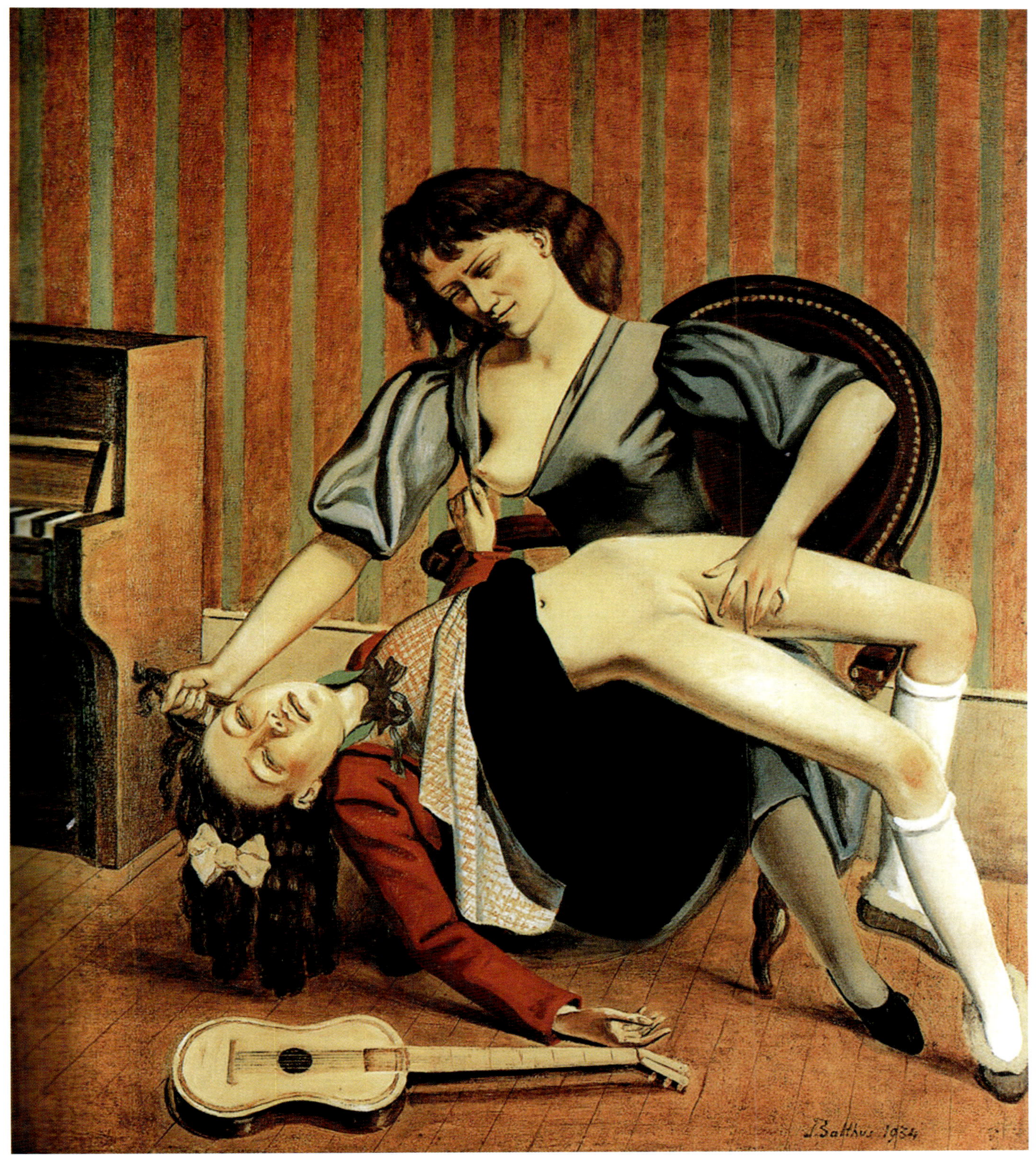

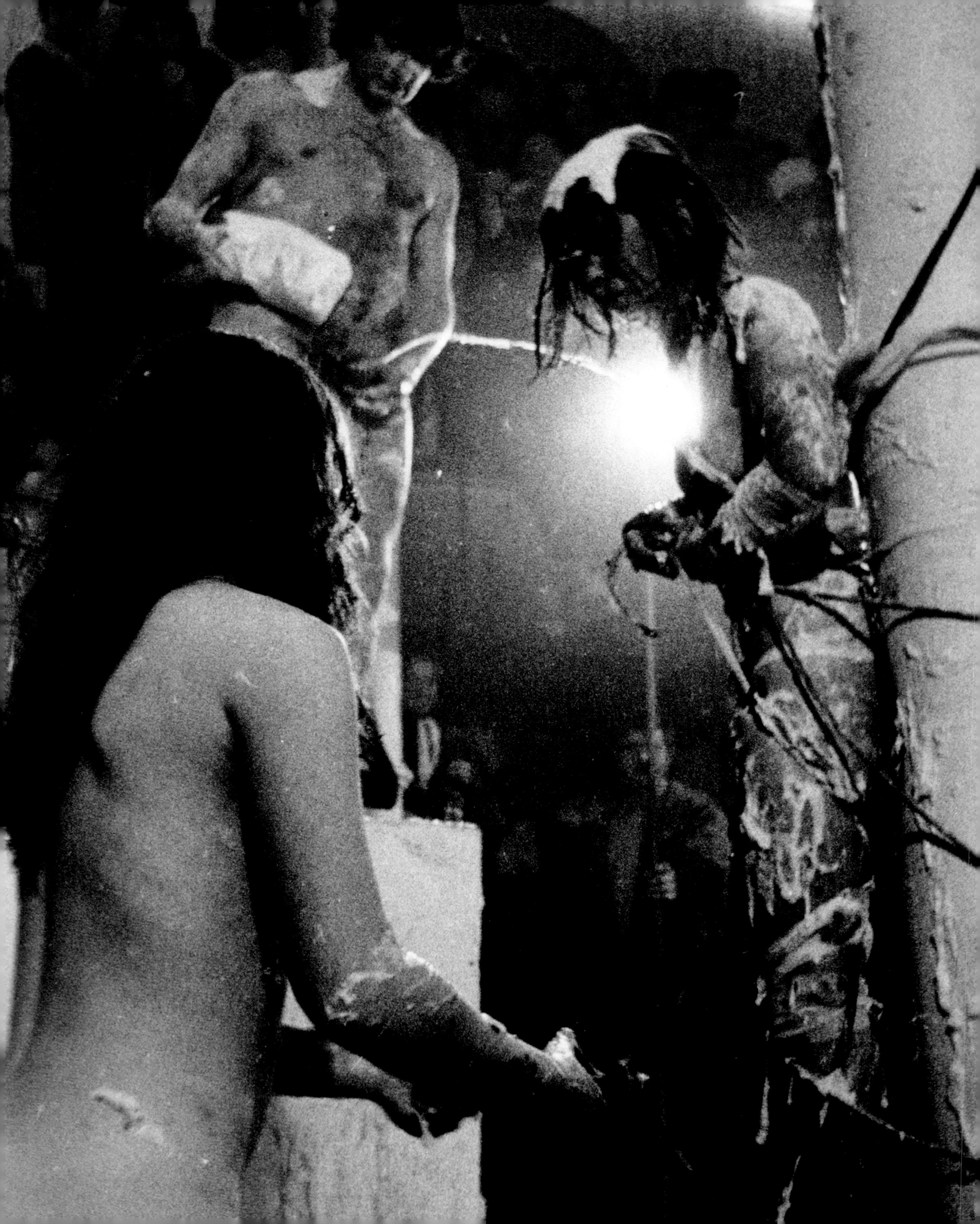

THE ABJECT AND THE LAW

The performances of the Viennese Actionists were concerned with transgressive acts, which consisted above all in making contact between the body and various bodily products – blood, semen, feces, urine – as well as entrails, food, and various objects. These actions, always radical and provocative, were closely watched by authorities and frequently censured.

Otto Muehl was one of the cofounders of Viennese Actionism. This movement, born in the 1960s, had the goal of liberating the subconscious from its chains by shocking the brain. The Austrian artist's performances were often followed by a conviction: fourteen days in prison in 1963, and two months in 1968 for having organized the *Art and Revolution* action at the University of Vienna. That is where his friend Günter Brus made a memorably provocative performance: after his torso and thighs had been slashed, he swallowed his own urine, defecated and spread his excrements over his body, and then masturbated while singing the Austrian national anthem. Some of the performers were later arrested.

During Muehl's imprisonment, several of his works were confiscated and destroyed by the authorities. In 1970, the *Happening and Fluxus* exhibition was held at the Kunsthalle in Cologne. Slaughtered fowl, blood, and feces smeared over bodies, Muehl and his assistants having intercourse with a female model: all of these ingredients were mixed together to create a scandal of the first magnitude! Some of the museum staff went on strike, newspapers and politicians condemned the work, and anonymous callers threatened to burn down the gallery or kill the fleeing artists. The Kunsthalle immediately put an end to the retrospective.

In 1971, Muehl founded a commune based on sharing everything (property, sexual partners, the education of the children...). However, the model did not work and the group dissolved in 1990. Muehl, who went too far in imposing himself as the "father" of the brotherhood, was sentenced to seven years in prison for "psychological manipulation" and "moral misdemeanors." Since his release until his death in May 2013, he has lived in Portugal, where he continues to follow his utopian ideals.

Otto Muehl (1925–2013), *Christmas 70*,
action on 16 December, 1970,
R. Jaeggli Gallery, Berne

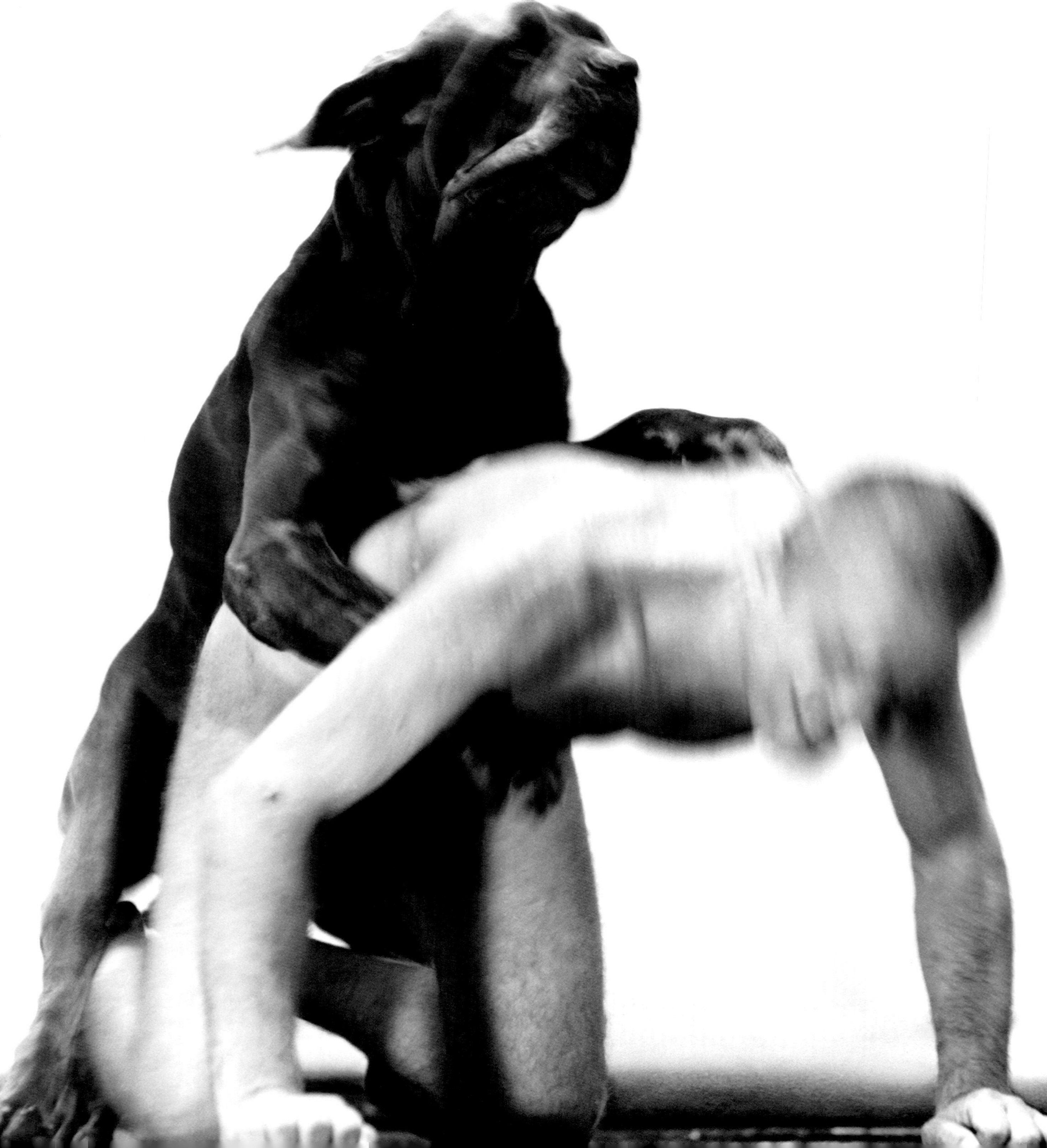

IT'S A DOG'S LIFE

Although Oleg Kulik started exploring the theme of animality in 1991, it was not until 1994 that he actually transformed himself into an animal for the first time when he realized the performance *Mad Dog, or Last Taboo Guarded by Alone Cerberus.*

The first performances by this Russian of Ukrainian origin were inspired by the brutality in his country in the 1990s after the end of the Soviet era. The artist resented that West Europe treated the citizens living there "like dogs." Okay, Lulik said to himself, let's push it to its limits! That led to the birth of several works and the nickname he was given: "man-dog."

In 1996, a case of surprising zoomorphism created a scandal in Stockholm. Tied up and completely naked, Oleg Kulik gave a masterly interpretation of *Mad Dog* in front of the entrance to the *Interpol* exhibition. He took his role as a guard dog completely seriously and *really* attacked and bit visitors who entered into his territory. Even worse, simulating the wild animal, he also attacked some works on display. This action was a reflection on the foundations of Kulik's art. In fact, he never stops questioning the notion of being human. Could one reverse the process and return to the state of "original" – meaning non-reflective – animals? According to the artist, we simply must not hide behind our "humaneness" and that is why he metamorphoses into a bird, a bull, a fish, or a dog in his performances. Kulik awakened the beast lying dormant in him in his *Family of the Future* series by letting his instinct get the upper hand over reason, hence the zoophile character of certain pictures. However, at the FIAC (International Contemporary Art Fair) in Paris in 2008, these photographs were not censored, while those showing *Mad Dog* were.

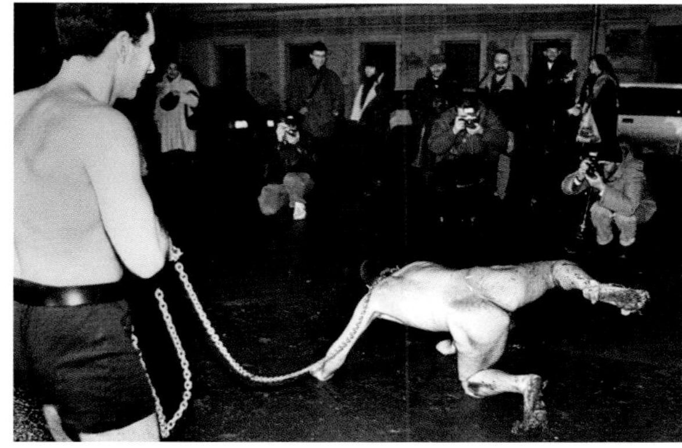

Under instructions from the Public Prosecutor, the French police confiscated those "images of a pornographic or violent character or a character seriously violating human dignity." His censors probably never knew that Kulik said: "I have never been a man."

Left: **Oleg Kulik (1961–), *Family of the Future*, 1997–1998,**
Moscow region

Above: **Oleg Kulik (1961–), *Mad Dog, or Last Taboo Guarded by alone Cerberus* (in association with Alexander Brener), 23 November 1994,**
Yakimanka Street, opposite the Guelman Gallery, Moscow, Russia

PUBLIC FUNDING FOR IMMORALITIES?

Robert Mapplethorpe was a photographer who worked in an academic style and whose technical mastery was matched only by the classical rigor of his stagings. In 1989, only a few months after his death, his erotic works were at the center of a controversy over the public funding of art in the United States.

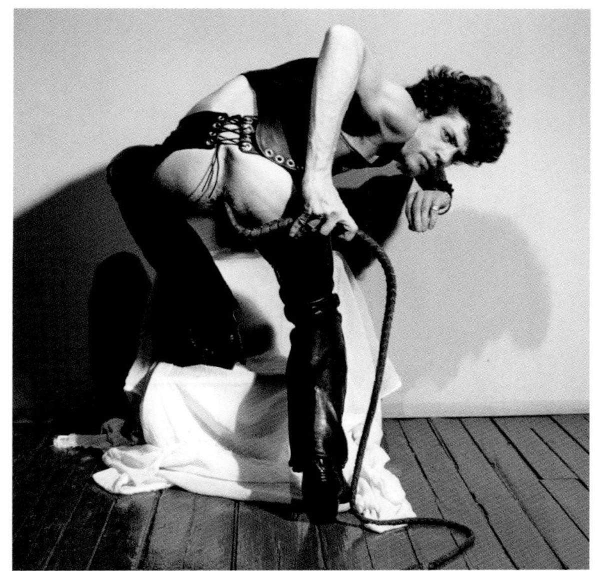

From 1971, the very first year of his activity as an artist, to his death in 1989, Robert Mapplethorpe cultivated the art of the photographic self-portrait. As with the other genres of his pictures, his self-portraits are a mixture of refinement and brutality. The body, far from being treated as something shameful, appears glorious and triumphant, displaying all its sexual and orgasmic potential. Mapplethorpe mainly focused on the representation of body openings, as is the case in this *Self-Portrait* from 1978, in which, dressed as a *leather man* (uniting the ideas of homosexuality, sadomasochism, and leather), he displays his anus with a whip inserted into it. Although appearing contemptuous, Mapplethorpe is actually much more cheeky. This image is a kind of parody on a stereotypical fantasy.

At the end of the 1980s, the American Senator Jesse Helms – supported by President George Bush – went to war against the deceased Mapplethorpe and attempted to track down even the most insignificant of his photographs of an erotic nature, with those showing homosexual and sadomasochistic practices at the top of the list. He threatened those museums benefitting from governmental support from the National Endowment for the Arts (NEA) with taking away their privileges if they undertook any actions to display the works of the subversive photographer.

For a time, the question was even raised of introducing a law forbidding the NEA from providing any support to organizations displaying any works of a homosexual character! Although this last proposition fell through, the Republican Party was still able to celebrate a small victory when – under pressure – the prestigious Corcoran Gallery of Art in Washington refused to host the exhibition *Mapplethorpe: The Perfect Moment.*

As with the affair around *Piss Christ* (see p. 34), this controversy led to a close re-evaluation of the role of the NEA.

Robert Mapplethorpe (1946–1989), *Self-Portrait*, 1978

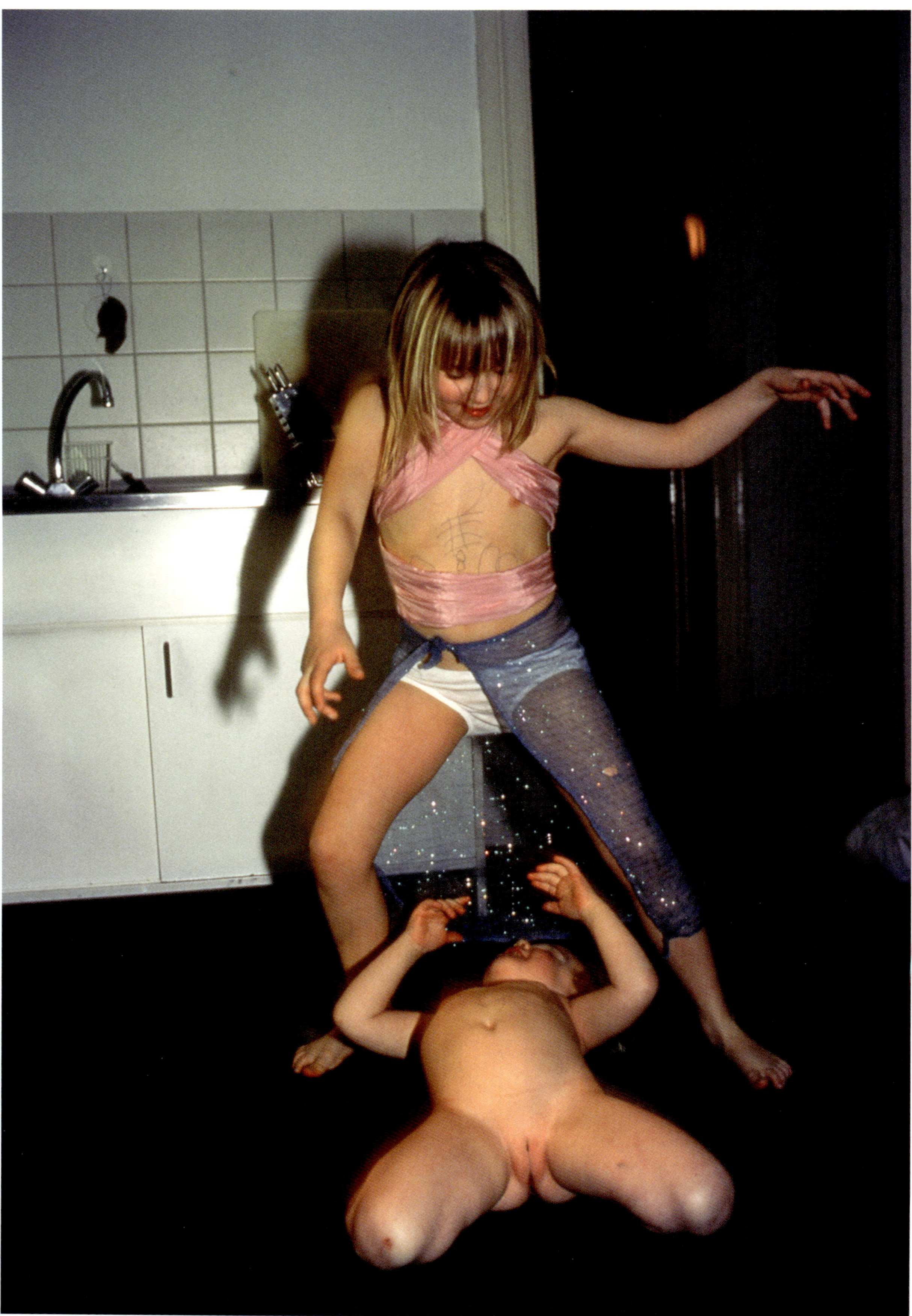

WHEN THE PORTRAYAL OF CHILDHOOD OFFENDS

One could ask if the (often real) threat of pedophilia does not blur the artistic judgment of some people. That is the problem highlighted by *Klara and Edda Belly Dancing, Berlin,* a photograph that was censored on several occasions as if it were a sordidly obscene shot.

Two little girls are playing. One is standing, dressed as an Oriental dancer. The other is completely naked and leaning back on her heels; her legs are spread revealing her smooth genitals. Nothing perverse about the shot; it is in keeping with the American photographer Nan Goldin's overall style. Her work is founded on capturing the intimate, off-guard moments of everyday life.

But some subjects are more enraging than others. Since the end of the twentieth century, the censorship of representations of children has been particular strict. Two cases in particular bear witness to this. The exhibition *Presumed Innocent*, shown at the Museum of Contemporary Art in Bordeaux in 2000, was devoted to the role of the child in modern visual arts and presented works by Robert Mapplethorpe, Christian Boltansky, and Cindy Sherman under this heading. The three curators of the exhibition were subsequently accused in a complaint lodged by an association for the protection of minors. It was not until 2011, after more than ten years of court cases, that those incriminated were cleared.

Another country, another scandal: in 2007, *Klara and Edda Belly Dancing* was seized on the day before it was to be exhibited in Gateshead in England. It was the management of the museum itself that called in the police on the day prior to the opening to ask their "advice" before showing this "work." The photo was forbidden but it formed an inseparable part of the series of 149 images and the owner – the singer Elton John – outraged by this liberticidal act, finally refused to lend his personal collection, in this way depriving the public of being able to experience one of the major works of the twenty-first century. And it began as a simple game being played by children.

Nan Goldin (1953–), *Klara and Edda Belly Dancing, Berlin*, 1998, photograph, private collection

FROM RUSSIA WITH LOVE

In 2005 the Blue Noses decided to pay homage to the British street artist Banksy. They took up and reinterpreted the motif of his famous *Two Bobbies Kissing*, a stencil showing two London policemen greedily embracing each other. The Russian government did not appreciate the message and impounded the photograph.

The Blue Noses are a collective of Russian artists formed around the two principal members Viasheslav Mizin and Alexander Shabukov. With their videos, performances, and photographs, these provocative clowns draw their audience into an absurd, poetic universe. The crazy goings-on target academic art, mass culture, and political institutions. In 2007, the Maison Rouge in Paris organized a historic exhibition devoted to the Russian Sots Art movement. Certain works were sadly missing. They had been held back at the Russian border by the government on the pretext that they created a negative image of the country. *An Epoch of Clemency (Kissing Policemen)*, which the Minister of Culture Alexander Sokolov judged to be a "pornographic" photograph and a "political provocation," was among them. In this, technically masterful, image with its harmonious staging, two men wearing the uniform and badge of the Russian military are shown embracing tenderly and, to top it off, kissing passionately! It is clearly sensual love. Around them, a forest of birch trees covered in snow, which is not insignificant, recalls the stiff posture of the two policemen and their hypothetical – but highly probable – erections.

Homosexuality has been decriminalized in Russia since 1993 but in reality it is hardly tolerated and the state has a reactionary attitude towards the subject. In January 2013, a law was proposed to punish any public activity that could constitute "propaganda for homosexuality among minors" and was adopted by the Duma, one of the chambers of the Russian parliament. This makes one lose hope of seeing *An Epoch of Clemency (Kissing Policemen)* being given a visa one day so that it can be shown in more welcoming countries.

Blue Noses (collective established in 1999),
An Epoch of Clemency (Kissing Policemen),
from the series *The Era of Mercy*, 2005,
color photograph, 75 x 100 cm, edition of 10

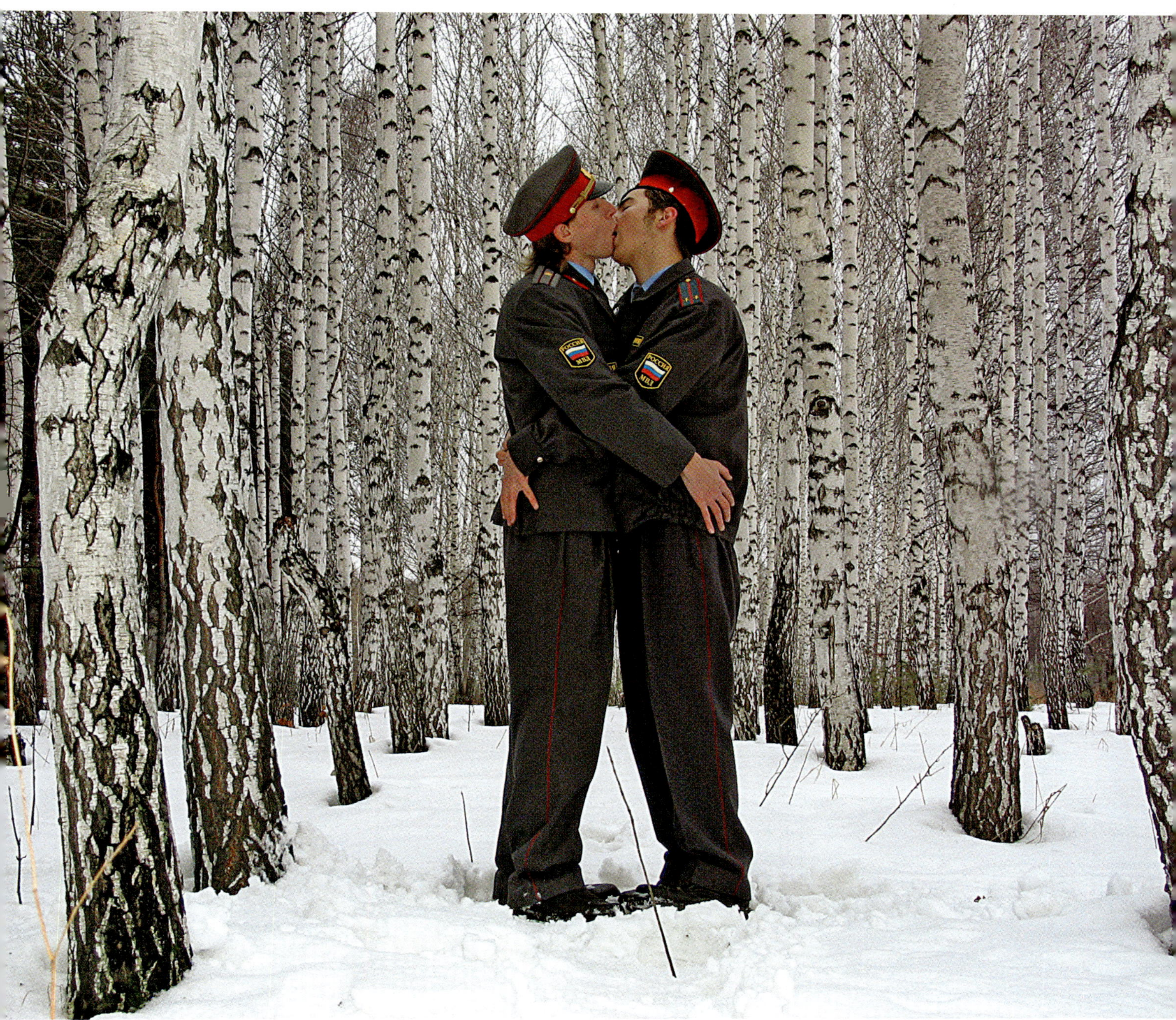

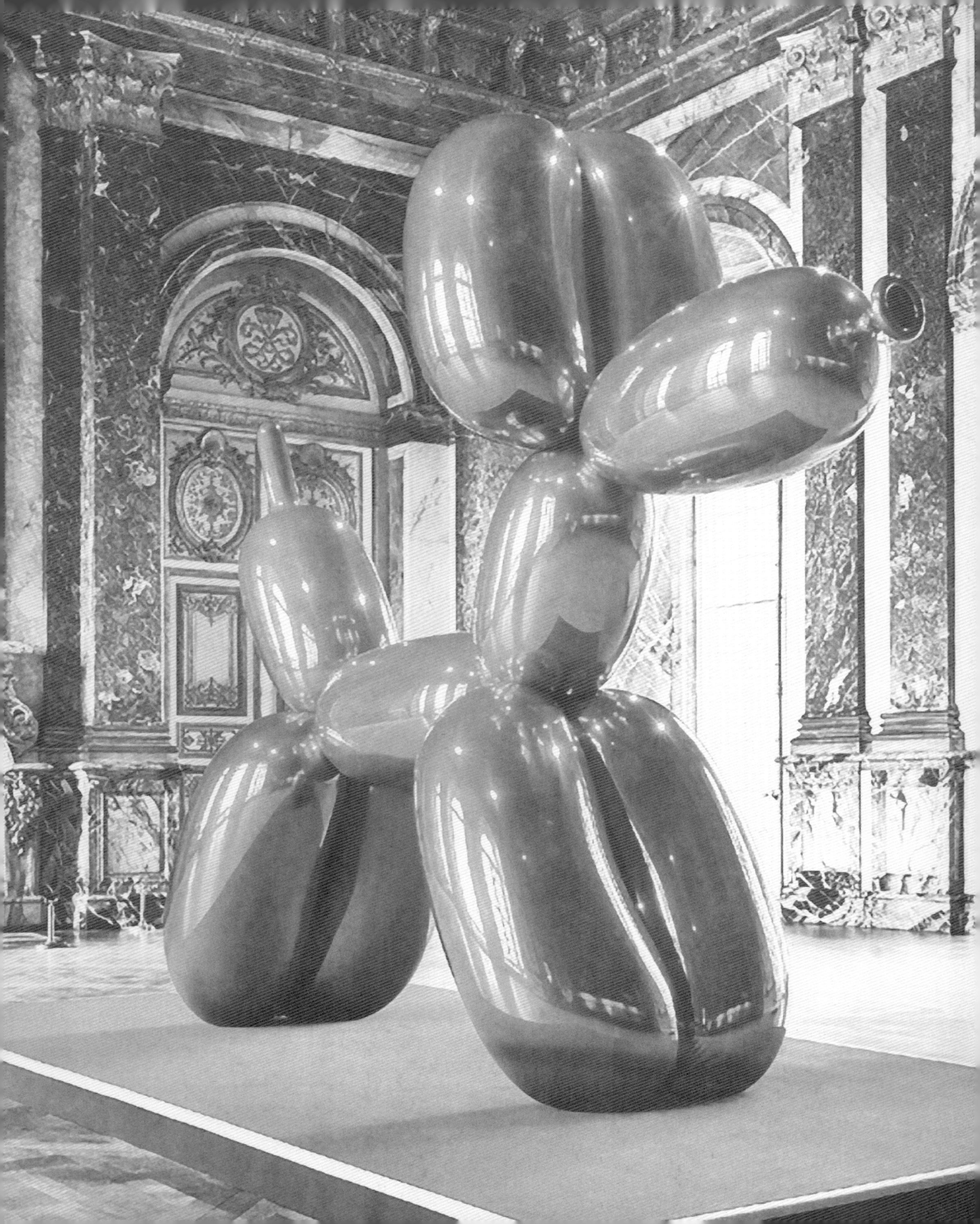

TRANSGRESSIONS

REMBRANDT

GUSTAVE COURBET

JOSEPH MALLORD WILLIAM TURNER

AUGUSTE PRÉAULT

AUGUSTE RENOIR

PABLO PICASSO

MARCEL DUCHAMP

JEAN DUBUFFET

JACKSON POLLOCK

PIERO MANZONI

DANIEL BUREN

JOSEPH BEUYS

WIM DELVOYE

DAMIEN HIRST

MARCO EVARISTTI

JEFF KOONS

XIAO YU

GUNTHER VON HAGENS

MR. BRAINWASH

**"Beauty is a way of death.
The newness, the intensity, the strangeness;
in a word, all of the values of shock supplant it."**
Paul Valéry

Breaking the basic rules of art amounts to overstepping the conventions of representation and creative production. For centuries, all aesthetic activities were structured according to explicit canons. Artists had only a limited amount of freedom and autonomy, their work being rigorously controlled by the Church or the State, the academy or patrons. It was difficult under these conditions to give free reign to one's rebellious imagination and to sweep aside all artistic – and social – rules.

Starting in the nineteenth century, artistic controversies became more frequent. Romanticism invested the artist with the status of a leader of men, of a rebel and prophet – a responsibility that artisans in the Middle Ages and the artists of the Renaissance never had. Gradually, the influence of the Church and European monarchies decreased, leaving room for greater freedom and making it possible to question the relevance of the traditional precepts of beauty and good taste. Certain artists, completely absorbed in their search for a new way of seeing, emancipated themselves from their benefactors and official circles. Although they had more freedom, many found themselves in terrible poverty. They were also exposed to the rebuke of formidable new adversaries: the critics and judges of official exhibitions, who determined what was considered good taste and, by so doing, the artistic – and financial – value of a work.

The spectator was not always aware of the internal controversies raging in artistic circles. Even today, we have a tendency to block out those turbulent moments in the history of art: Who still remembers and argues about the scandals created by the first Impressionists and Cubists?

From that time on, scandals seemed to become par for the course. While artists previously attempted to expand the field of representation by overstepping the boundaries of conformity and convention, they now deliberately attempt to provoke. Scandal pays off. Even more, it is possibly even essential to assure success, to be noticed and remembered. It is impossible to count all the artists who have made a name for themselves with an exhibition that shocked or offended. The media, greedy to report on this kind of provocation, are the perfect allies of those clamorous personalities with a lust for publicity. Faced with this new dimension of art, one cannot help but notice the profusion of works that shock. This development can be disquieting, for it not only presents the public with a bewildering succession of ever-more disturbing and demanding challenges, it also raises a deeper concern: Is provocation the new unbending and unchallenged norm to which all creativity has to conform, the sole aim being to scandalize?

THE COCQ COMPANY GETS CONNED

When Rembrandt received the commission for *The Night Watch* he was at the peak of his success. Paid a small fortune to create a group portrait, he effectively deceived his clients. Full of mysteries, which have still not been resolved to this day, the painting pays no heed to the conventions of the genre.

In the seventeenth century, group portraits were very fashionable with the Dutch bourgeoisie. Each person shown paid a part of the price of the work in keeping with his importance and so his place in the picture. Around 1640 the company of musketeers led by Captain Cocq ordered a painting from the famous Rembrandt. When it finally appeared, it was greeted with bewilderment: it does not show a series of individual portraits but a bustling scene, a slice of life in which the mystery of human existence is exposed. Not all of the members who had paid appear, and others, in the shadows of the background, are hardly recognizable. Offended, they had a crest with a list of the members of the guild added to the painting. But that undoubtedly did little to calm their feelings when they were confronted with this strange portrait of the group. Instead of showing a dignified, well-organized militia and glorifying the qualities of its members, the painter had staged a lively, merry crowd that the captain, who has given the signal to start marching, can hardly control. At the second level, behind Captain Cocq, a man starts in surprise. This is because somebody has just let off an untimely shot immediately in front of him – smoke can still be seen coming out of the barrel of the firearm. To add to the confusion and noise, a dog barks at the man playing the drum. And what is the child, bathed in a ray of sunlight that sparkles on her extravagant clothes, and with a chicken hanging from her belt, doing here? It is actually not at all contradictory to talks about sunlight in *The Night Watch*. The painting, darkened by dirt and varnish, was named incorrectly; the scene takes place in the morning. The artist's disregard of the artistic canons of the period shocked. This marked the start of a series of misfortunes in Rembrandt's life that finally led to his bankruptcy.

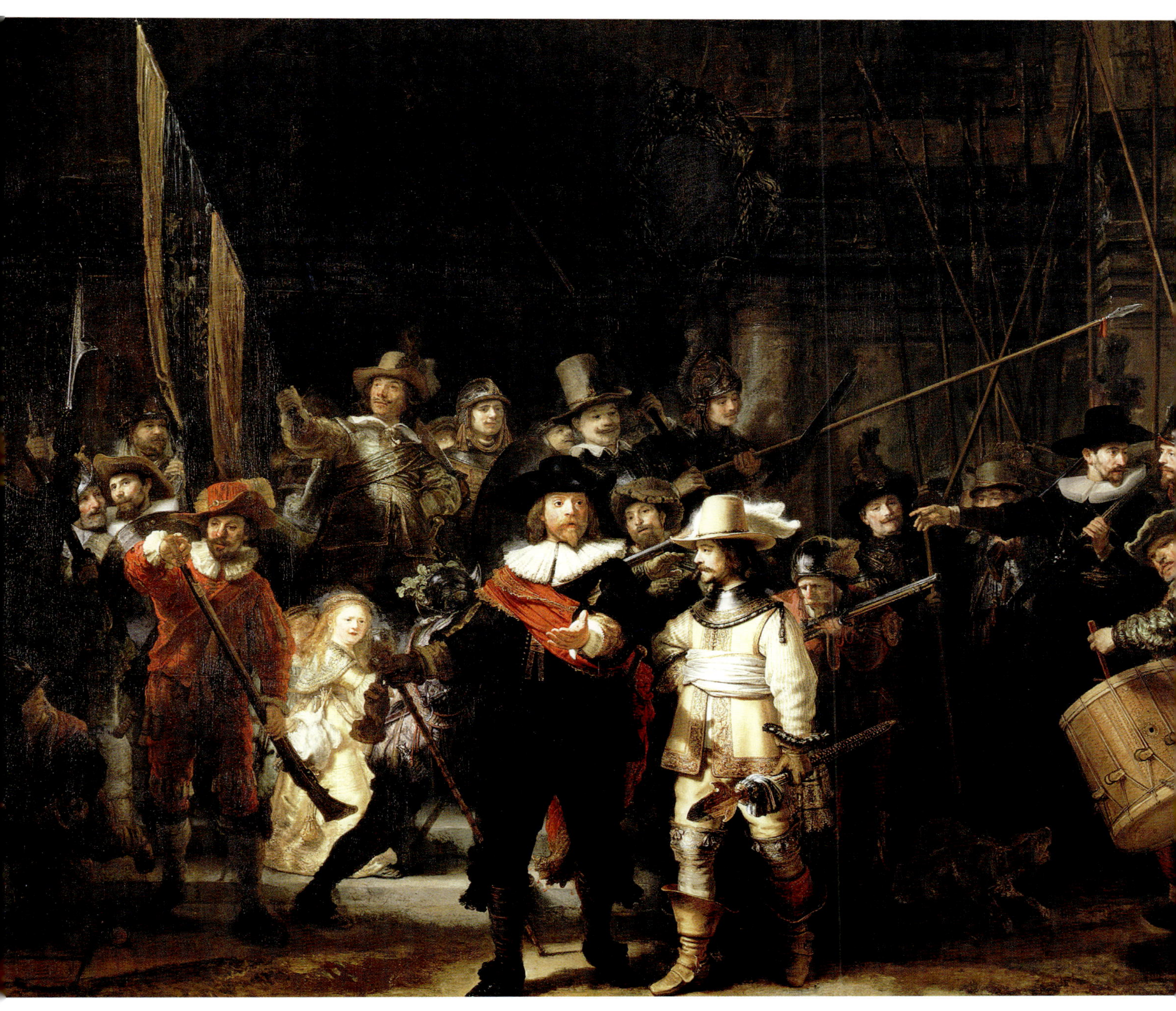

Rembrandt Harmenszoon van Rijn (1606–1669),
***The Company of Frans Babbing Cocq and Willem van Ruytenburch*, called *The Night Watch*, 1642,**
oil on canvas, 363 x 437 cm, Rijksmuseum, Amsterdam

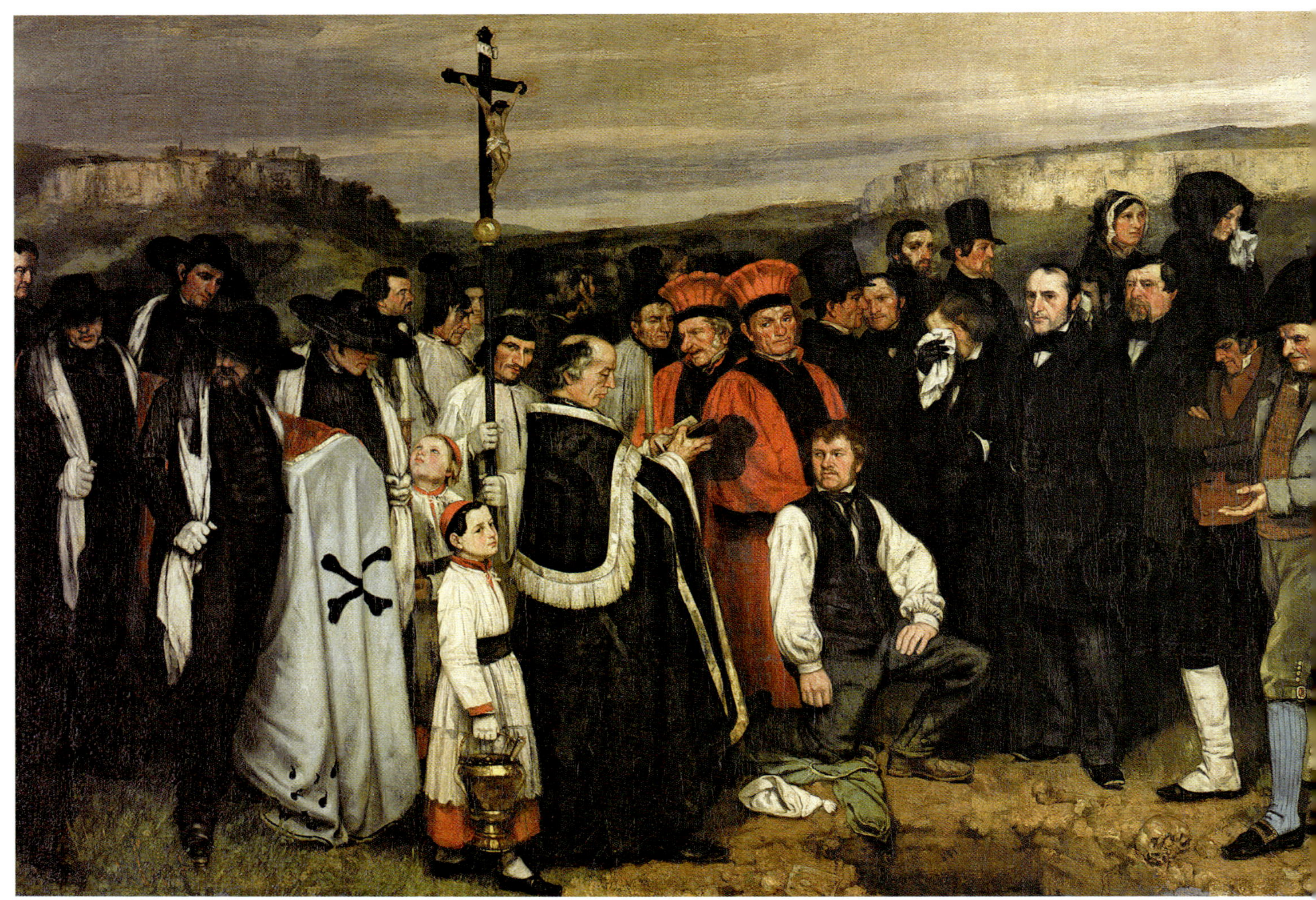

THE ART OF THE BANAL

Gustave Courbet reveled in his status as a scandalous painter, a status that made it possible for him to gain the reputation he so ardently sought. His aim was to revolutionizing the history of art, and his programmatic *A Burial at Ornans*, rejected at the 1855 Paris World Exposition, was calculated to strike the first blow in his struggle to establish himself.

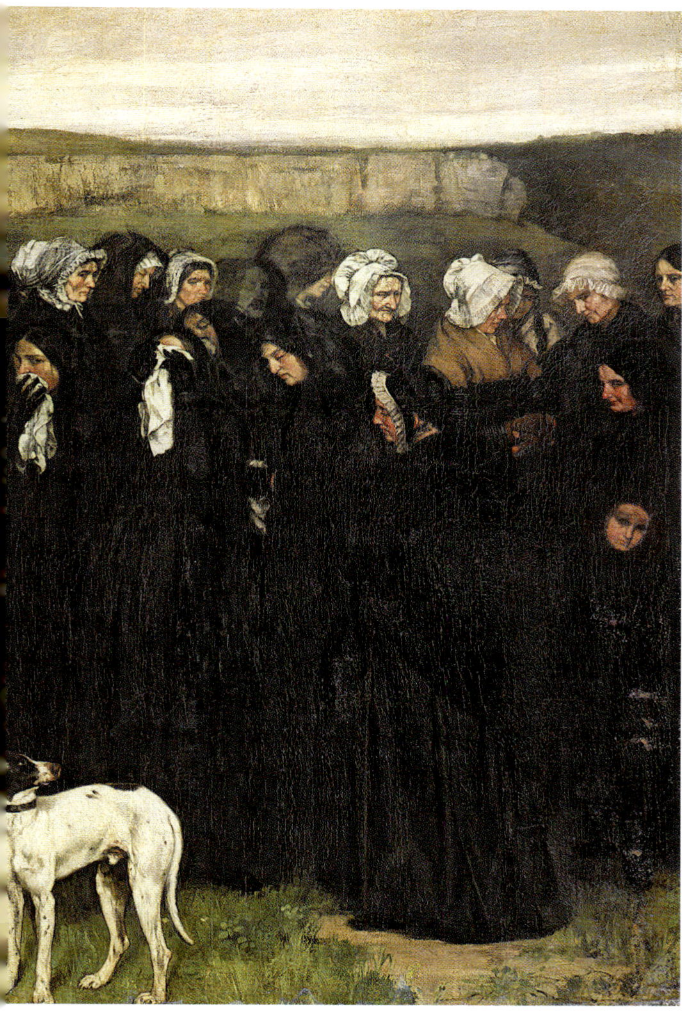

Gustave Courbet (1819–1877),
***A Burial at Ornans*, also known as**
***A Painting of Human Figures, the History of a Burial at Ornans*,**
1849–1850,
oil on canvas, 315 x 668 cm, Musée d'Orsay, Paris

Many were outraged at the 1850 Salon: *A Burial* was considered to be a celebration of the banal and the ugly. Those who were able fully to understand the spirit of this work made the controversy even more contentious. Today, we see a simple rural funeral, the austerity of which is underlined by the somber colors. But at the time, people took up arms against the work: Courbet had painted an everyday scene in a large format even though the academic tradition reserved such huge canvases for elevated subjects such as mythological, biblical, or historical scenes. The arrogant young painter had chosen to make a big splash by painting the inhabitants of the village of his birth, Ornans, as the mourning protagonists of the work. Aiming at neither the sublime nor the allegorical, he simply had his fellow citizens and members of his family pose. What a lack of good taste, people exclaimed at the time; he dares to depict reality in all of its meanness: the vergers red-faced and drunk, the family heavy and gracelessness. Far from being devastated by the hatred he aroused, Courbet drew strength from it and defended his artistic choice by loudly proclaiming that painting had to show "real things as they exist." This work was a manifesto of Realism, the movement of which Courbet was the principal founder and undisputed leader.

The scandal it created was not limited to the sphere of art. Some accused the artist of being anticlerical for having painted man alone confronted with death in a scene made oppressive by the yawning grave below, the bleak landscape in the background, and the gray sky above. Others discovered a political message in the representation of a community united around its civic leaders. And indeed, Courbet, a passionate Republican who would play an active role in the bloody Paris Commune in 1871, defined his realism as "democratic art."

FROM THE CLASSICAL TO THE MODERN

His contemporaries thought both Turner and his paintings "eccentric." They were uncomfortable with his humble background, his competitive spirit, but above all his progressive experiments in representing nature that, at the end of his life, pushed him towards an almost abstract formlessness.

In his book *Modern Painters* (1843), John Ruskin argued that Turner's faithfulness to nature came about in defiance of the works of the past. The painter, in spite of his deep admiration for the Old Masters, brought about a complete break with the past. He could have been content with his early fame: from humble origins, he was elected to the Royal Academy at the age of twenty-six, something that was unprecedented at the time. Enchanted by the art of the French painter Claude Lorrain (c. 1600–1682), Turner became a popular, respected landscape artist even though some people always regarded him as a parvenu from the proletarian heart of London. But, far from resting on his laurels, he sought to innovate and experiment. He opened his own gallery in order to be able to exhibit his most daring paintings, though he continued to measure himself against his peers in exhibitions organized by the Royal Academy. New pigments started to appear on the market. Turner integrated them into his work to the great displeasure of the public who, unaccustomed, criticized the originality of his new style. He did not hesitate to make sketches in the open air on the banks of the Thames to capture the light and nature in all its aspects. Increasingly hazy, his canvases moved in the direction of a subjective abstract vision that stood in stark contrast to the clear forms of traditional art. *Rain, Steam and Speed*, exhibited in 1844, is a graphic representation of the blurred sensation experienced by a traveler sitting in a train hurtling through a shower of rain, his perception becoming a hazy fusion of rain, steam, and movement. Fascinated by nebulous landscapes, Turner became estranged from the taste of the public and his paintings, which were increasingly radical and increasingly difficult to sell. Constable, one of his illustrious rivals, was able to understand and admire his colleague from the Royal Academy: "Turner seems to paint with tinted steam, so evanescent and so airy." One recognizes how Turner influenced the Impressionists, who were also searching for a more direct expression of feeling, movement, and the natural world. Incidentally, Claude Monet and Camille Pissarro also took up the subject of the steam locomotive.

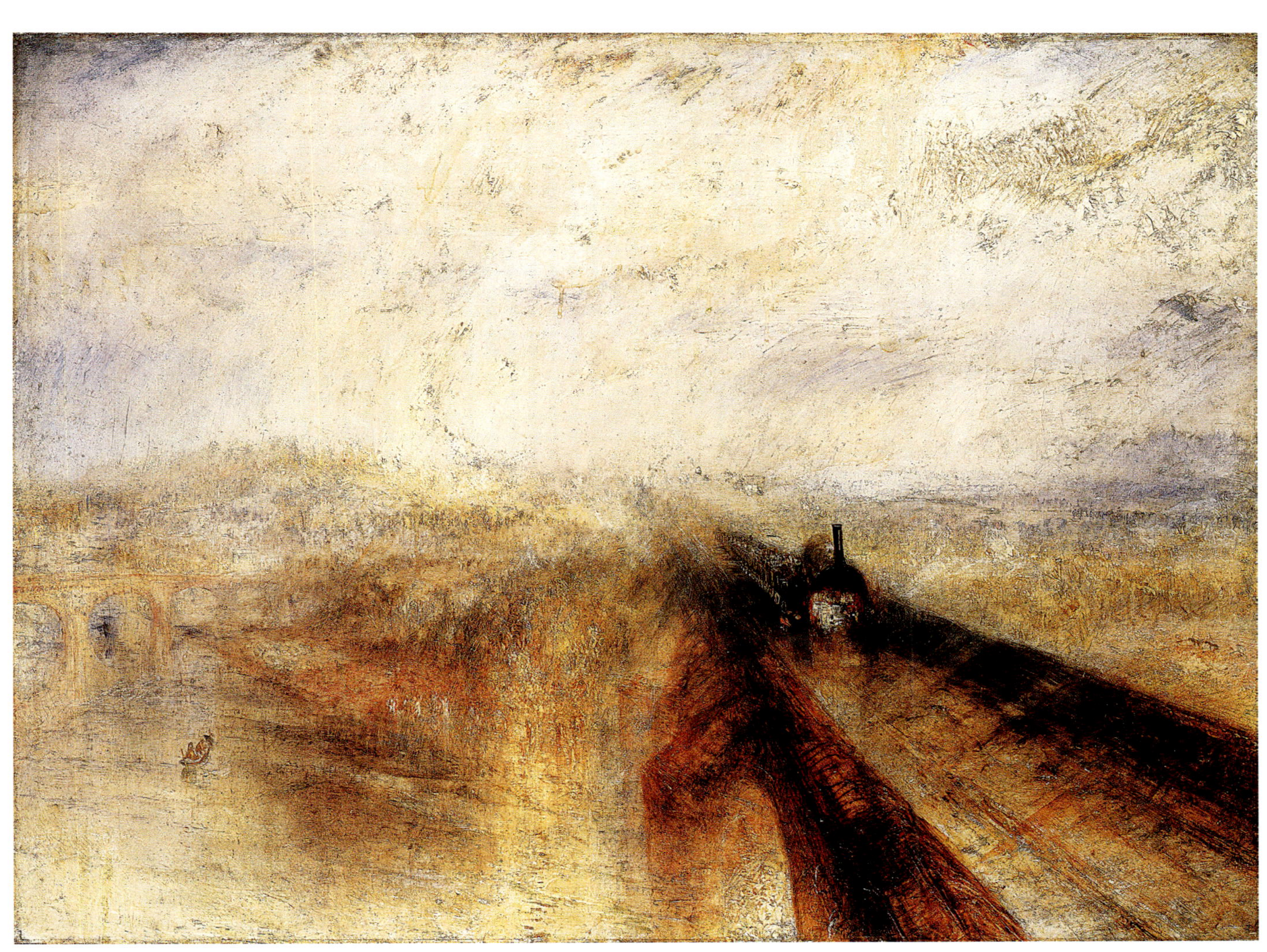

Joseph Mallord William Turner (1775–1851),
Rain, Steam and Speed – The Great Western Railway, **1844,**
oil on canvas, 91 x 121.8 cm, National Gallery, London

FINAL VICTORY

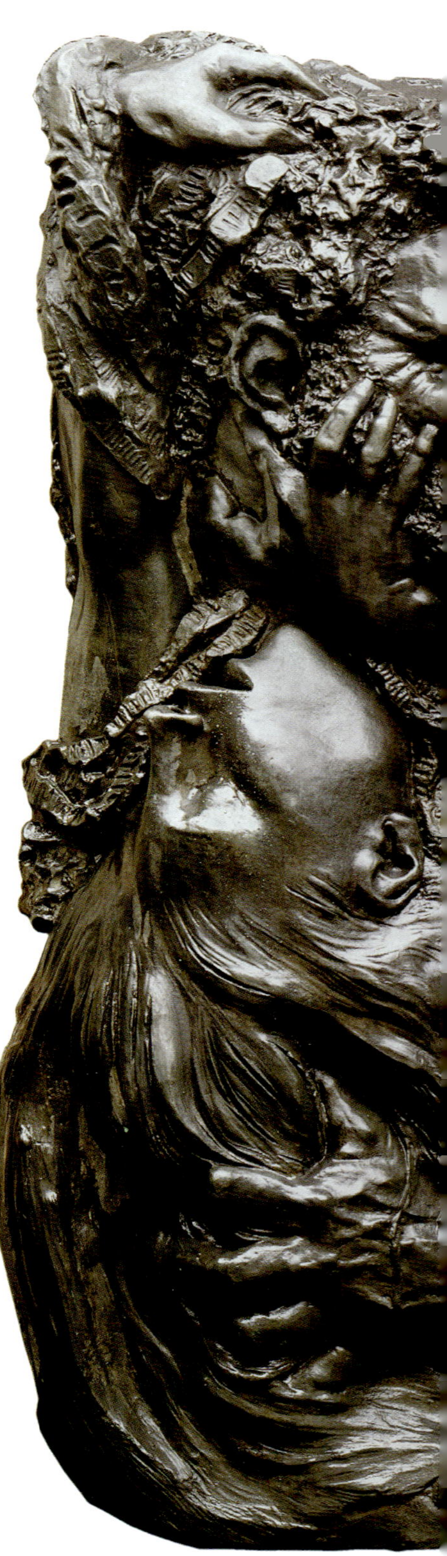

The Romantic sculptor Auguste Préault was impatient and temperamental by nature and his work was marked by the restless spirit that drove him. He spent virtually his whole life striving to get his work shown in the Salon, despite being faced with jurors who were repelled by the apparent chaos and unfinished nature of his work.

Auguste Préault first unveiled his work to the public at the Salon of 1833. It was largely through the good offices of influential friends such as Victor Hugo that he succeeded in being accepted. His work met with a universally hostile reception from critics, who dismissed it as ugly. He was criticized for exhibiting what seemed more like preliminary sketches than finished sculptures. Writing in *Le Constitutional* on 26 April 1833, one reporter described Préault's work as "going beyond ugly to hideous, with expressions that would not be out of place in an emergency ward in a hospital or at a hanging." He added that he could not assess Préault's talent as a sculptor until he "made a whole figure, rather than odds and ends of human body in colored plaster." Préault persisted with his style, however, and of five works submitted to the Salon in 1834, only *The Killing*, a nightmare vision of violence, was accepted. It was included as a counterpoint to beauty. Préault's admirers and detractors were polarized: the poet Charles Baudelaire could not praise *The Killing* highly enough, while critics were incensed by the truncated bodies and the incomprehensible mass of faces with no apparent meaning. Préault continued his struggle to get his work into the Salon. He was accepted in 1837, but was rejected year after year after that for over ten years and had to use all his wits to secure enough commissions to save himself from penury.

In an article in *Le National* on 26 June 1849 a journalist declared that Préault had been "a victim of the most savage persecution ever inflicted by an academic jury." Success finally smiled on Préault in the Salon of the same year; without changing the way he worked in any way, he eventually became well known and prosperous. At his death his close friends celebrated his long battle and final victory over the Académie des Beaux-Arts.

Auguste Préault (1809–1879), *The Killing,* **1834–1850,** bronze relief, 109 x 140 cm, Musée des Beaux-Arts, Chartres

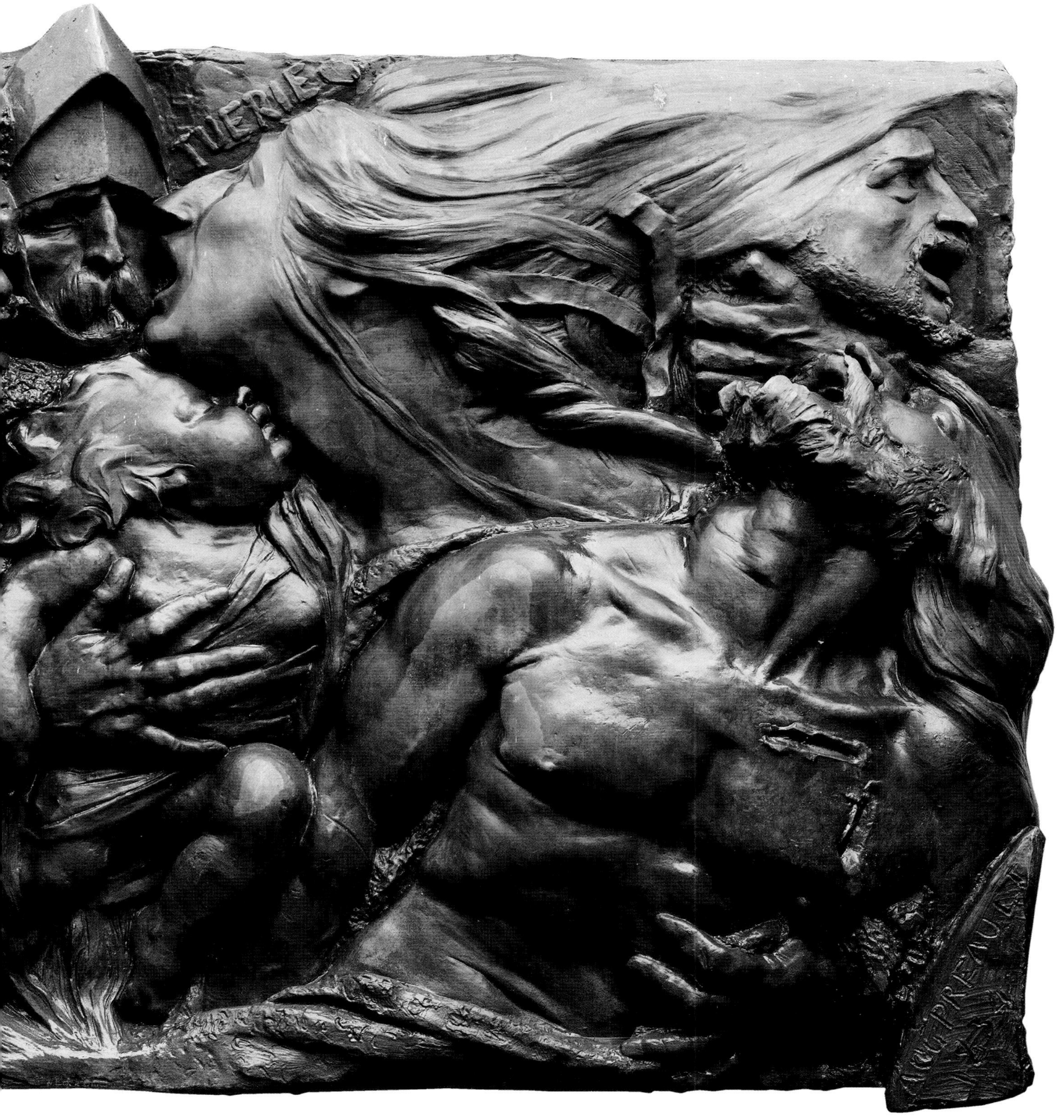

MAKING A POOR FIRST IMPRESSION

In 1876, Renoir set up his studio on Montmartre; that is where he painted many of his most important canvases, including the *Bal du Moulin de la Galette*, in which he brought together all of his Impressionist experiments. But the main problem was that only a few visionaries supported this movement, which – initially at least – gave rise to incomprehension, mockery, and even hate.

The Impressionist Exhibition of 1876 was a scandal. The critic Albert Wolf raged in *Le Figaro*: "The unsuspecting passerby … enters, and a cruel spectacle opens up in front of his appalled eyes. Five or six lunatics, one of them a woman, a group of unfortunates blinded by the folly of ambition, have a rendezvous here to display their works. There are some people who burst into laughter at the sight of those objects. For my part, my heart sank. These so-called artists call themselves the *intransigents, impressionists*; they take a canvas, paint and brushes, throw some colors haphazardly on it and then sign the thing."

Renoir was definitely one of the painters targeted in this condemnation; but in the same year he painted the *Bal du Moulin de la Galette* – and without making the slightest concessions to his critics. Contrary to what he was accused of, he did not chose his colors "haphazardly." He attempted to reproduce that which delights the eyes when viewing a scene of this kind: the dappled light, the sense of spontaneity and movement. With the invention of photography, painters were no longer the only ones able to capture a moment, a face. Artists then looked for the vision that only they could capture. And this is how Renoir diligently painted the crowd of people at a dance for ordinary folk glittering in the sunlight. Art lovers were accustomed to coming close to the canvas to inspect each and every detail; but Impressionism forced them to change their habits, to abandon attention to detail and to clearly defined contours and forms. Look at a crowd outdoors, in the daylight: the reflections which produce unusual nuances, the hazy background that your eye has difficulty focusing on … all of this justified the Impressionist experiment. And in fact Impressionist images are actually more realistic, in terms of our perception of the world, than academic painting, with its precise brushstrokes.

Auguste Renoir (1841–1919): *Bal du Moulin de la Galette*, **1876,** oil on canvas, 131 x 175 cm, Musée d'Orsay, Paris

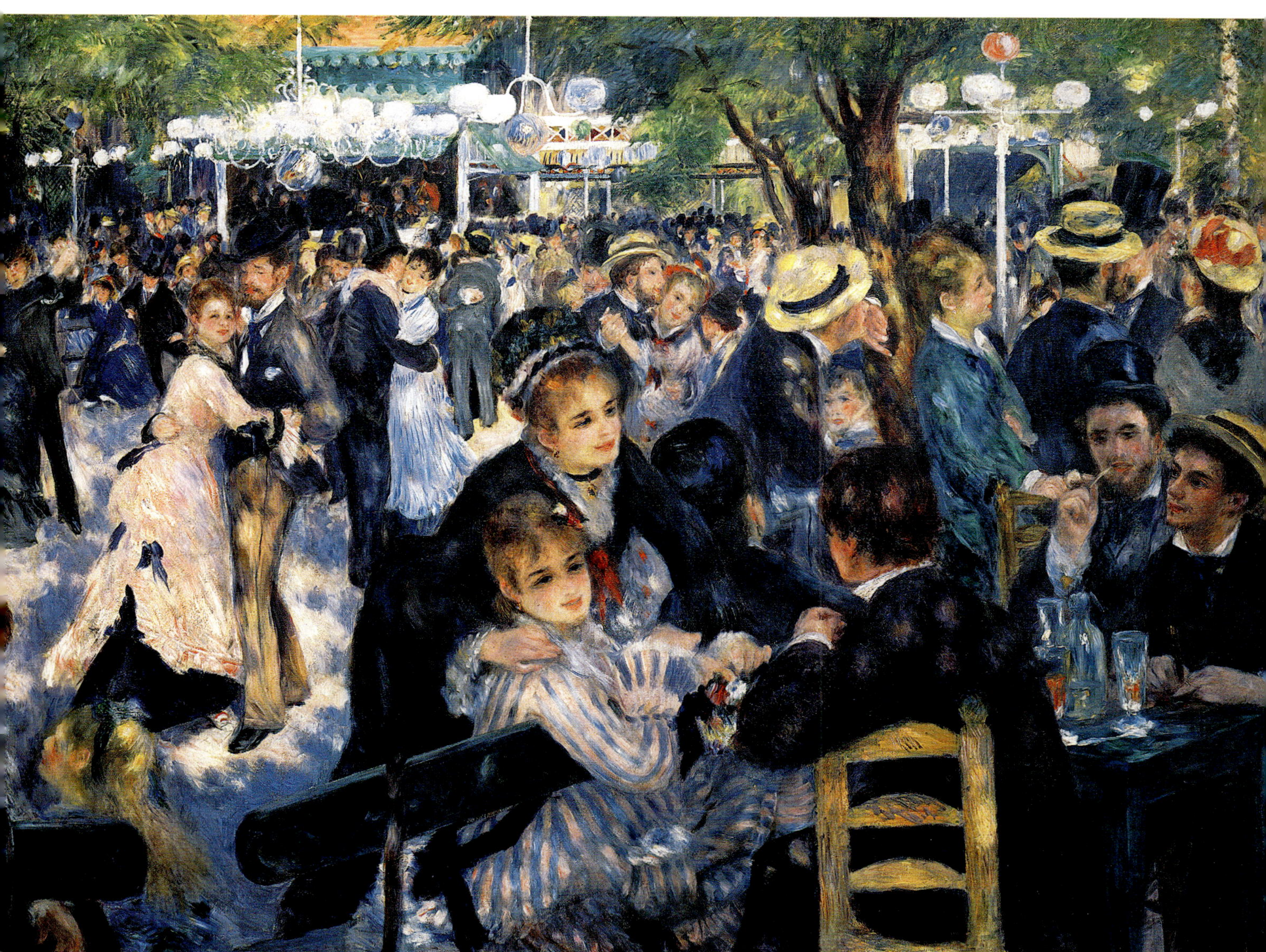

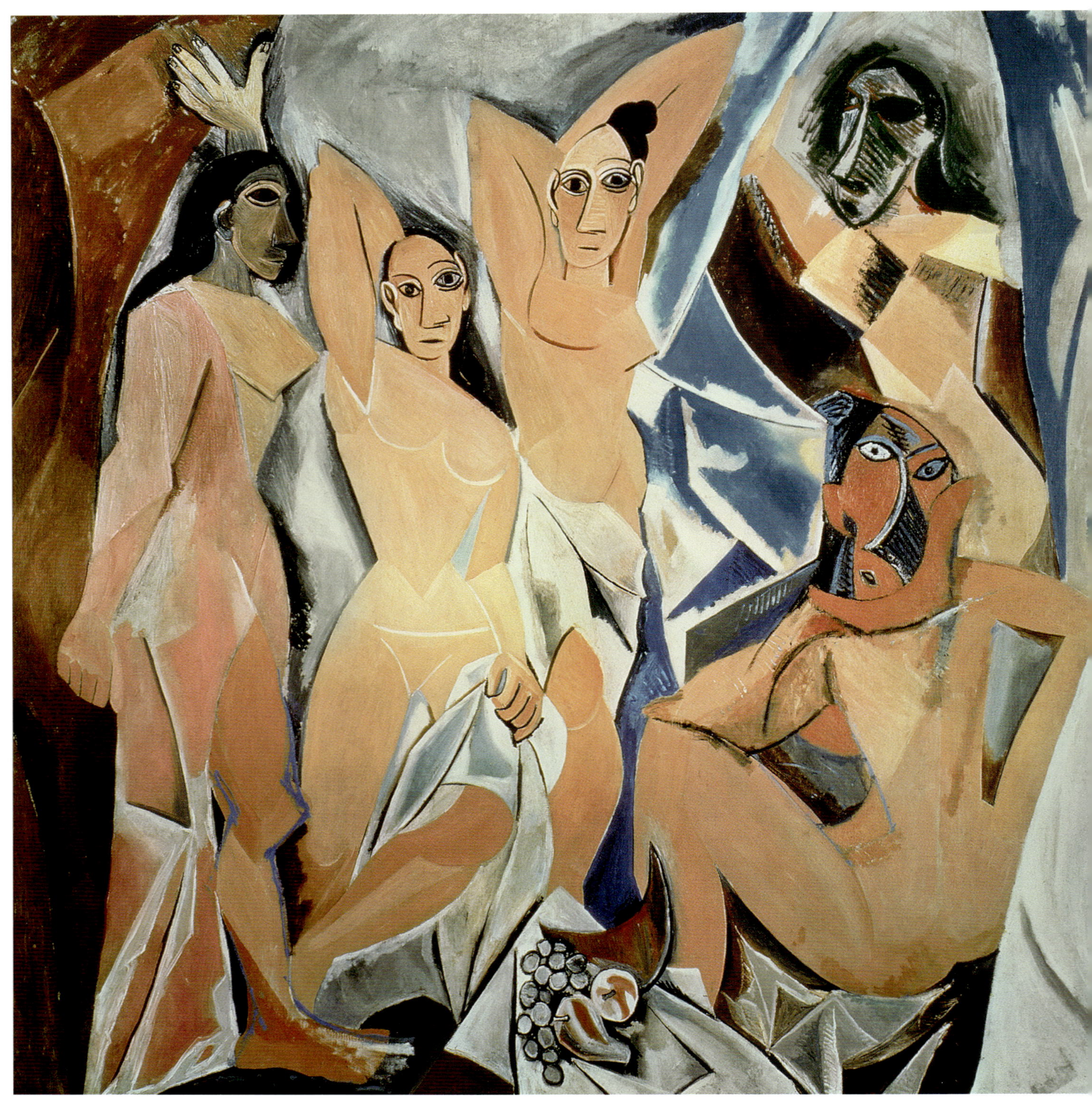

THE PHILOSOPHY OF THE BROTHEL

In 1907, Picasso's friends had the privilege of seeing his latest painting: *Les Demoiselles d'Avignon*. This small select audience was mainly made up of radical artists who had also caused scandals – but even they struggled to come to terms with it: Georges Braque was shocked and Matisse burst into laughter. There was almost a complete inability to comprehend this primitive, aggressive work.

It has been said that this work, which marked a radical break with the past, was the starting point of Cubism. For Picasso it was an "exorcism canvas." He put all of his rejection of decadent civilization, the prevailing fear of sexually transmitted diseases that linked love and death, and his experiences in the Barcelonan brothel in the Carrer de Avinyó (Avignon Street) into the painting. One also discovers traces of numerous other works that influenced the painter: Iberian and African sculpture in the mask-like faces of the women on the right, El Greco, Cézanne and even Ingres' *The Turkish Bath* (see p. 100) in the body of the crouching woman. Picasso was not fond of the title under which the painting was known; he would have chosen *Le Bordel Philosophique (The Philosophical Brothel)*.

In an attempt to explain the specific character of his work, he stated: "We love, all of us, prehistoric paintings; there is nothing like them!" He also declared that he did not choose his representations, they imposed themselves on him. All the same, he made more than 700 preliminary sketches leading up to the painting itself. Initially, the group also included two clients but Picasso removed them to concentrate on this exhibition of female bodies. However, one can still make out traces of a male anatomy in the prostitute on the left lifting the curtain to reveal the indecent scene to our eyes. They hide nothing, these women in their daring poses. However, although a sexual atmosphere reigns supreme, there is no sensuality about these curveless hookers with their frightening, empty, searching eyes that make the viewer feel ill at ease.

This work remained in obscurity for a long time and did not become famous until it was acquired by the Museum of Modern Art in 1947. By then it ad become the symbolic masterpiece of modern art.

Pablo Picasso (1881–1973), *Les Demoiselles d'Avignon*, 1907, oil on canvas, 243.9 x 233.7 cm, Museum of Modern Art, New York

THE ART OF THE COMMONPLACE

Who would have thought that a simple urinal could have triggered one of the scandals that changed the course and concept of art? Marcel Duchamp might have sensed that something like this could happen to what was originally planned as a prank, but nobody could have imagined the incredible fate waiting for this piece of porcelain.

In 1917, the Society of Independent Artists in New York promised to exhibit any work for a fee of six dollars. However, the members of the hanging committee were perplexed when they were presented with an upside-down urinal with the title *Fountain* signed "R. Mutt." It was a false name that hid the identity of the president of the committee: Marcel Duchamp. The group was divided: the majority who refused to consider the object as a work of art clashed with those who accused them of not respecting their basic principle of exhibiting without passing judgment. Finally, the object that had caused this conflict was hidden behind a partition and disappeared never to be seen again … except in the form of replicas: other urinals were chosen to recreate *Fountain*.

Duchamp tried to strike a blow against good taste as well as the sacralization of art by selecting an everyday object that he transformed into art and then duplicated. This was the *ready made*, a concept invented by the nonconformist artist, who explained: "Whether Mr. Mutt modeled the fountain with his own hands or not is in no way important. He CHOSE it. He took an article familiar in everyday life and made its utilitarian significance disappear behind a new title. From this point of view, he invested it with a new meaning."

In 2006, the artist Pierre Pinoncelli attacked the version in the Centre Georges – Pompidou with a hammer. He described this as an artistic gesture that was meant as a wink at Dadaism and its lack of respect. According to him, this act magnified the iconoclastic character of the urinal. He was still given a three months' suspended sentence and ordered to pay more than 14,000 euros for the restoration.

Whether one of the major icons in the renewal of art, or a permanent scandal, *Fountain* has lost none of its potential to surprise and even offend a century after the joke that gave birth to it.

Marcel Duchamp (1887–1968), *Fountain*, **1917/1964,** glazed earthenware, paint, 61 x 48 x 36 cm, replica created after a photograph of the original taken in 1917 by Alfred Stieglitz, Israel Museum, Jerusalem

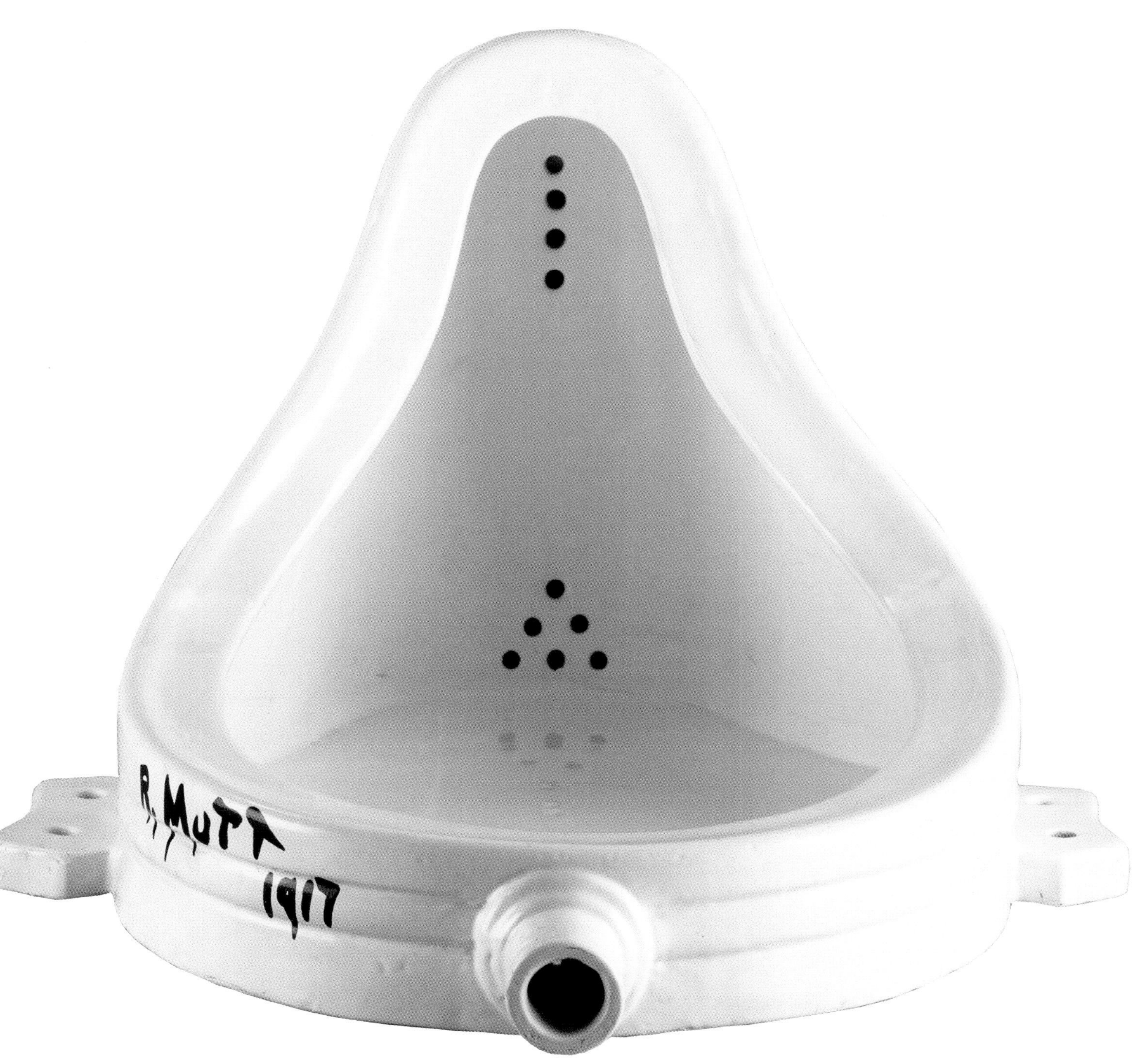
R. Mutt
1917

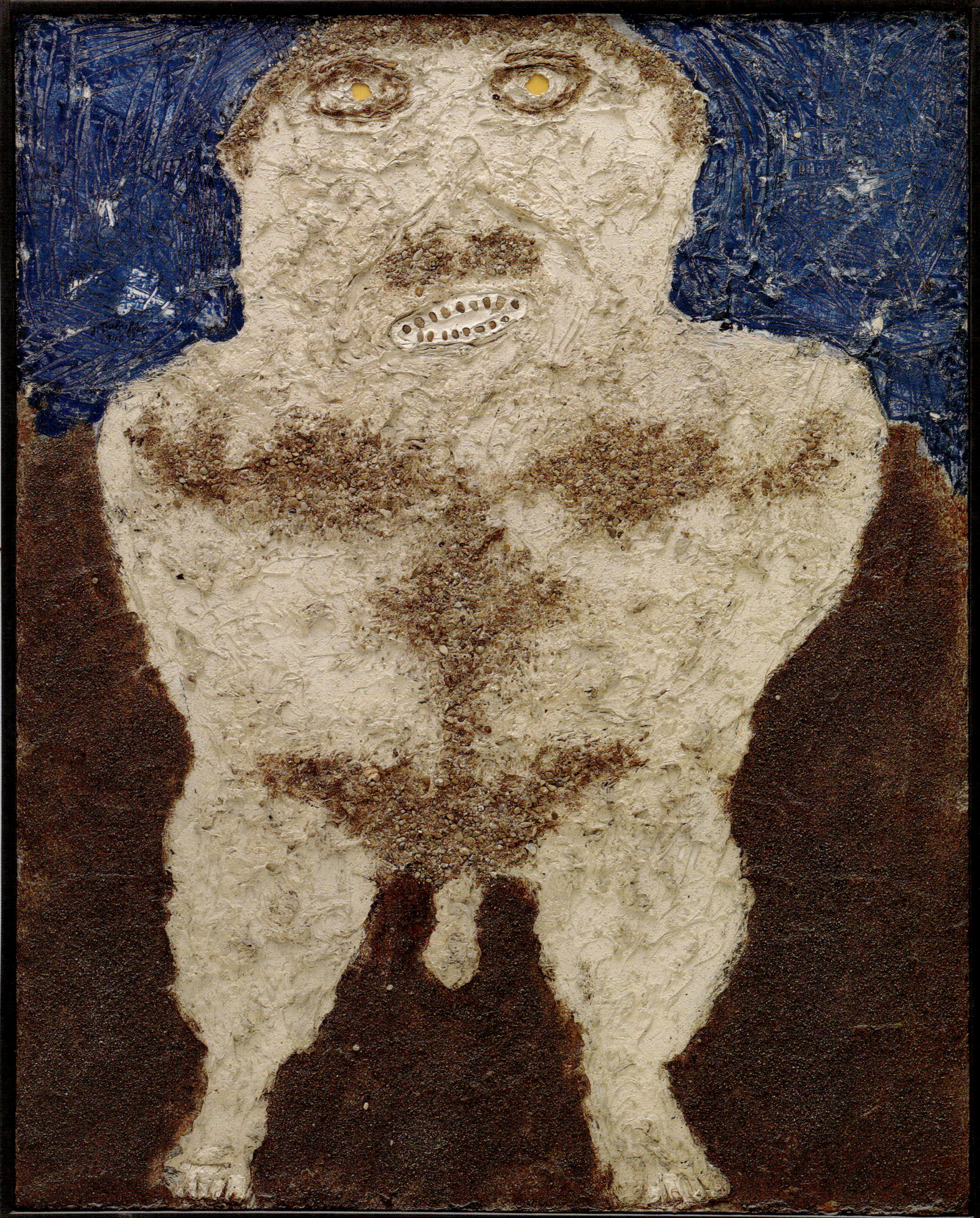

WHEN ART FORGETS ITS OWN NAME

Jean Dubuffet executed a savage form of art in which instinct and passions reign supreme. This iconoclast, free of any -isms, succeeded in bringing down the wrath of all Paris in the 1940s by presenting his intentionally "clumsy" paintings.

Dubuffet's most innovative artistic period came relatively late: it was not until the 1940s that he rebelled against any pre-existing concept of art and set out to look for beauty in what was commonly rejected not only by the general public but also by the cultural community.

His first solo exhibition was held in Paris, in the René Drouin gallery, in 1944. The visitors were shocked by his maladroit canvases painted in thick, gaudy paint. He had flouted all of the codes of painting! The following year, this practitioner and theoretician of *art brut* (raw art) went even further with the exhibition *Mirobolus, Macadam et Cie*. He maintained the same naïveté until 1944 but abandoned color to be able to experiment with textures: plaster, sand, gravel, dust, and cord became his main materials. He covered his canvases with a mixture of different materials to form a paste that he then scratched away to arrive at a motif. The critics found these examples of *Haute Pâte* ("thick paste," usually translated as Matter Paintings), as he called them, intolerable and united in their violent condemnation of the works.

In *Volonté de Puissance (Will to Power)*, a kind of satire on fascist authority, a man emerges out of magma; his thickened flesh merges with the landscape. They are made of the same dense material with an irregular contour. The absence of any perspective, the absence of arms ... a child could not have done it better. Dubuffet used a row of little pebbles to signify the teeth; he chose fragments of glass for the man's eyes. This painting demonstrates how he refused to be stifled by convention. As he said: "Art doesn't go to sleep in the bed made for it; it would sooner run away than say its own name: what it likes is to be incognito. Its best moments are when it forgets its own name."

Jean Dubuffet (1901–1985), *Volonté de Puissance (The Will to Power)*, January 1946,
oil, pebbles, sand, glass and rope on canvas, 116.2 × 88.9 cm, Solomon R. Guggenheim Museum, New York

MORE AT EASE ON THE FLOOR

Jackson Pollock became the trailblazer of modern art in the United States after the Second World War. He totally redefined painting, mainly with his *dripping* and *pouring* techniques, which consisted of letting paint flow or drop directly onto the canvas. This novelty alarmed people and certain critics were incensed: Pollock not only professed a belief in radical abstraction, he also attacked the fundamental techniques of painting.

Jackson Pollock (1912–1956), *One: Number 31, 1950*, **1950,**
oil and enamel paint on ungrounded canvas, 269.5 × 630.8 cm,
Museum of Modern Art (MoMA), New York

A t the end of the 1940s, Jackson Pollock finall started to become known on account of h astonishing *drip painting*. There were mixed feelings about this new style of painting that exclude any direct contact with the canvas. Going even further, Pollock worked horizontally: he tacked his canvas to the floor before moving around and pourin trickles of paint onto it as if in a kind of trance. H stated: "On the floor I am more at ease. I feel neare more part of the painting, since this way I can wal around it, work from the four sides and literally be *i*

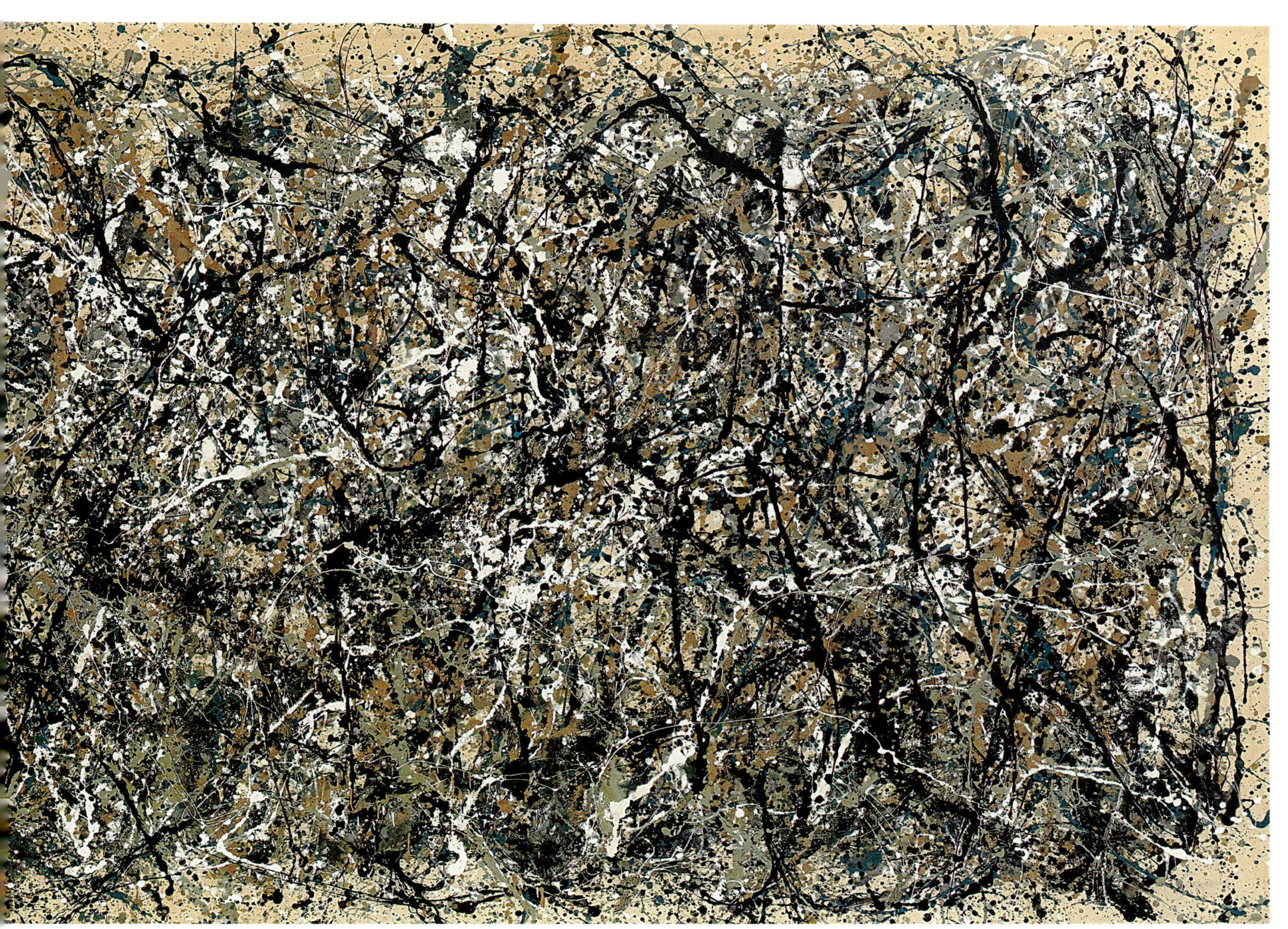

the painting." This marked a total break with established traditions.

Abstraction was not limited to the contrasting lines and areas of color; it was also evident in the titles of his paintings. In 1948, he began numbering his canvases, without worrying about order or chronology, so as not to distract the viewer with words.

Starting in 1945, the critics began a war of words in polemical articles. The famous influential American art journalist Clement Greenberg heaped praise on the artist and paid tribute to Pollock's vitality. His main opponents were Harold Rosenberg and Eleanor Jewett. The latter wrote in the *Chicago Daily Tribune* on 6 March 1945: "His paintings seem to be based on the theory according to which the more they resemble a child's doodles, the more significant they are."

In 1950, Hans Namuth made a film of the controversial painter at work, a film that played a key role in defining the public's perception of the artist and his work. His struggle with alcoholism and his death in an automobile accident six years later put the finishing touches to his romantic image.

ART DOES NOT STINK

A provocateur in the extreme, Piero Manzoni produced ninety cans that he guaranteed contained his own excrement. The scandal did not stop at that: they were sold at the price of gold. It was a deliberately provocative act that shattered all of the taboos of art – and that for some was a fitting commentary on the character of contemporary art.

t is said that the artist's father gave him the idea for these cans when he supposedly said: "Your work is shit!" Be that as it may, Manzoni was proud to present *Merde d'artiste* in 1961. The yellow cans are numbered consecutively and signed. Even more, one can read – in Italian, English, French, and German – "Artist's Shit, CONTENTS: 30 gr net, FRESHLY PRESERVED, PRODUCED AND TINNED IN MAY 1961."

The work is in fact a contract of confidence between the artist and purchaser, who cannot open a can without changing its nature and destroying its artistic – and commercial – value. What really is in the cans? The outraged skeptics assure that it could not be excrement, and some suggest sausage meat. But in 1989 an artist dared the act of sacrilege: he opened the relic and overstepped the unspoken ban. After he had broken open his example of the work, Bernard Bazile found another can, wrapped in cotton. A joke of Manzoni's or an act of caution to guarantee impermeability? In any case, this was obviously a wise precaution because Bazile refrained from going any further and discovering the truth.

Another important controversy started a few years before, in 1971, the year the director of the National Art Gallery in Rome acquired a *Merde d'artiste*. A declaration by twenty-four disgusted major art authorities was published in the Italian newspaper *Il Messaggero*. In 1974, a citizen brought the matter before the Italian parliament. Tenaciously, but with humor, he complained that public money had been misused on buying a can that possibly did not contain what it promised; according to him, it would have been better to catch the public's eye by using the money to repair the sewers, which were causing a real stink. The director was acquitted; but for many his works still stands condemned.

Piero Manzoni (1933–1963), *Merde d'artiste Number 31*, 1961, tin, paper, 5 x 6.5 cm, Musée National d'Art Moderne – Centre Georges – Pompidou, Paris

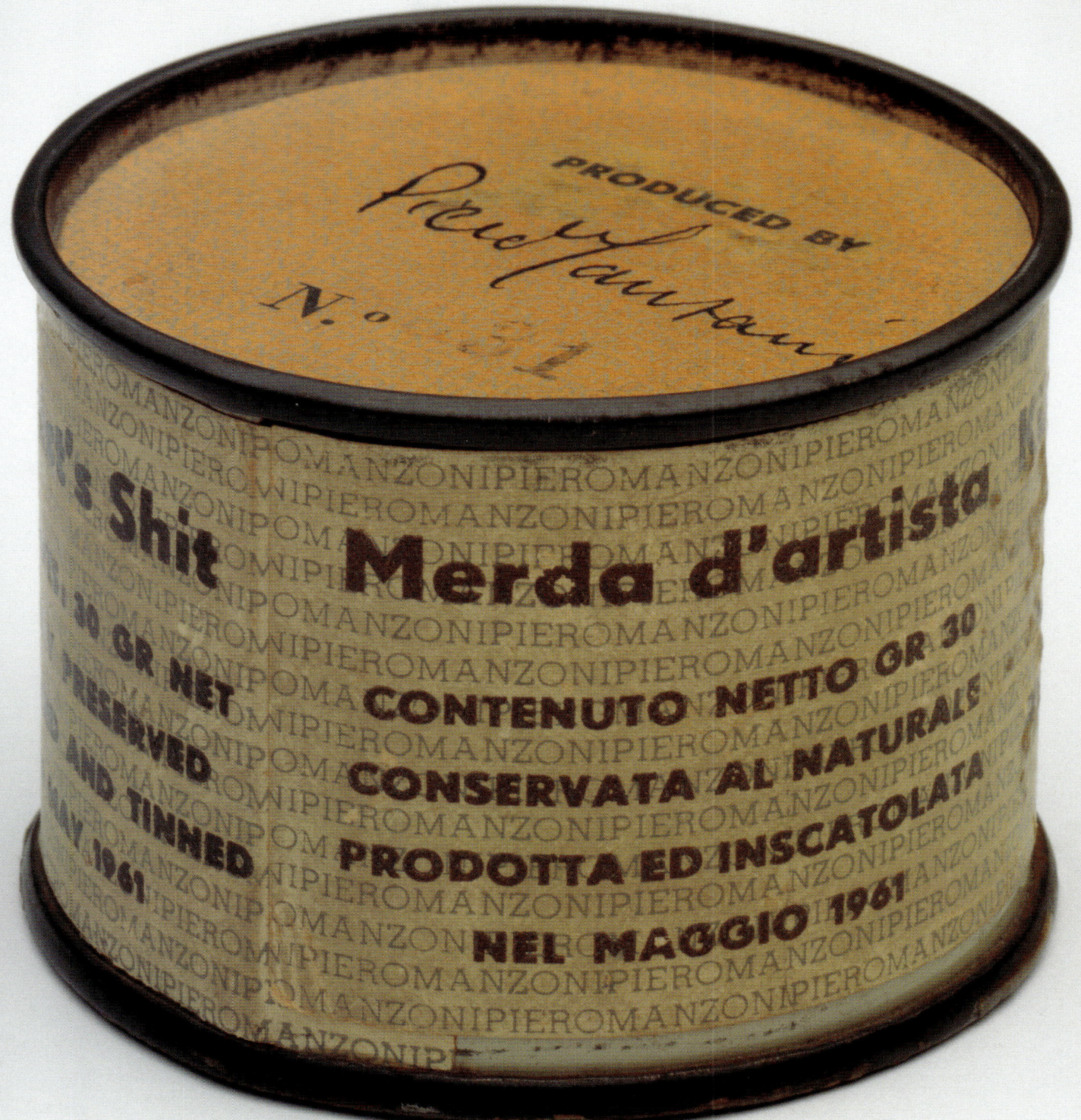
PRODUCED BY
N.o
's Shit
30 GR. NET
PRESERVED
AND TINNED
MAY 1961
Merda d'artista.
CONTENUTO NETTO GR 30
CONSERVATA AL NATURALE
PRODOTTA ED INSCATOLATA
NEL MAGGIO 1961
PIEROMANZONIPIEROMANZONI

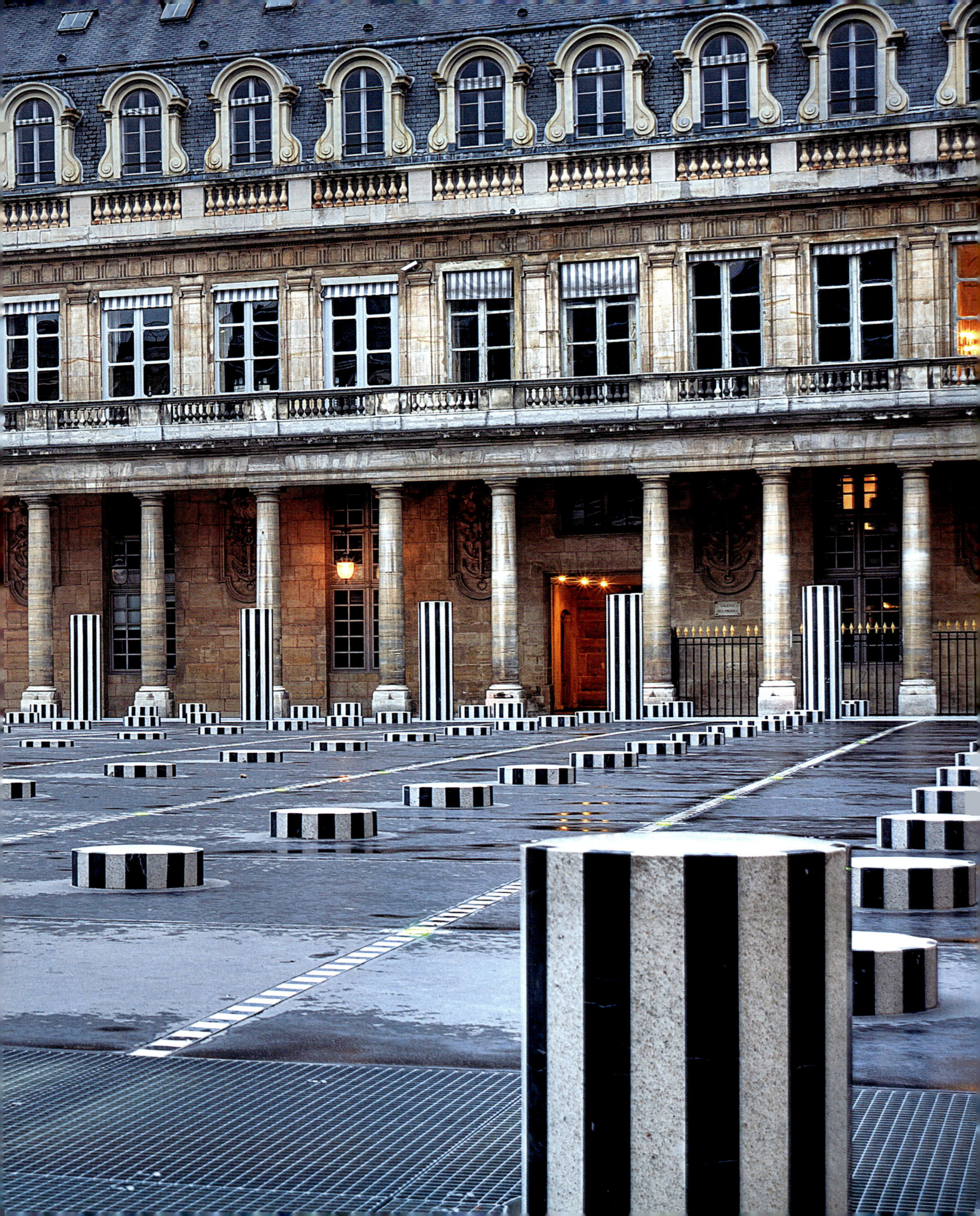

CONTEMPORARY ART AND CULTURAL HERITAGE

The plans for the Palais Royal in Paris were originally drawn up in 1629. This dignified building then hosted the royal family until Versailles was constructed. In the early 1980s, Jack Lang, the Minister of Culture, handed over the Court of Honor, which was then used for parking, to the artist Daniel Buren as an enormous artistic worksite. There was an immediate outcry: an unbelievable coalition was formed to put a stop to the "disfiguring" of a historic location.

In 1967, Buren moved out of the miserable cellar that had served him as his studio. The rents in Paris had become too high for the artist to be able to even hope for a decent space, and so he decided to work in situ. He produced his ephemeral creations, which were displayed only at a specific place and could not be used again anywhere else. Bold stripes, which he calls his "visual tools," became characteristic of the major part of his work after he had bought some striped fabric in the year 1965. It is therefore not at all surprising that he chose columns – as a reference to classical art – of black-and-white stripes for his work at the Palais Royal. The complex installation was not limited to that, however: a play of light and a fountain were the finishing touches. Motivated by what was his first commission from the state, Buren planned a magnificent space. But that was without taking into account the scandal that this kind of project creates. Articles in the newspapers, petitions, insulting and threatening letters, offensive graffiti on the fence hiding the work in progress, and heated political polemics... Buren later admitted that he had been severely affected by these hateful attacks, which were also directed at Jack Lang.

Finally, *Photo-souvenir: Les Deux Plateaux (Photo Souvenir: The Two Levels)*, more commonly known as *Buren's Columns*, was handed over without any official opening ceremony. But it was soon accepted by Parisians and tourists on account of its aesthetic appeal and playfulness; one could sit on the columns or play leapfrog over them, and coins were even thrown into the fountain.

Twenty-four years later there was another scandal: Buren accused the government of negligence and spoke of "vandalism by the state." His work, he claimed, had been allowed to fall into ruins. This time, and with a great deal of support, he pushed for a restoration that was enough to cause yet another pained outcry: estimated at 5.3 million euros, it was more expensive than the original work.

Daniel Buren (1938–),
***Photo-souvenir: Les Deux Plateaux*, 1985–1986,**
260 marble columns, water, seen from
the Court of Honor of the Palais Royal, Paris

A WALK ON THE WILD SIDE

Joseph Beuys was one of the most remarkable artists active from the 1960s to the 1980s. For a long time he was considered a charlatan or a fool. His radical theories on art, together with the strangeness of his works, made him deeply controversial – but also a rallying point for younger artists.

For Beuys art was not merely a studio activity, it was a way of life, and he made his memories, thoughts, anxieties, and political convictions visible through it. When he proclaimed that "each person is an artist" he was making the claim that no kind of training was necessary for one to become a painter or sculptor, a claim that incensed those conservative spirits who swore by the values of the Art Academy in Düsseldorf, a venerable institution that in fact employed Beuys as a professor. Incidentally, he was dismissed in 1972 for having attempted to reform the enrolment system: he maintained that everybody had a right to participate in the courses. Beuys was unsettling because each of his works questioned the very foundations of art. In May 1974, he enacted a controversial performance for the opening of the René Block Gallery in New York. The arrival of the artist was a spectacle in its own right. Determined not to set foot on American soil in protest of the USA's presence in Vietnam, the artist was transported from the plane to the gallery first of all on a stretcher and then in an ambulance. And then he lived together with a coyote captured in the desert in Texas for three days and two nights (or a full week,

according to certain sources). The artist created a kind of ritual of initiation with the aim of reconciling nature and humanity. This disquieting *happening* was also an opportunity for evoking the pre-colonial world of Native Americans. Beuys endowed art with a new mystical dimension by becoming, in effect, a shaman. This characteristic, which can often be found in his work, perplexed the art theoreticians of the period, who were astounded when confronted with a challenge of this kind.

His contemporaries thought of Beuys as a "shocking" artist on account of his efforts to expand the concept of art. However, since his death in 1986 there has been a worldwide boom in retrospective exhibitions devoted to his works, a re-examination that shows there was not the slightest trace of affectation or insincerity in his pioneering oeuvre.

Joseph Beuys (1921–1986),
***I Like America and America Likes Me**, 1974,*
week-long action with coyote at the
René Block Gallery, New York, USA
Photo: Caroline Tisdall
Courtesy Ronald Feldman Fine Arts, New York/
www.feldmangallery.com

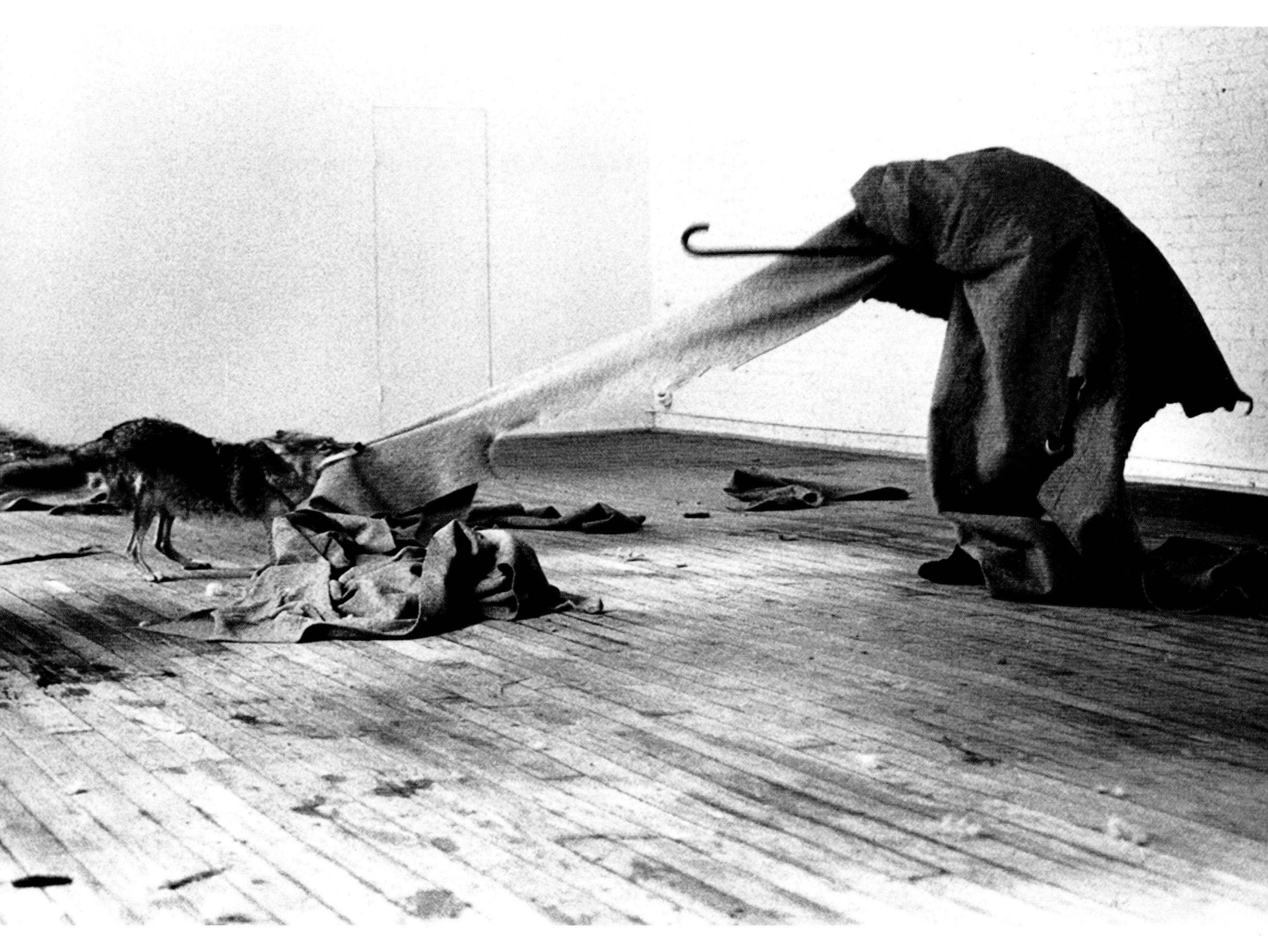

PEARLS BEFORE SWINE

Wim Delvoye is a great admirer of old art; however, he does not attempt to measure himself against his masters – they are inimitable. The Belgian concept artist centers his art on reorientation and irreverence. But as soon as it is suspected that animals have been mistreated, the farce comes to a sudden end.

This is an artist who has never been at a loss for ideas. Since *Cloaca* (2000), the famous "machine à caca" (shit machine) that made him famous, he has strung together a series of works that are just as provocative as they are eclectic: pornographic stained-glass windows, bird nests decorated with sado-masochistic accessories, and even an x-ray of fellatio.

This kind of irreverence can either annoy or make one smile. But when Delvoye seemed to mistreat animals, a flood of sordid accusations followed. Interested in the mechanism of globalization, the artist became the proprietor of a farm in China where he installed some pigsties. There he raised some piglets that had an extraordinary fate awaiting them. At the site, a team tattooed the animals with a pattern designed and then faxed by Delvoye while they were still young; they were slaughtered when they weighed 200 kilos (440 pounds). The skin was frozen to be shipped to Belgium, where it was tanned by a professional. It was then framed to become the final work. Sometimes Delvoye had the pig stuffed. In 2010, the exhibition of seven of these tattooed pigs at the Museum of Modern and Contemporary Art in Nice aroused the indignation of the supporters of animal rights, who planned to protest. The museum issued a communiqué in an attempt to calm things down: "Saved from the food-processing industry, the piglets were anesthetized before being tattooed. During their lifetime, the animals were pampered, treated like stars, and had freedom of movement." However, Delvoye's detractors continued to point out the suffering that the animals must have felt as they were only lightly anesthetized. In 2008, the artist sold a tattooed man, Tim Steiner. For the sum of 150,000 euros, a gallery owner has him at his disposal for several weeks a year to exhibit him; he can also reclaim Steiner's skin after his death. It is somewhat bizarre that people were no more offended than they were by the pigs.

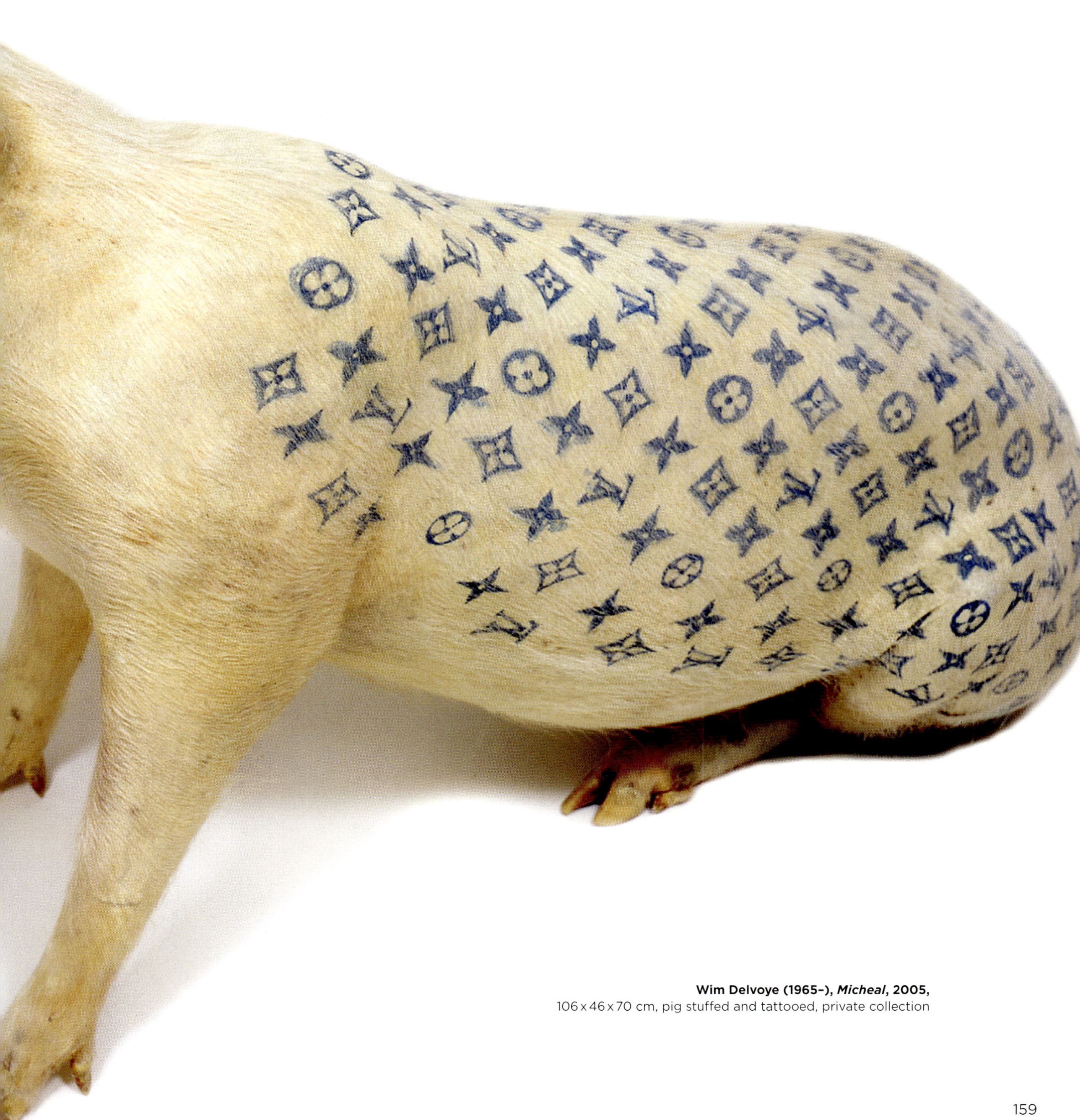

Wim Delvoye (1965–), *Micheal*, **2005,**
106 x 46 x 70 cm, pig stuffed and tattooed, private collection

DIAMONDS ARE A BOY'S BEST FRIEND

He has been called vain, a provocateur, a cynical opportunist, and an arch self-promoter. His overproduction and sense of marketing make the players on the art market nervous and his works regularly hit the headlines. He just does not stop: the man who is known as a "shockaholic" continues to be his own number one fan and surfs on the waves of artistic controversy with brio.

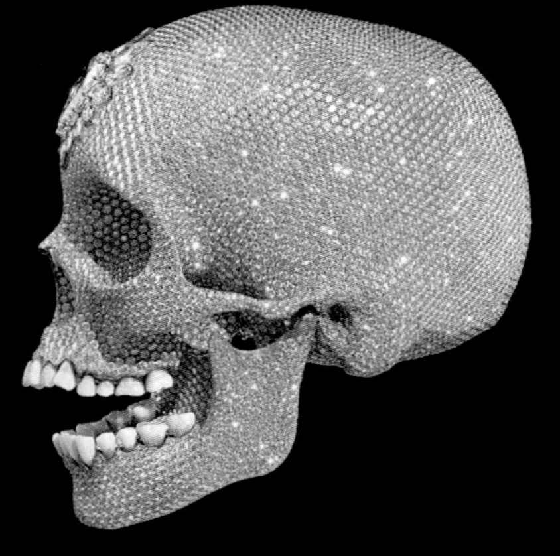

Damien Hirst (1965–),
***For the Love of God*, 2007,**
platinum, diamonds, human teeth,
17.1 × 12.7 × 19.1 cm;
photo: Prudence Cuming Associates
© Damien Hirst and Science Ltd.
All rights reserved, DACS 2012

In June 2007, Damien Hirst, who was at the peak of commercial success at the time, made a big splash. He presented a platinum cast of a skull studded with more than 1,100 carats of diamonds at an exhibition in the White Cube Gallery in London. *For the Love of God* was skillfully staged in a separate room to which only a few spectators – armed with a special ticket – were admitted at a time; they were allowed only two minutes to view the work before being gently moved on by the attendant. Cleverly orchestrated, the exhibition of *For the Love of God* triggered a controversy. An artwork that cost close to 15 million euros to produce was simply inconceivable! And, in addition, Hirst never even got his hands dirty: he went so far as to pride himself on having delegated all the work to his assistants and a famous jeweler! Once again, this astute businessman was accused of having produced a "publicity" stunt devoid of any artistic content. And the icing on the cake – *For the Love of God* soon found a buyer: it was purchased by a group of investors – Hirst among them – for 75 million euros!

The following year, the *enfant terrible* of contemporary art found himself the talk of the town once again when he personally consigned 223 of his works to auction. In this way, he thumbed his nose at his art dealers and the art market in general!

More recently, he once again caught everyone's attention by presenting a smaller version of *For the Love of God* in *For Heaven's Sake* (2008), a similar work realized using a child's skull covered with 8,000 diamonds. This time family associations, who considered this an insult to those who had lost a child, were the ones who were furious.

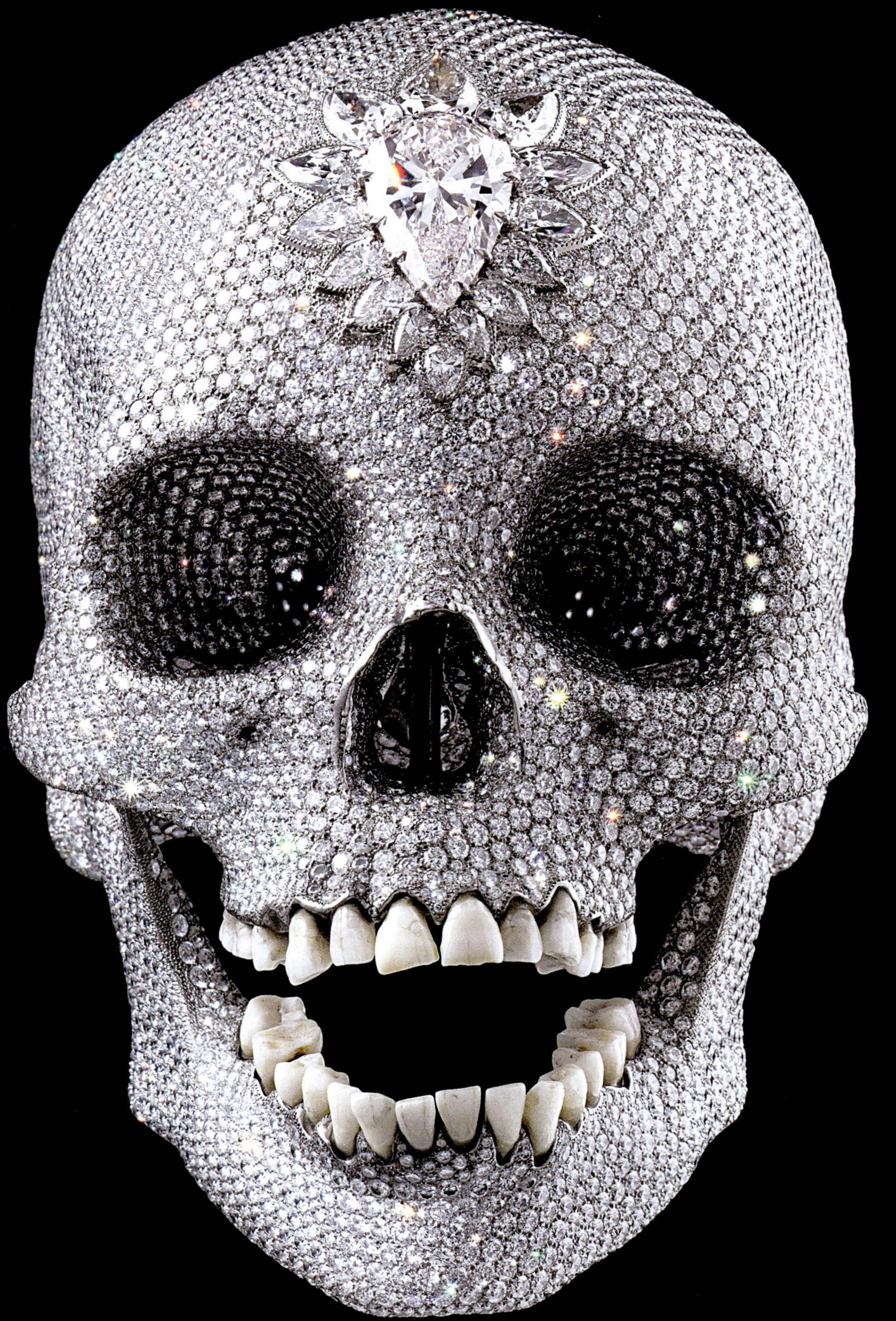

BLENDING ART AND LIFE

To what extent is it permissible for contemporary artists to use live animals? This is the question posed by *Helena*, a work by Marco Evaristti, in which goldfish take part in an unprecedented way. It is actually up to the viewer to decide whether these innocent creatures should live or die.

Helena is an installation in which food mixers take the place of goldfish bowls. The apparatuses are clearly connected to an electricity supply. Therefore the visitor understands that it would be sufficient to press a yellow button for one of the animals to be immediately ground up. Evaristti ensures that there is no distance between art and his public who, in this way, become an integral part of the work. This staging aimed at drawing in three categories of spectators: the "idiot," who would press the button; the "voyeur," who would watch him do it and enjoy it, and the "moralist." The work is open: what happens when an ordinary viewer finds himself alone with his conscience?

Helena was shown at the Trapholt Art Museum in Kolding (Denmark) on 10 February 2000, on the occasion of the opening of the *Eyegoblack* exhibition. One hour after the opening, a visitor pressed one of the buttons and irretrievably put an end to the life of a fish. The police intervened immediately and ordered that the electricity supply to the museum be cut off. Peter S. Meyer, the museum's director, was taken to court and accused of cruelty to animals; he was fined around 300 euros. He appealed and experts were consulted: a Moulinex engineer pointed out that the power of the machine made it possible to kill a fish in less than one second and a veterinarian assured that the animal would not have suffered in that amount of time. It was established that the fish had been killed "instantaneously" and therefore "humanely." Meyer was acquitted.

Helena – the title refers to the woman who caused the Trojan Wars – continued to be shown and started a war in the media. Many visitors are said to have pushed the yellow button.

Marco Evaristti (1963–), *Helena*, 2000,
10 Moulinex Optiblend 2000 mixers, water, goldfish,
artist's collection

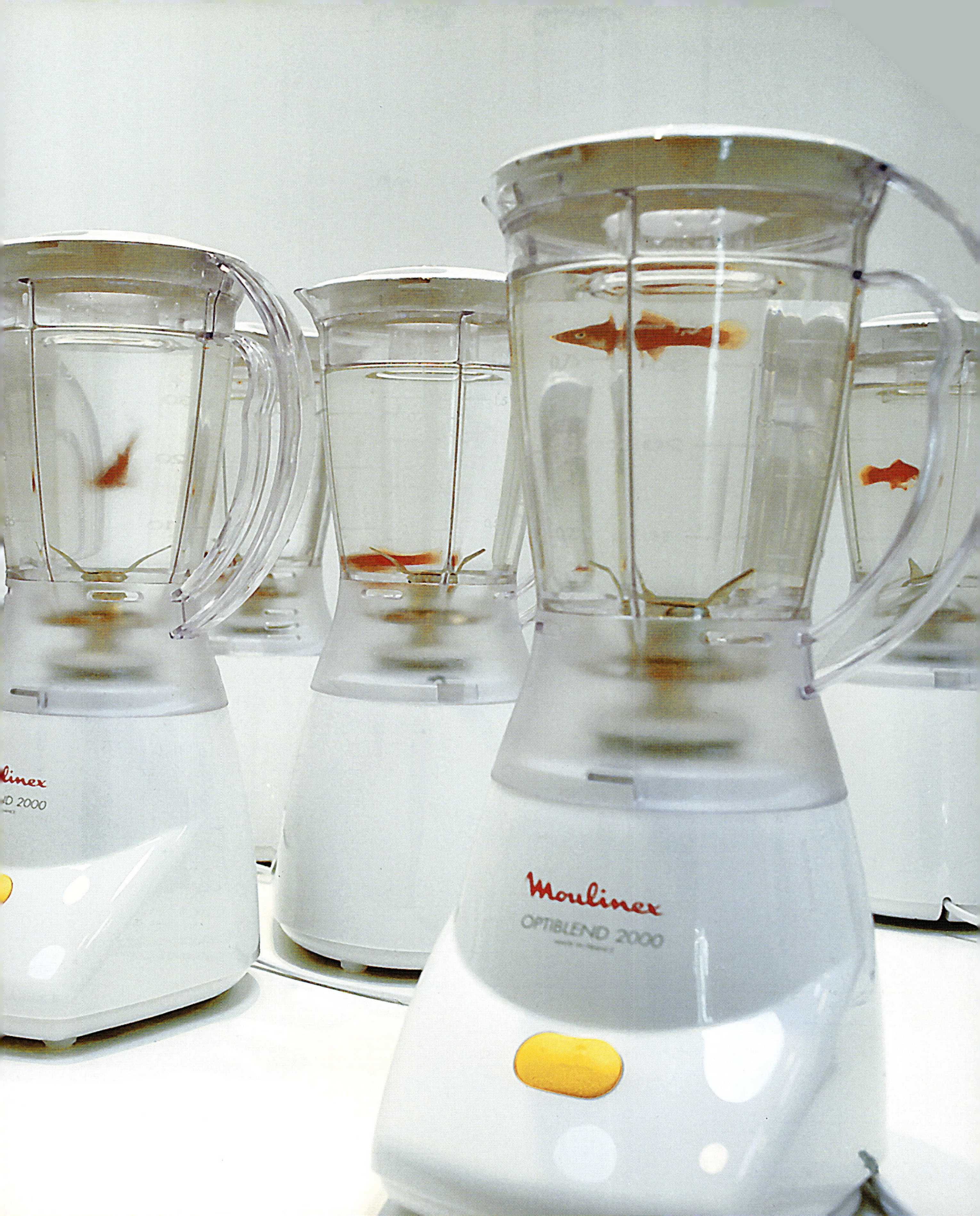

Moulinex
OPTIBLEND 2000
ND 2000

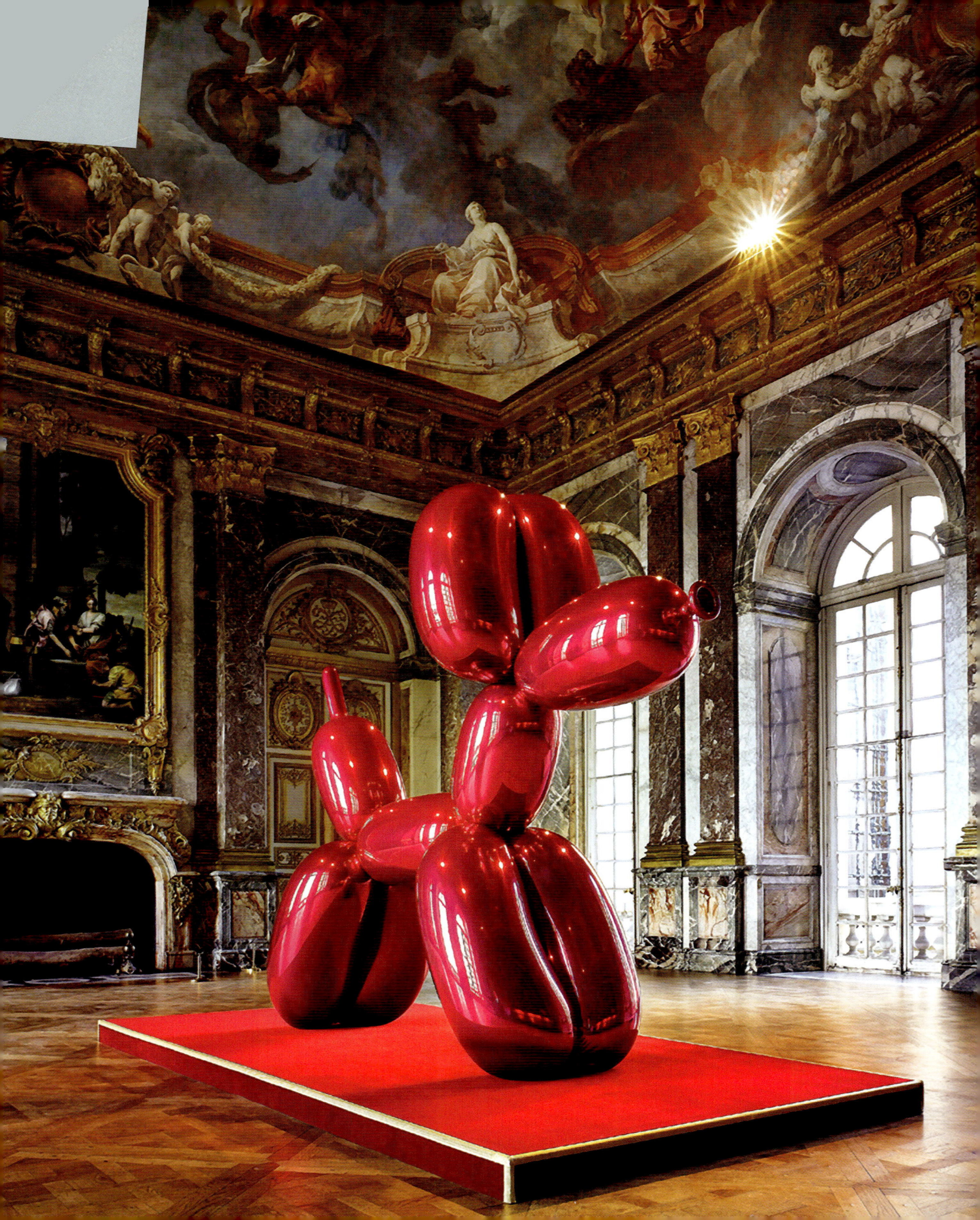

CLASSICAL CULTURE AND CONTEMPORARY KITSCH

A "risk" and an "ephemeral folly" – just two of phrases used by the curators of the *Jeff Koons–Versailles* exhibition to characterize the event they themselves had organized! To enthrone the king of kitsch and neo-pop in the residence of the monarchs of France proved itself not to be to the taste of all.

Just imagine: a gigantic polychrome aluminum lobster, a pink porcelain panther embracing a pretty blond, or a three-meter-high balloon dog in the midst of all the marble, mirrors, gilding and sumptuous fountains of the palace. Welcome to the *Jeff Koons–Versailles* exhibition, which caused a scandal with the lovers of Versailles – grouped together in organizations such as the Coordination for the Defense of Versailles and the National Union of French Writers – even before it opened to the public in September 2008. In their opinion, Koons' crazy ideas were "non-art" and his bad taste clashed with the classical, Baroque elegance of the estate. In addition, the critics were deeply concerned that erotic works dating from the period when the artist was married to the Hungarian pornographic film actress and politician Ilona Anna Staller, better known as Cicciolina, would also be shown.

Charles-Emmanuel of Bourbon-Parma even took the dispute to court! This descendent of Louis XIV bought charges against the organizers of the exhibition for "desecration and violation of the respect due to the deceased." His case was dismissed.

On top of the aesthetic controversy, there were suspicions of a conflict of interests. Jean-Jacques Aillagon, president of the public organization responsible for the Château of Versailles, had previously been the director of the Venetian Palazzo Grassi owned by François Pinault, a major collector of Jeff Koons' works.

There is no need for Jeff Koons to feel that he was the only artist who was personally attacked: after him, Takashi Murakami in 2010 and Joana Vasconcelos in 2012 were also faced with heated controversy when they exhibited in Versailles.

Jeff Koons (1955–), *Balloon Dog (Magenta)*, 1994–2000,
stainless steel with chrome, with transparent colored layer, 307.3 x 363.2 x 114.3 cm, main apartments of the Château de Versailles (Hercules Salon), Paris, photo: Laurent Lecat

THE CASE OF THE FETUS IN THE JAR

Ruan, Xiao Yu's installation, was like a time bomb: created in 1999, it was not until it was shown in Berne in 2005 that it triggered off a scandal for the first time by posing the question of the limits to using humans in art.

In June 2005, an exhibition of contemporary Chinese art, *Mahjong*, was held in the Kunstmuseum in Berne in Switzerland. *Ruan* – a series of six containers filled with formalin in which floated the bodies of animals that had been previously dismembered and reassembled by the artist – was among the works presented. One of the jars was especially singled out for criticism: the one in which the body of a seagull, the head of a human fetus, and the eyes of a rabbit were united as a kind of hybrid puzzle or freak.

Voices were raised. One journalist in particular, close to the extreme right politically, took offense and pressed charges against the artist, the museum, and Uli Sigg, the former Swiss ambassador to China who had loaned *Ruan*, a work form his private collection. The plaintiff evoked articles from the Swiss penal code that had been offended, notably those concerning cruelty to animals and disturbing the peace of the dead. Where did the fetus come from? Was the infant possibly killed for the work? Had Yu decapitated it himself? These were the macabre questions asked by the opponents of *Ruan*.

Xiao Yu dispelled the most unsavory doubts: the head had been bought at an auction organized by a museum of natural history in Peking. He also tried to explain his approach: for him, *Ruan* is an artistic reflection on genetics and the abuse of the human being in the matter of techno-sciences. He also reckoned that his creature had made it possible for the seagull and fetus "to have a second life."

No further legal action was taken, and a committee was quickly formed to decide the fate of the work: it was reintegrated into the exhibition.

Xiao Yu is not the first contemporary artist to examine the role of science. However, the scandal in Berne rekindled reflection on the limits of art and its ethics.

Xiao Yu (1965–), *Ruan*, 1999,
installation

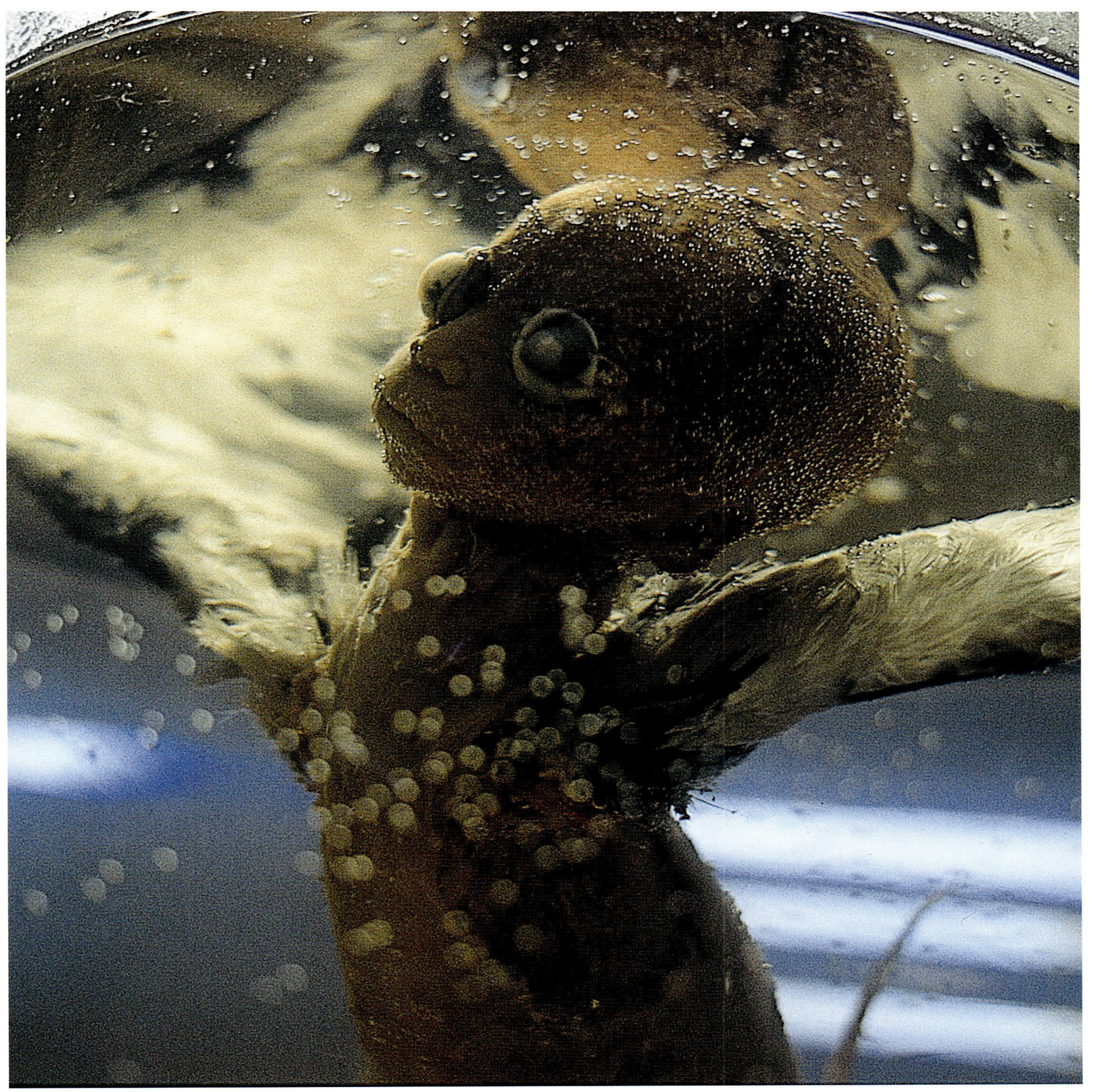

BODY ART

It amounts to the end of the inviolability of the human body. Desecrated, from this point on, it is open, analyzed, dismembered … often in the name of science but sometimes also in the name of art, and that can certainly scandalize!

Until the fifteenth century, the physical and spiritual were considered to be inseparable: it was completely out of the question to dissect a corpse – unless this was done clandestinely. It was not until the Renaissance, and principally the work of Flemish physician Andreas Vesalius (1514–1564), that the study of the human anatomy became permitted, leading to major advances in science.

Similar to the scientists and artists of the Renaissance, the German anatomist Günther von Hagens is fascinated by the human body and how it functions. In 1977, he invented "plastination," a process making it possible to preserve the body intact after death. All the fluids (water, blood, fat) are removed and replaced by silicone in order to stop decomposition and to solidify the remains (human or animal). Muscles, veins, arteries, intestines, tendons are visible, as if the body had been dissected. More than simply solidifying the bodies, Günther von Hagens stages them in a particular scene or position. Pole-vaulter, chess player, acrobat, saxophonist … the corpses in the *Body Worlds* exhibition appear to be enjoying themselves to their heart's content.

This exhibition, which was launched in 1995, was an immediate triumph in several countries. However, its success is just as marked as the controversy surrounding it. The main problem is one of classification: is it a scientific or artistic event? Attacked from all sides, Günther von Hagens takes an ambiguous position on this subject: with scientists, he emphasizes the aesthetic character of his plastinates, but emphasizes scientific interest when a "But that is not art!" is flung at him. What is it then, a major advance in science or voyeuristic craving designed to draw in the masses? The debate remains open and the controversy only increases. In any case, business is going well for Professor von Hagens: his Institute for Plastination has already received thousand of promised donations.

View of one of the bodies plastinated by Gunther von Hagens (1945–), 6 May 2009, on the occasion of the *Body Worlds* exhibition in Berlin

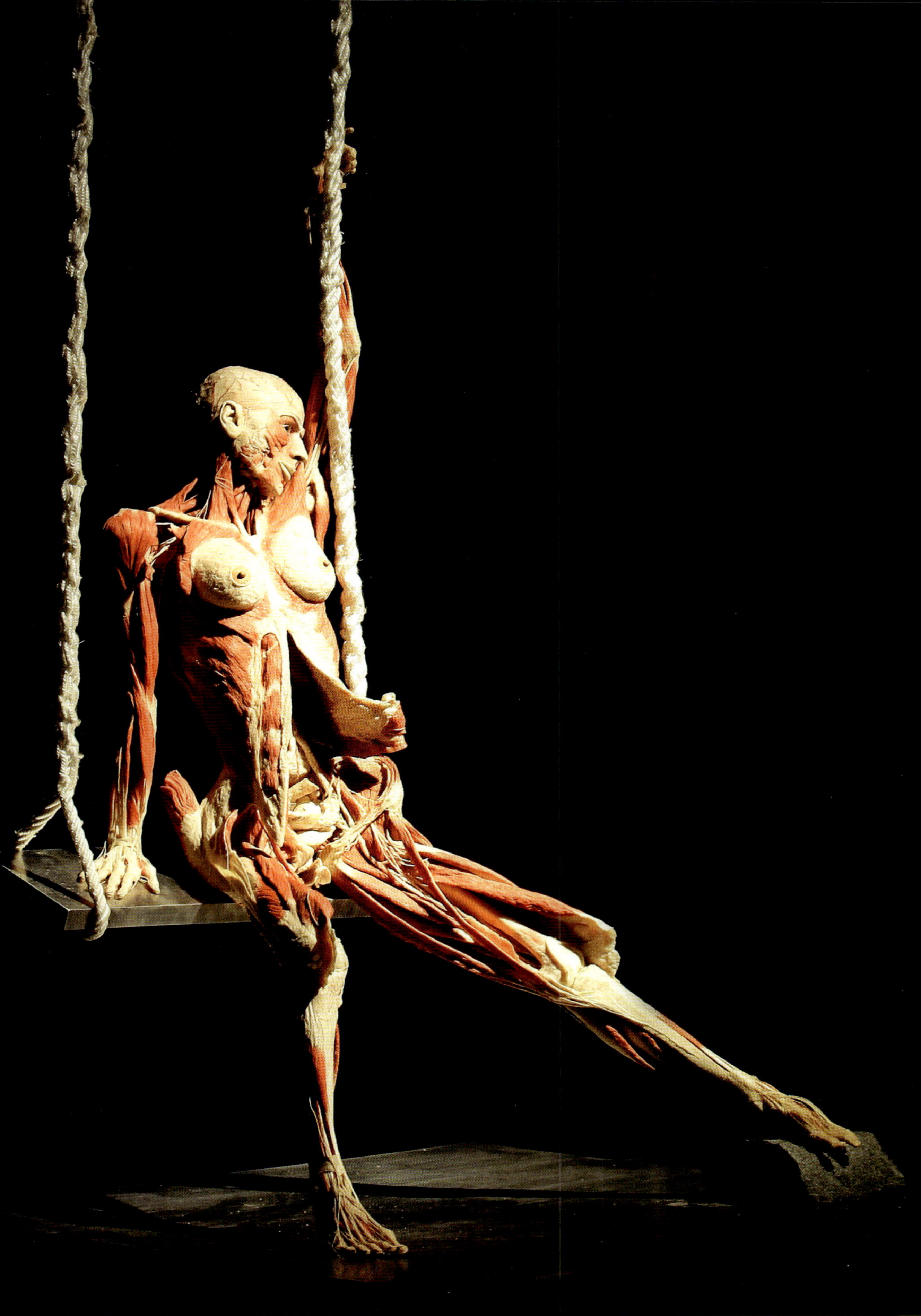

ANONYMOUS CELEBRITY

Thierry Guetta, alias Mr. Brainwash (MBW), is a mysterious phenomenon. Most of the information we have on him comes from Banksy's film *Exit Through the Gift Shop* released in 2010. There he appears too incredible to be true. But whether it is a prank or not, it must be noted that works stamped "MBW" have flourished in auctions and galleries from that time on.

Thierry Guetta is first and foremost a video maker. He incessantly films everything around him. With the concept of making a documentary, he succeeded in penetrating into the secret world of street art. The major stars in the field (Banksy, Shepard Fairey...) accepted that the scatterbrained Frenchman follow them with his camera. The film proved to be a fiasco and Guetta, influenced by the company he was keeping, dreamed of starting a career as a street artist himself: he became Mr. Brainwash. Hardly concerned about what people say, he unashamedly takes inspiration from his friends and has become completely at ease with his social climbing. In the style of Damien Hirst, he has his works produced in industrial quantities by an army of assistants. To make each piece unique, he sometimes hastily throws a few spots of paint on them.

In 2008, while he was still unknown to the public at large, he decided to go the whole hog and organized a gigantic personal exhibition in Los Angeles entitled *Life Is Beautiful*. Thanks to his nicely packaged advertising campaign, the artist drew in more than 7,000 visitors and sold dozens of works for more than a total of one million dollars. He is treated like a charlatan but he manages to keep his head held high: "Who isn't playing a role these days? Who says it is forbidden to copy? Who says that there are rules in art?"

Nobody knows who Mr. Brainwash really is and whether *Exit Through the Gift Shop* (in which he is said to be an French artist working in Los Angeles) is to be taken at face value or not. The artistic journey of MBW, as well as the role Banksy possibly plays in his success, is the subject of constant debate. Fraud or not, it is one of the most monumental nose-thumbings the art market has faced in recent years.

Right: **Mr. Brainwash (1966), *Obama Superman*, 2008,** silk-screen print (print run of 500 copies), 111 x 81 cm
Following pages: **Mr. Brainwash (1966),** view of the exhibition entitled "Mr. Brainwash" (in presence of the artist), held from 5 August to 31 August 2012 at the Old Sorting Office, London

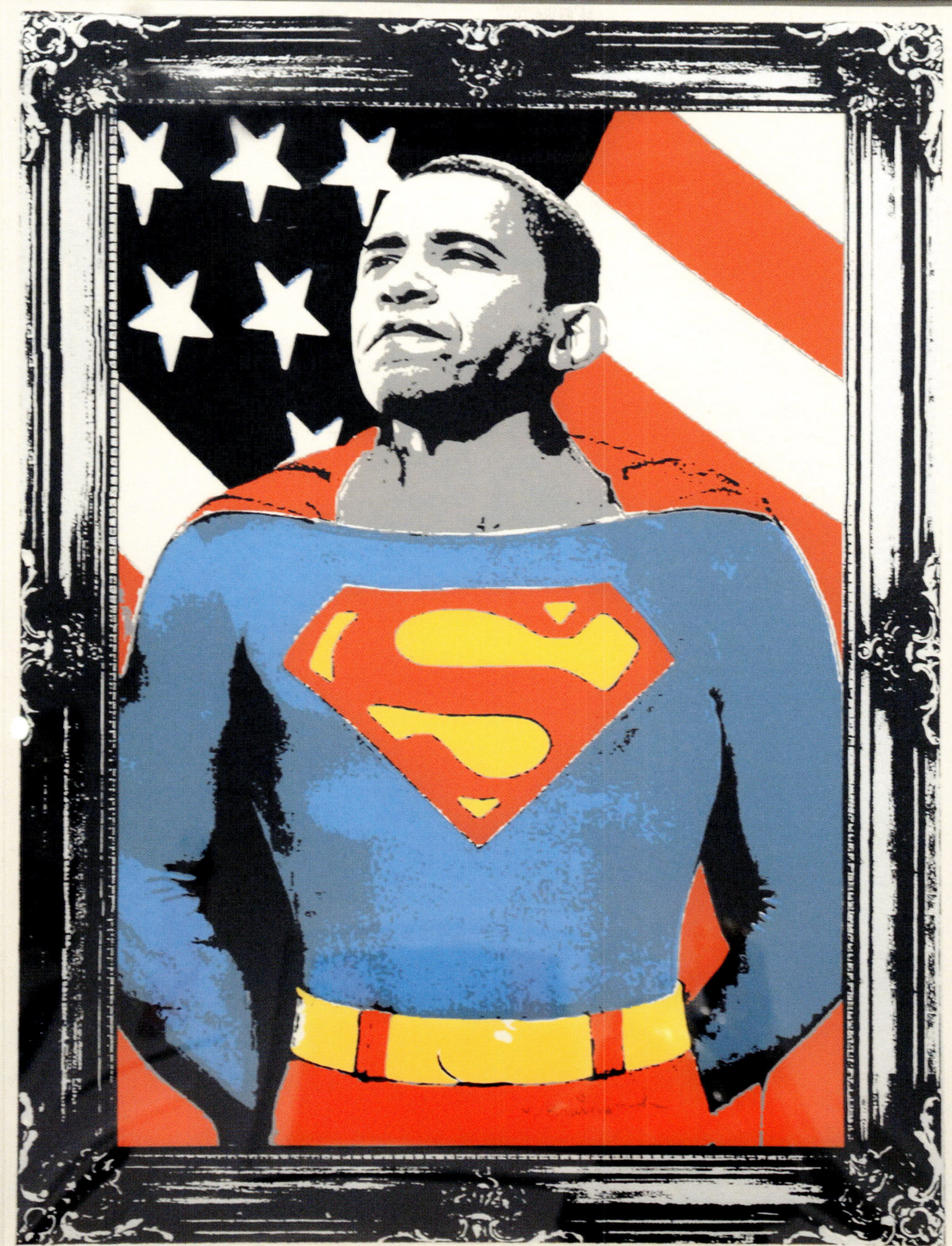

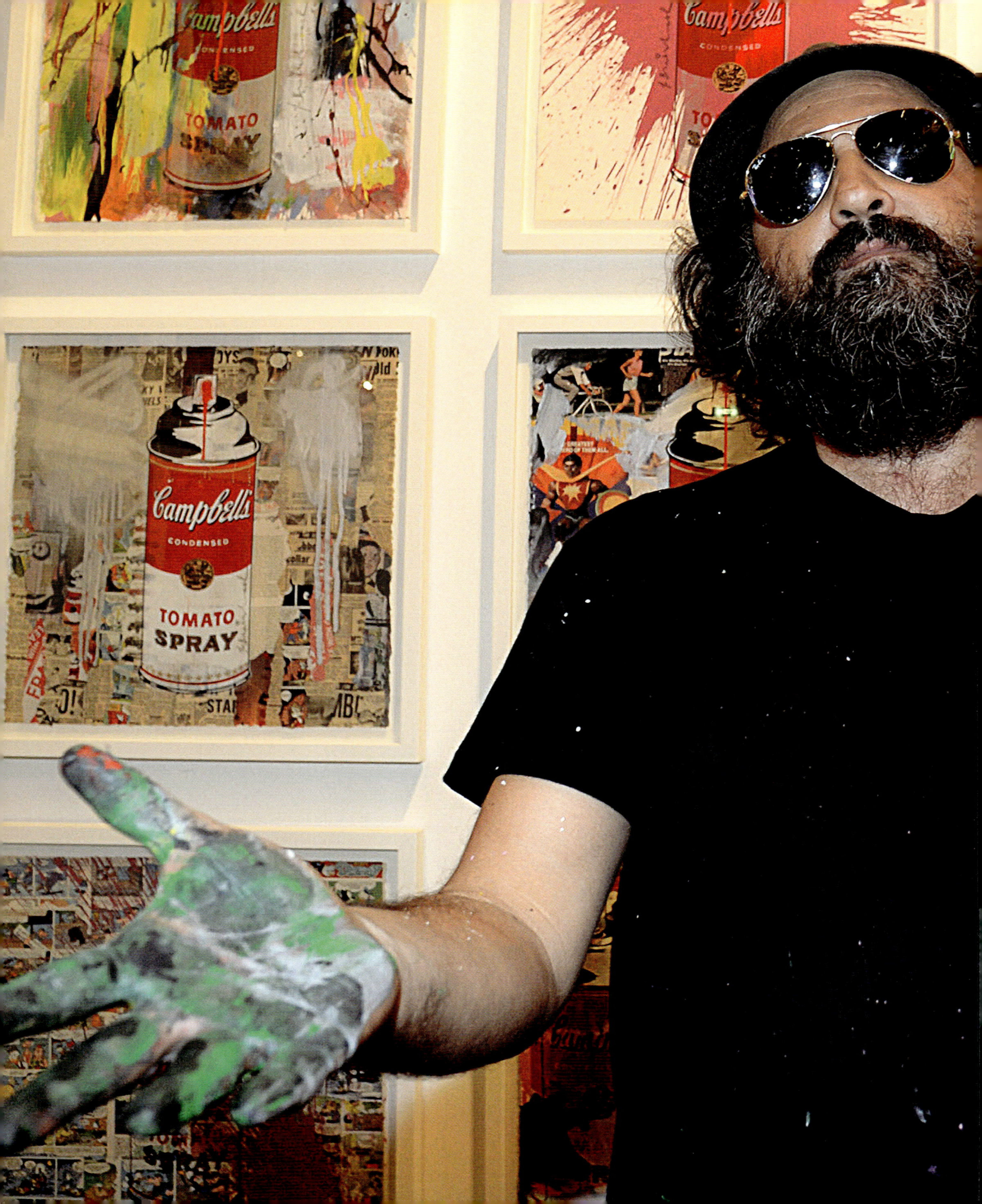
Campbell's
CONDENSED
TOMATO
SPRAY
Campbell's
CONDENSED
TOMATO
SPRAY
Campbell's
CONDENSED

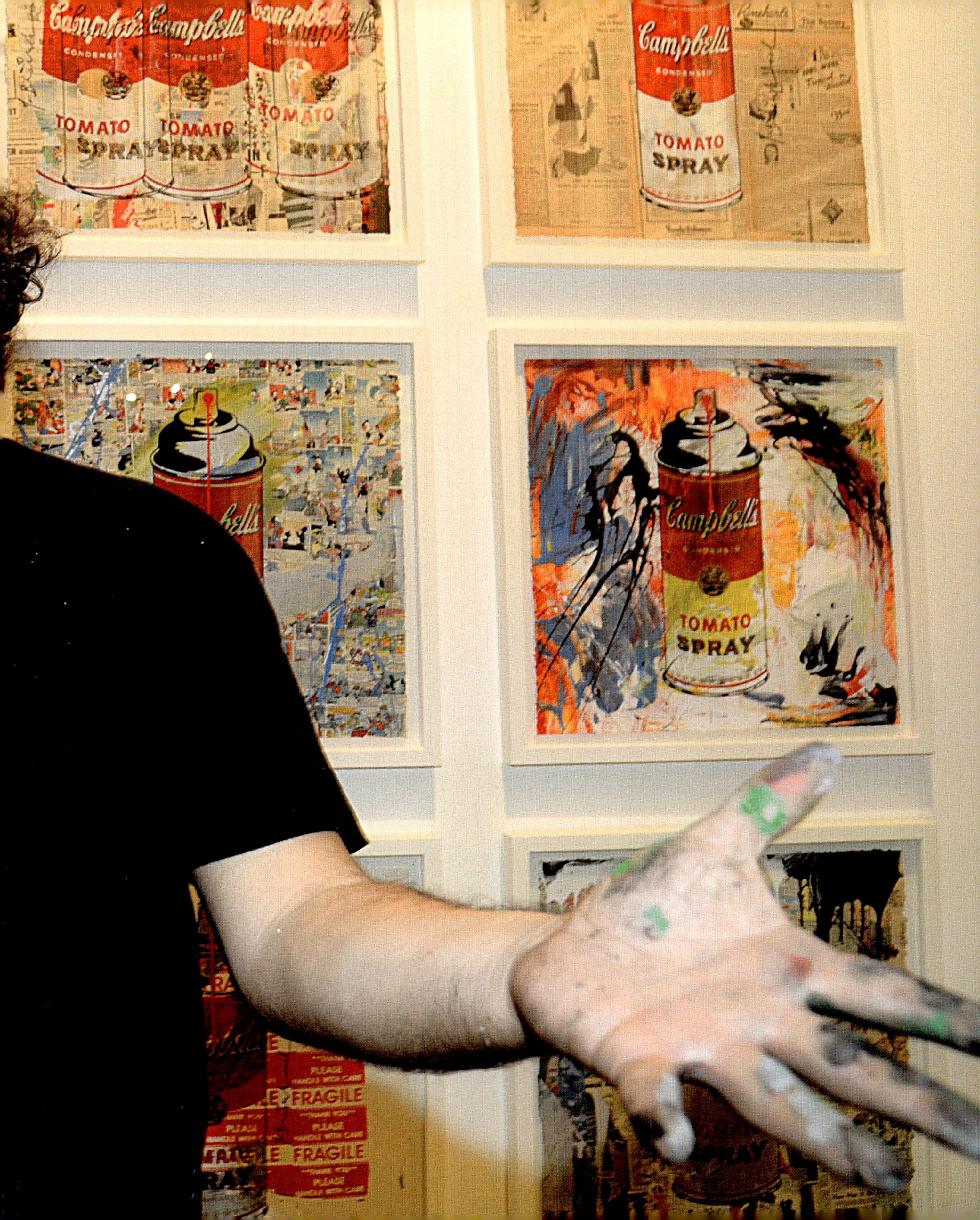

Campbell's Campbell's Campbell's
CONDENSED CONDENSED CONDENSED
TOMATO TOMATO TOMATO
SPRAY SPRAY SPRAY
Campbell's
CONDENSED
TOMATO
SPRAY
Campbell's
CONDENSED
TOMATO
SPRAY
Campbell's
CONDENSED
TOMATO
SPRAY
PLEASE
HANDLE WITH CARE
FRAGILE
PLEASE
HANDLE WITH CARE
FRAGILE

INDEX OF ARTISTS

PHOTO CREDITS

Cover: © Courtesy Maurizio Cattelan's Archive

© **Adagp, Paris 2013 for all the works by its members:** Alexander Kosolapov p. 38; **mounir fatmi** p. 43; **Otto Dix** pp. 73, 74–75; **Marc Chagall** p. 76; **Constantin Brancusi** p. 111; **Hans Bellmer** pp. 116–117; **Otto Muehl** p. 120; **Jean Dubuffet** p. 148; **Jackson Pollock** pp. 150–151; **Piero Manzoni** p. 153; **Joseph Beuys** p. 157; **Wim Delvoye** pp. 158–159; **Marco Evaristti** p. 163

Tamara de Lempicka p. 115: © 2010 Tamara Art Heritage/ADAGP, Paris 2013; **Marcel Duchamp** p. 147: © succession Marcel Duchamp/ADAGP, Paris 2013; **Daniel Buren** p. 154: © DB – ADAGP, Paris 2013; **Damien Hirst** pp. 160, 161: © Damien Hirst and Science Ltd. All rights reserved, ADAGP 2013

pp. 8–9 © Courtesy of the artist and Yvon Lambert, Paris; **13** (left) © Giraudon/The Bridgeman Art Library; **13** (right) © The Bridgeman Art Library; **15** © akg-images/Rabatti – Domingie; **16–17** © The Bridgeman Art Library; **18–19** © The Bridgeman Art Library/Getty Images; **20–21** © Universal Images Group/Getty Images; **22–23** © Cameraphoto Arte Venezia/The Bridgeman Art Library; **25** © Giraudon/The Bridgeman Art Library; **27** © The Bridgeman Art Library; **28–29** © Dea/G. Dagli Orti/De Agostini/Getty Images; **31** © Archives Alinari, Florence, Dist. RMN-Grand Palais/Araldo de Luca; **32** © RMN-Grand Palais (Musée d'Orsay)/Hervé Lewandowski; **35** © Courtesy of the artist and Yvon Lambert, Paris; **37** © AP/Sipa; **38** © Alexander Kosolapov; **40–41** © Courtesy Maurizio Cattelan's Archive; **43** © Courtesy de l'artiste et Galerie Hussenot, Paris; **44–45** © Peter Willi/SuperStock/Getty Images; **49** © Index/The Bridgeman Art Library; **50** (left) © Index/The Bridgeman Art Library; **50** (right) © The Bridgeman Art Library; **51** (left and right) © Index/The Bridgeman Art Library; **52–53** © The Bridgeman Art Library; **55** © Peter Willi/SuperStock/Getty Images; **56–57** © Roger-Viollet; **59** © RMN-Grand Palais (Musée d'Orsay)/Jean Schormans; **61** © The Bridgeman Art Library/Getty Images; **62** © The Bridgeman Art Library; **65** © RMN-Grand Palais/François Vizzavona/reproduction RMN; **67** © The Bridgeman Art Library; **68** © Charles F. Olney Fund/The Bridgeman Art Library; **71** © The Bridgeman Art Library; **73** © BPK, Berlin, Dist. RMN-Grand Palais/image BPK; **74–75** © BPK, Berlin, Dist. RMN-Grand Palais/Jürgen Karpinski; **76** © Photo Scala, Florence; **79** © Collection Walker Art Center, Minneapolis T. B. Walker Acquisition Fund, 2009. Courtesy: SCAI THE BATHHOUSE; **81** © Courtesy Maurizio Cattelan's Archive; **83** © The Artist/Courtesy James Cohan Gallery, New York/Shanghai; **84–85** © Ai Weiwei; **86–87** © Casey Caplowe; **88–89** © Giraudon/The Bridgeman Art Library; **93** © Alinari/The Bridgeman Art Library; **94–95** © Giraudon/The Bridgeman Art Library; **96–97** © The Bridgeman Art Library/Getty Images; **98** © British Library Board. All Rights Reserved/The Bridgeman Art Library; **101** © Giraudon/The Bridgeman Art Library; **103** © Giraudon/The Bridgeman Art Library; **104** © Giraudon/The Bridgeman Art Library; **107** © RMN-Grand Palais (Musée d'Orsay)/Thierry Ollivier; **108–109** © Imagno/Hulton Archive/Getty Images; **111** © Centre Pompidou, MNAM-CCI, Dist. RMN-Grand Palais/Adam Rzepka; **112** © Photo Scala, Florence; **115** © Mondadori Electa/The Bridgeman Art Library; **116–117** © Centre Pompidou, MNAM-CCI, Dist. RMN-Grand Palais/Georges Meguerditchian; **119** © DR; **120** © Centre Pompidou, MNAM-CCI, Dist. RMN-Grand Palais/Image Centre Pompidou, MNAM-CCI; **122** © Oleg Kulik; **123** © Oleg Kulik; **125** © Robert Mapplethorpe/Art + Commerce; **126** © Nan Goldin; **129** © Blue Noses; **130–131** © Jeff Koons; **135** © Dea Picture Library/De Agostini/Getty Images; **136–137** © The Bridgeman Art Library/Getty Images; **139** © Dea Picture Library/De Agostini/Getty Images; **140–141** © RMN-Grand Palais/Agence Bulloz; **143** © Dea/A. Dagli Orti/De Agostini/Getty Images; **144** © Giraudon/The Bridgeman Art Library and © Succession Picasso 2013; **147** © Vera & Arturo Schwarz Collection of Dada and Surrealist Art/The Bridgeman Art Library; **148** © Solomon R. Guggenheim Museum, New York; **150–151** © Digital image, The Museum of Modern Art, New York/Scala, Florence; **153** © Centre Pompidou, MNAM-CCI, Dist. RMN-Grand Palais/Philippe Migeat; **154** © Harald A. Jahn/www.viennaslide.com/akg-images; **157** © Courtesy Ronald Feldman Fine Arts, New York/www.feldmangallery.com; **158–159** © Wim Delvoye. Courtesy Galerie Perrotin, Hong Kong & Paris; **160** © Handout/Getty Images; **161** © Handout/Getty Images; **163** © Evaristti Studios; **164** © Jeff Koons; **167** © M+ Sigg Collection; **169** © Andreas Rentz/Getty Images/AFP; **170** © Kevin Mazur/WireImage/Getty Images; **171–172** © Kevin Mazur/WireImage/Getty Images